LONDON CLERICAL WORKERS, 1880–1914: DEVELOPMENT OF THE LABOUR MARKET

PERSPECTIVES IN ECONOMIC AND SOCIAL HISTORY

Series Editor: Andreas Gestrich
                   Steven King
                   Robert E. Wright

TITLES IN THIS SERIES

FORTHCOMING TITLES

LONDON CLERICAL WORKERS, 1880–1914: DEVELOPMENT OF THE LABOUR MARKET

BY

Michael Heller

LONDON AND NEW YORK

First published 2011 by Pickering & Chatto (Publishers) Limited

Published 2016 by Routledge
2 Park Square, Milton Park, Abingdon, Oxfordshire OX14 4RN
711 Third Avenue, New York, NY 10017, USA

First issued in paperback 2015

Routledge is an imprint of the Taylor & Francis Group, an informa business

BRITISH LIBRARY CATALOGUING IN PUBLICATION DATA

Heller, Michael.
London clerical workers, 1880–1914 : development of the labour market. –
(Perspectives in economic and social history)
1. Clerks – England – London – Social conditions – 19th century. 2. Clerks – England – London – Social conditions – 20th century. 3. Clerks – England – London
– Economic conditions – 19th century. 4. Clerks – England – London – Economic
conditions – 20th century. 5. Labor market – England – London – History – 19th
century. 6. Labor market – England – London – History – 20th century.
I. Title II. Series
305.9'65137'09421-dc22

ISBN-13: 978-1-138-66133-2 (pbk)
ISBN-13: 978-1-8489-3054-4 (hbk)

Typeset by Pickering & Chatto (Publishers) Limited

CONTENTS

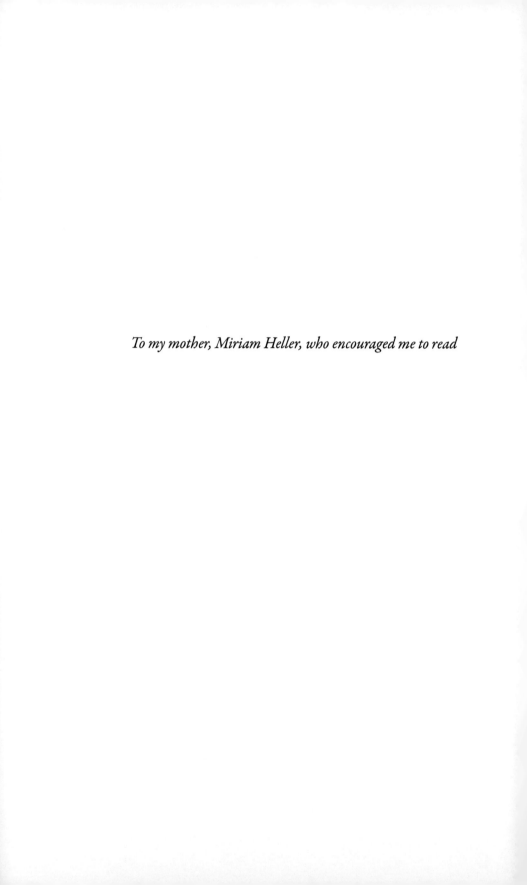

To my mother, Miriam Heller, who encouraged me to read

ACKNOWLEDGEMENTS

I would like to thank my PhD. research supervisors Professor David French and Professor Catherine Hall at The Department of History, University College London for the invaluable help, advice and support that they gave me whilst carrying out research which became the basis for this study.

In relation to the actual research, I would like to thank all the archivists, librarians and organizations that have assisted me and allowed me to look at their material. In relation to the latter, I would particularly like to thank the Royal Bank of Scotland Group and the Prudential, and their archivists Philip Winterbottom, Clare Bunkham and David Carter. I would also like to thank the staff at the British Library, the National Archives, the London Metropolitan Archives, the Essex Records Office and the staff of the local history libraries in the London Boroughs of Hackney, Southwark and Redbridge. I would also particularly thank Jim Hancock whose sharing of his and his father's memories of office work at the Westminster and later National Westminster Bank has been of invaluable help to this study.

I would also like to thank my family and friends for their help and support which was has been essential. In particular I would like to thank my wife Kaoruko Kondo, and my close friends Adrian Casillias, Martin Percy, John Prowle, Rico Dent and Stephie Courlet. Their often long conversations with me on the subject of my thesis and help they furnished were of great assistance.

LIST OF TABLES

INTRODUCTION

The emergence of the modern clerical worker in London between 1880 and 1914 transformed the metropolis. Many aspects of the life and development of this great city were inextricably linked with the rise in its white-collar inhabitants. Whilst clerical workers had lived in London for centuries, they were always a marginal group. It was their rapid rise in the latter half of the nineteenth century that witnessed their arrival as a social, economic and political force. The politician and writer C. F. G. Masterman commented on them in 1909, 'They are the creations not of the industrial, but of the commercial and business activities of London. They form a homogeneous civilization, – detached, self-centred, unostentatious, – covering the hills along the northern and southern boundaries of the city, and spreading their conquests over the quiet fields beyond'.[1] In the capital the number of male commercial clerks increased from 58,278 to 82,027 between 1881 and 1911 and the number of female commercial clerks from 2,327 to 32,893. Adding civil servants, local government officers, bank, insurance, law and railway clerks this figure rose from 80,109 to 140,847 for men; and for women from 3,101 to 39,847.[2] In 1911, this represented 10 per cent of male workers in London and 5.2 per cent of female workers. Amongst occupied males, clerical workers were the largest single professional category in London. In the same year there were a further 46,860 male clerks living in Middlesex, 42,473 male and 7,582 female clerks living in Essex, 25,315 in Surrey and 14,782 living in Kent. Many of these lived in the Metropolitan areas which had sprung up around London's borders.[3] By 1911 there were an estimated 200,000–250,000 clerks living and working in London and its metropolitan surrounding areas. Writing in 1904 on commercial education, Sidney Webb bore witness to this vast concentration of office workers and the myriad commercial and governmental concerns in which they worked,

> London is above all other cities, the city of office. It has not only far more clerks, and more kinds of clerks, than any other city, but probably more also in proportion to its total population ... London, too, is, in nearly every business, the head office of the world. Great banks, insurance companies, railways and international enterprises of every kind ... have their principle centres, in the 'five million city.'

Then there is the great and growing service of public administration. There are
20,000 civil service or municipal clerks and offices in London ... There are 30,000
merchants, brokers, factors, commercial travellers, etc. The bankers and their
clerks number over 8,000 whilst those involved in the great businesses of insurance exceed 5,000, and there are no fewer than 8,000 clerical offices at work in
the administration of railways. These large numbers are irrespective of the great
army of merely commercial or business clerks, not further defined, of which there
are in London over 100,000. We have thus a total of at least 200,000 persons at
work in London offices, before we begin to count the dealers, manufacturers, and
shopkeepers themselves.[4]

For London the growth in such numbers was revolutionary. Villages were
transformed into thriving suburbs with tens of thousands of inhabitants.
This included Metropolitan Essex to the east of London with suburbs such
as Ilford, Leyton and East Ham, and Tottenham and Edmonton to the north
in Middlesex.[5] Within London proper clerks led demand for inner-suburban
development in Hackney, Lewisham, Camberwell, Lambeth and Wandsworth.[6]
More central areas such as Battersea and later Maida Vale were filled with unmar-
ried clerks, many newly arrived in London. Such residential developments
spurred the development of suburban railway networks, electric tramways, buses
and underground trains. Masterman succinctly described London's hordes of
clerks as being daily, '... sucked into the City at daybreak, and scattered again
as darkness falls. It finds itself towards evening in its own territory in the miles
and miles of little red houses in silent streets, in numbers defying imagination.'[7]
Clerks and the wider lower-middle class to which they belonged emerged as a
political force within the capital. Conservatism flourished in the suburbs.[8] The
1907 victory of the conservative Moderate Party in the London County Council (L.C.C.), removing the liberal Progressives who had controlled the L.C.C.
since its inception in 1889, was attributed to the political power of London's
outer domiciles and their white-collar inhabitants.[9] Masterman compared it to
being butted by a sheep![10] The impact of London's clerks, however, went much
further than its physical and political fabric. Clerical workers received stable and
growing incomes. They restricted family size, had disposable money and were
not subject to the vagaries of unemployment and unforeseen and uninsured illness which so afflicted London's working-classes.[11] The result was the rise in a
critical-mass of inhabitants who had leisure and money (however limited) to
spend.[12] The effect on London was profound. The period witnessed the growth
of a popular press, literature and music which catered to the cultural needs of
this class.[13] Department stores, shops, restaurants, tea-houses, parks, skating
rinks, theatres and latter cinemas flared up across the capital in response to their
demand and custom.[14] Sport, clubs, associations and adult educational institutes
grew at an unprecedented rate.[15] Holiday resorts erupted across the South-East

coast for the annual ritual of the weekly summer holiday of the clerk and his family.[16] What was gradually emerging in London was the slow growth of a consumer society which would transform the very fabric of the city.

Sadly this book does not concern itself with these wider issues. This will have to wait for a further study. This work focuses more narrowly on the professional lives of male clerks in London between 1880 and 1914. It is a study of the working lives of these men and the offices in which they worked. Its aim is to question the dominant argument in current historiography that these workers were in crisis in terms of income, job stability and promotion. It also aims to historically examine the lives of this key group of London workers who have so far escaped the notice of historians. In relation to occupation, it seeks to examine a number of areas including the work these men executed, the expectations they had towards this, and the impact of changes which took place during the period of study on their professional lives such as the rapid growth in the employment of female clerks and the growing application of technology. It also aims to analyse the late Victorian and Edwardian office. Relations between employers and employees, amongst the staff as a whole and between the institution and individuals, will be important areas of discussion. In addition, the impact of the growth of modern bureaucracies and the labour markets which they entailed will be examined. All were new to this era, and the strategies, ideologies and routines which clerical workers developed in relation to these, such as, for example, a stress on vocational education and qualifications, set important precedents for the future. It is these structural changes in office work in London which are key to the narrative of this study.

Literature Review of British Clerical Workers *c*. 1870–1914

Central to any discussion of the historical literature on the working lives of clerical workers in the late-Victorian and Edwardian period is the fact that it is pre-dated by a large corpus of social research. Before historians became interested in clerical workers there was an established academic vocabulary and field of reference for this group of workers which was broadly accepted by these writers. Research and debate by historians on the topic has consequently been informed by and is to a large degree an extension of a prior sociological discourse. Any review of the historical literature would therefore be incomplete without an examination of this academic commentary.

The central text in this debate, and perhaps the one which has academically introduced most individuals to clerical workers, are the writings of the German sociologist Max Weber. While Weber wrote little on clerical workers themselves, he was keenly interested in the modern breeding grounds of many of these individuals, the expanding bureaucracies in which they daily worked.[17] Weber was one of the first writers who perceived bureaucracies, both in the public and private sector, as a vital, transformative structure which was pivotal in the emergence of modern society. For Weber, bureaucracies and their rational goal-driven mechanisms were both institutional manifestations of modernity and a means by which this modernity could be realized. An understanding of the former could consequently disclose elements of the latter.

Weber argued that bureaucracies were the modern means of transforming social action – whether this was wealth creation or governance – into rational, organized action, which was superior to any other form of collective behaviour.[18] This rationality manifested itself in a number of ways. Bureaucracies were governed by abstract principles and formal rules rather than the sporadic whims or wishes of any one individual. The governance of bureaucracy was thus based on authority (itself earned by merit, qualifications and experience) rather than individual power. In terms of performance the rationality of bureaucracies displayed itself in their efficiency, controllability and calculability. This led to superiority in terms of decisionmaking processes, allocation of responsibilities, speed, precision, storage and retrieval of information, discipline, unity and continuity.[19] In addition, Weber discussed the relationship of the individual employee to the bureaucracy, the importance of the career within the bureaucrat's life and the centrality of academic qualifications for promotion. Many of these themes will be discussed in detail in this book, and, indeed, have formed the cornerstone of any academic discussion of bureaucracies and their clerical employees.

The first individual to produce a comprehensive survey of clerical workers in Britain was B. G. Orchard, a clerk from Liverpool and former head of the Liverpool Clerks' Provident and Annuity Association. Orchard's work, *The Clerks of Liverpool*, published in 1871, provided an in-depth contemporary study of Liverpool's office workers.[20] It presented information on the number of clerks working in the city, their social background, education, work opportunities, incomes, apprenticeships, employment agencies and associations, and their complaints. Orchard's chief aim was to refute those commentators who claimed that the clerical profession in Liverpool was in crisis. The study was filled with statistics and quotes from newspaper articles, individual clerks and employers, and tried its utmost to provide objective information.

Orchard's work was the first systematic study of clerks in Britain, and acted as a template for later research. Many of the areas he examined, such as the incomes of clerks, their promotional opportunities, the growth in scale of the office, qualifications and clerical combination were addressed by future historians and social commentators. Furthermore, much of the evidence he produced was used by authors such as Gregory Anderson to demonstrate decline in direct opposition to his original purpose.[21] This is ironic and ahistorical, given the intention of the work.[22]

In the 1930s an important book on clerical workers was published by the Marxist sociologist F. D. Klingender, The Condition of Clerical Labour in Britain. This argued that since the 1870s clerks, middle-class in origin, had undergone a process of downward mobility and by the mid-1930s had become working-class or 'proletarianized'.[23] Thus began the 'proletarian debate'. The debate was important to Marxists such as Klingender since it was seen as a major test of the accuracy of Marx's social prognostications. The rapid rise in clerical work in Britain made the work doubly relevant to this group.

Marx had argued that with the development and expansion of capitalism, divisions between capitalists and the proletariat would become more marked and openly aggressive.[24] In addition, the working class, in part with the absorption of pre-industrial groups such as the peasantry, small farmers, the petit bourgeoisie and independent craftsmen, would expand, and, conversely, the bourgeoisie would contract. These developments would hasten the revolution which would usher in Marx's communist utopia. In such a social nexus the rapid expansion of clerical workers since the latter half of the nineteenth century clearly posed a dilemma. How could the bourgeoisie be withering away when one of their key components was expanding every year? The answer to this conundrum was that clerks and clerical labour, always a vulnerable group on the fringe of the bourgeoisie, were with time, incrementally, but systematically, becoming more and more proletarianized.

Klingender, often relying heavily on the literature of clerical unions, used several basic arguments to demonstrate the social decline of office workers. He argued that with the increase in the scale of production of offices, their rationalization and the application of technology, clerical work had become deskilled. In relation to working conditions and remuneration, Klingender tried to show that vis-à-vis the working classes, clerks had suffered gradual, relative decline. Additionally, one of the chief benefits of clerical work, its stability, had in his opinion become a myth. Clerks, like the rest of the working classes, had become vulnerable to unemployment. For Klingender, the clear sign of the 'proletarianization' of clerical workers was their increasing attraction to trade unionism, a sure indication of their rejection of bourgeois values. It was this and the experience of the Slump and prolonged depression of the thirties which convinced him of the social demise of clerks.

A riposte to Klingender's argument came after the Second World War from the sociologist David Lockwood's, The Blackcoated Worker: A Study in Class Consciousness.[25] Reminiscent of Orchard's earlier work, Lockwood argued for the distinct status of clerical workers, their superiority to skilled worker and against any sign of social deterioration. Using a Weberian social critique based on notions of class, status and party, Lockwood argued that in terms of market situation – i.e. wages, job security and promotion prospects, work situation – i.e.

social relations between employers and managers and more junior staff, and status situation – i.e. the degree of prestige enjoyed by groups of workers in society, white collar workers enjoyed distinct advantages over blue collar workers. Clerks earned more, had greater security, received more perks such as company pension plans, had greater opportunities for promotion, enjoyed better relations with senior management, worked in smaller groups with more autonomy and received greater social respect. There was, hence, no evidence of proletarianization.

In addition to his research on clerical workers in the 1950s, in his opening chapter Lockwood wrote a brief historical account of clerical workers in the Victorian and Edwardian periods. He argued that many of the advantages that he had enumerated for blackcoated workers in the 1950s had been present half a century earlier. Clerks were more educated than blue-collar workers, they usually came from higher social backgrounds, their work was clean and involved the exercise of brain and not brawn. Their dress distinguished them from the mass of ordinary workers, they worked more closely with their superiors, enjoyed better chances of promotion and security, and were entrusted with more confidential work. As Lockwood noted, '... If economically they were sometimes on the margin, socially they were definitely part of the middle class. They were so regarded by the outside world, and they regarded themselves as such'.[26]

Klingender and Lockwood established the parameters for the academic discourse on clerical workers from the nineteenth century to the present. It was one which was primarily concerned with class, and which gravitated around the question of social decline. Were clerical workers on a downward social path, as a result of the onslaught of capital accumulation, rationalization, feminization and technology, or were they able to maintain barriers between themselves and the working classes beneath them? It was, and remains, a hotly contested debate as for many what was and is at stake is the nature of class society and its implications.[27] The whole debate was revitalized in particular by the publication of Harry Braverman's *Labor and Monopoly Capitalism*, which, while essentially repeating Klingender's arguments in the context of the United States, was greeted with broad acclaim and met with wide interest.[28]

Given the academic weight of such a debate it is hardly surprising that when historians finally began to look at clerical workers in the 1970s many of the above issues were incorporated into their studies. The first such work was Gregory Anderson's *Victorian Clerks*, a study of clerical workers in Liverpool and Manchester from the 1870s to 1914.[29] Anderson relied heavily on previous studies, and in relation to theory and to some extent content, his book was broadly a more modern rendition of Klingender. Anderson argued that clerks had earlier in the nineteenth century been an exclusive group, rewarded socially and financially for their command of the relatively scarce skills of literacy and numeracy. With the onset of a more intense stage of capitalism in the 1870s, however, clerical workers began to lose this privileged status. The rapid growth in the numbers of clerks, the use of youths and women, the Great Depression of the late 1870s, the growth and rationalization of work, the establishment of universal education, and the application of technology all contributed to this. Clerks' attempts to stave off their fall via associations and commercial education were dismissed as useless. By 1914, with a decline in income due to an over-supply in the clerical market, increased unemployment and deskilling, the difference between clerks and the working classes, particularly artisans, had been greatly narrowed.

No other major historical research devoted exclusively to clerical workers appeared until 1998 with the publication of R. Guerriero Wilson's *Disillusionment or New Opportunities? The Changing Nature of Work in Offices, Glasgow 1880–1914.*[30]

Wilson's work is effectively a transfer of Anderson's Victorian and Edwardian Liverpudlian and Mancunian clerical workers to Glasgow. Apart from some work on the changing nature of accountancy, the effect of increased Governmental regulation of clerical work, and the struggle between businessmen and educationalists over the direction of commercial education in Scotland, there is little to distinguish Wilson's basic argument from Anderson's. The story is the established one of decline and fall. The usual suspects of bureaucratization, office machinery, female clerks, falling incomes, unstable positions, and failed dreams of promotion all make their appearances. Invidious comparison between clerks and artisans is the warp and weft of its entire analysis. There is also a serious absence of reference to previous research on clerical workers, particularly in relation to the feminization of office work.

The entry of women in office work from the 1880s has attracted historical interest, especially from those interested in gender related issues. One of the first books to address the issue was Lee Holcombe's *Victorian Ladies at Work.*[31] Holcombe devoted two chapters of her book to female clerks in commercial offices and the civil service. She concentrated on the work which women carried out in offices, their working conditions, opportunities, and the salaries they received. The close connection between the feminization and mechanization of the office was highlighted, with the majority of women becoming typists. Holcombe also drew attention to the growth of commercial education which prepared many female clerks for office work and argued that, partly as a result of this, many of the first female clerks came from the middle classes. Female clerks' grievances, particularly their low pay and excessive hours were also discussed. Gregory Anderson's edited collection of essays on women clerks, *The White-Blouse Revolution*, expanded on many of the themes Holcombe had covered.[32]

Work on the feminization of the office has been developed to a much greater extent by the American social scientist Samuel Cohn in his work, *The Process of Occupational Sex-Typing.*[33] The study is a detailed historical analysis of the feminization of office work in two British businesses, the Great Western Railway and the Post Office, between 1870 and 1939. As the title suggests, Cohn was primarily interested in occupational sex-typing, the process by which work becomes gendered. As Cohn argued, clerical work is an excellent area to study as it is a good example of a profession which switched its sex-type from predominantly male in the nineteenth century to female in the twentieth.

Cohn applied dual labour-theory to clerical work, the idea that within work there are usually two cadres of employees. On the one hand there is normally a smaller group of individuals carrying out more skilled and well-paid work with firm chances of promotion, while on the other there exists a larger group of workers performing mechanical and low-paid work with few chances of mobility. Cohn argued that a gendered dual-labour market became established in the two companies he examined. Men moved into more skilled and better remunerated positions, while women were relegated to low-paid, and on the whole, relatively unskilled clerical positions. This thesis was investigated by Ellen Jordan in relation to the Prudential Life Assurance Company in London between 1870 and 1914, and was broadly corroborated.[34]

While Cohn's research was concerned primarily with the feminization of clerical work, it also produced important findings which directly contradicted the pessimistic research of Anderson and Wilson. Cohn's work suggested that male clerks' positions actually improved as a result of employing women. Promotion for male clerks was regular and incomes were increasing, not going down as has been almost universally accepted. In addition, in relation to the application of office machinery, Cohn argued that there was no overall deskilling affect. Whereas some items such as adding machines and filing systems may have replaced older skills, others, such as typewriters introduced new ones. In addition, much of the new machinery performed mechanical, routine work, thus leaving clerks free to concentrate on more demanding tasks.[35]

Cohn's work is important in the historiography of clerical workers as it shows that there are alternative accounts to those which support the proletarianization thesis argued by writers such as Anderson and Wilson. Such work is more akin to the work carried out by Lockwood. Such a positive view is also supported by historians who have concentrated on individual organizations and have paid attention to clerical workers in this period in such concerns as the Home Office, the Hong Kong and Shanghai Bank and the London County Council.[36] In these important case studies there is no evidence, either in terms of income, promotional aspects, feminization, or the introduction of technology that male clerks were suffering or were undergoing any form of proletarianization. In many respects the opposite was indeed the case.

The most complete rejection of Anderson *et al's* account of decline is an article written by Paul Attewell, 'The Clerk Deskilled: A Study in False Nostalgia'.[37]

Attewell's article challenged the theory of the deskilling and degradation of clerical work in the latter half of the nineteenth century on several major levels. His most important argument was that theories of decline advocated by Braverman and other writers have blurred the distinction between the clerks in crisis in the closing decades of the nineteenth century and the more prestigious, exclusive clerks of an earlier period. For Attewell much of what has been written on these earlier clerks was pure nostalgia, based on the experience of an atypical group of more affluent clerks. Citing comments on pre-1880s clerks, Attewell argued most clerical work had always been routine, repetitive and deadening. In addition, he argued that divisions of labour within the office and rationalization took place much earlier. In this sense, Attewell threw into question the whole bifurcated genealogy of clerks which was so central to the doctrine of the proletarianization of office work.

Attewell's and Cohn's work is important. Just as in the case of debates amongst sociologists concerning clerks and office work, there exist strong grounds for rejecting the claims of those who argue for the proletarianization of clerical workers towards the end of the nineteenth century. Cohn's work, for example, contains statistical evidence which demonstrates salary increases and career mobility in the General Post Office and Great Western Railway, something which is not reflected in the works of Anderson, Wilson and most other clerical *declinist* writers. But as yet, no full-scale study has been carried out to demonstrate this. Indeed, chapters and articles have continued to sporadically appear advocating decline, particularly in terms of career mobility.[38] There is thus a solid case for research which could test and further investigate market positions of clerks, particularly for London, which has been so strangely neglected.

The need for such revision has received support from an interest taken into the emergence of the career in clerical writers, particularly from Michael Savage and Alan McKinley.[39] Both writers have pointed to the rise of the career amongst clerical workers in the latter half of the nineteenth century, Savage writing on the Great Western Railway and McKinley examining Scottish banks. What is highly original in both writers is the role of the career as a disciplining device. Heavily influenced by Foucault's concept of governmentality, both writers argued that the career was developed as a means by which clerical workers could be controlled and power exerted by bureaucracies and those who ran them.[40] The career created a milieu in which clerks could be externally observed and examined. McKinley, for example, writes in detail on the role of bank inspectors reports on employees conduct and performance, and internally self-regulated and inspected.[41] Clerks learnt to accept the control of an emerging managerial class and discipline themselves in the hope of career advancement, professional status and material prosperity. However, as both writers noted, such an arrangement came at the cost of a loss of individual autonomy, institutional straitjacketing, and the danger for employers that a failure to provide a realization of expectations in the form of promotions could lead to large scale disgruntlement amongst clerks.[42] While both writers by no means reject the argument that clerical workers were undergoing professional and economic decline, the focus on the career is certainly an interesting angle to re-examine the position of clerical workers, and indeed suggests that for many clerical careers (and hence upward mobility) were a reality.

Another endorsement for revision has come from the publication of Jonathon Wild's book on the portrayal of the clerk in English literature, which focuses on London and the period 1880 and 1939.[43] There are strong overlaps between Wild's book and this book. In his introduction Wild himself states that a motivation for writing his book was the surprising neglect of the (London) clerk in historical writings during a period in which this group emerged so strongly both as an independent socio-economic group and as a genre of English literature.[44] Wild's book is a study of the emergence and development of the clerical novel. Over the period of his study the literary world saw the onset of a genre of novel in which the clerk was the protagonist and his home and office the centre-stages of the fiction.[45] Wild points to a plethora of novelists such as Arnold Bennett, Walter Besant, the Grossmiths, Jerome K. Jerome, William Pett Ridge, Shan Bullock, Frank Swinnerton and E. M. Forster whose fiction focused on the London clerk and his milieu, and which were widely read at the time. While Wild acknowledges a critique of the clerks by some writers such as Gissing and Forster, who created narratives of emasculation, intellectual and cultural pretension and decline, he also draws attention to a far more positive and even affectionate depiction of this group, particularly from authors such as Pett Ridge and Swinnerton, who were formerly clerical workers themselves. Of particular interest is Wild's chapter on the depiction of the clerk in the Edwardian office. Here Wild points to the genesis of a new type of 'super-' or 'ueber' clerk in the Edwardian clerical novel.[46] These were clerks who were large, physically strong, capable, singular in their ambition, and successful in terms of career. While for some authors, these clerks were depictions of ruthless capitalism and thus degeneration, their existence sits uncomfortably with an overall picture of clerical decline.

Finally, while the debate on class and the nature of office work in a modern capitalist society inherited from the sociological discourse is clearly relevant, there is an equally valid historical need to investigate what was taking place in offices. In terms of research, there has been too much dependence on newspaper articles, the magazines of clerical unions and associations (which tend to produce one-sided views), and an entire literature of complaint, rather than a comprehensive analysis of actual offices and the experiences of clerks. By the use of detailed investigation on London offices and by using oral evidence and diaries this study hopes to redress this balance. Finally, there has been too ready an acceptance of these complaints and a lack of healthy, genuine scepticism. There is a need to cross-examine these sources in order to gain a better insight into the actual conditions of office life in the years running up to the First World War.

Key Questions of the Book

This study agrees with the literature reviewed that important structural economic and social shifts took place which altered the nature of office work. Capital accumulation, technological innovation, and feminization all had fundamental implications for clerks and their working environment. Related to these were important developments in London's economy. These included the integration of domestic and international markets via changes in transport, communication and distribution, and the emergence of London as an international centre which played a leading role in orchestrating an emerging global economy transformed the capital. As a consequence, clerical work rapidly expanded in London. Side by side with this growth, some organizations such as the railways, banks, insurance houses, and national and local government quickly expanded, and office work became more methodical, impersonal and bureaucratic.

Where this study differs from much of the existing literature is in its approach to the implications of these changes. The principle question of this study is whether the overall effects were as traumatic as has been portrayed in much of the literature, or rather are writers such as Cohn and Attewell more accurate in taking a less jaundiced view? In this respect, the study is 'traditional' in that it examines areas such as income, work relations, technology, feminization, education, and trade unionism and organization which have been examined before. It is different, however, in that it does not accept the grand narrative of writers such as Klingender, Braverman and Anderson that these changes invariably had such an egregious impact on clerical workers.

Related to this is the question of how both employers and employees, companies and clerks, reacted to these changes. What strategies were devised by the former, for example, to maintain harmony in their organizations, to integrate clerks into the office, and to ensure that work was smoothly carried out? In relation to the latter, what approaches were developed to negotiate this new working environment? How did clerks' attitudes change towards work and how in turn did this affect these workers both socially and individually? Important contributions are made here by this study in relation to the emergence of internal labour markets, the growing importance of sport and social activities in work, the role of commercial education and the professionalization and growing career opportunities for clerical workers.

One final important question for this research is what did these changes mean for clerical work in London? Throughout the period of this study London was the biggest city in the world and clerical workers were its largest male occupational group. Yet there has been no study of London clerks, despite similar studies having been done for Liverpool, Manchester and Glasgow. A large part of this research has consequently been historical mapping, particularly in sectors such as banking, the railways and local and national government. In addition, how London's education system changed to deal with the growth in office work is an important focus of study.

Outline of the Chapters

The study is divided into eight chapters. They are as follows:

Chapter 1

An introductory chapter. A definition of 'clerk' is given for this period, based on the contemporary usage of the term. The chapter examines how changes in London's economy had radical implications for clerks, especially in terms of the clerical labour market. In addition, it reveals how businesses and government offices altered in relation to these changes. The emergence of the specialized office worker is documented.

Chapter 2

An examination of working conditions. Trends in clerical salaries in London throughout the period, job security and promotion are all investigated. The principal aim of the chapter is to refute Anderson's claim, and that of other pessimists, that conditions were worsening, and to show that they were improving.

Chapter 3

This chapter shows how the working environment radically changed for clerical workers. It is divided into two parts. Firstly, it examines how relations changed between the clerk and his employer. It argues that this relationship evolved from a master/servant affair based on patronage and dependence to an employer/employee arrangement based on efficiency, company loyalty and income. In the second part working practices are examined. It is argued that the period witnessed the establishment of more tightly defined divisions of labour in the office which encouraged the development of specialization. Such changes should not, however, be seen as an unfavourable development. For many, there is evidence that clerks during their career passed through a number of positions, thus developing their professional skills. The implications of the introduction of sport and social clubs into the workplace and the actual working regime in the office are also considered.

Chapter 4

The attitude of the clerk towards work is discussed. In addition to the security which office work provided and the income it secured, the clerical worker invested his work with other positive characteristics. These were the non-manual character of clerical work, professionalism, service, character, the pride of working in London and promotion. Some of these factors evolved from an earlier period, some were new. All were associated with the new working environment discussed in the previous chapter. The issues of job satisfaction and occupational masculinity will also be considered.

Chapter 5

The mechanization and feminization of the office is examined. This is an area which has received relatively wide coverage. Much of the chapter is consequently a re-examination of the question based on a review of existing work and new material. Did the introduction of new technology into the office and the advent of female clerks pose the threat to male clerks that has been posited, or was it really an opportunity for these workers? The chapter argues that the extent of the danger that these posed to men has been exaggerated. Technology removed repetitive work, and women were often used to operate this technology. Freed from these tasks, male clerks were given greater chances to carry out more diverse and well-paid work.

Chapter 6

This chapter has two related themes. The first is the effects of the expansion of education on the clerical worker. The second is the change in recruitment for office work in this period. A traditional argument is that the expansion of education had a negative impact on clerical workers by diluting their relatively scarce literary and numerical skills and opening their work up to a much wider pool of people. This chapter argues that there is a more complex picture. While elementary education expanded, so did secondary education. Since secondary education was an increasing requirement for clerical work, the effects of the spread of elementary education were mitigated. In the second part recruitment is considered. The introduction of formal qualifications and their effects on clerical recruitment are investigated. In addition, the continued existence of formal ties and patronage are discussed. An important argument here is that recruitment into London's clerical market was highly regulated. It is this which partially accounts for the lack of any collapse in clerical incomes.

Chapter 7

This chapter discusses commercial education and the clerk. The period witnessed a massive expansion of its provision in the capital. The extension of commercial education, the institutions where it was provided and its impact on clerical work is examined. In particular, the Polytechnics, the evening schools, the London School of Economics and Pitmans Metropolitan School are discussed. The examination of the effects of commercial education on clerical work takes place within the context of the introduction of new technologies and techniques into the office, the breakdown of more traditional training techniques and the growing professionalism of the work itself. Finally, the attitude of clerks to commercial education is considered. Within the framework of the overall argument of the research, it is suggested that the growth of commercial education had a considerable impact on clerical work and should be examined from the perspective of the structural shifts that were taking place within office work.

Chapter 8

The final chapter examines clerical trade unions and professional organizations. The chapter questions to what degree traditional definitions of trade unions are adequate to describe clerical organizations. Organizations such as the Civil Service Assistant Clerks Association, for example, were not officially trade unions but certainly acted like these groups. The aims of clerical unions and professional organizations, the strategies they deployed to achieve their goals, the relationship between the clerical worker and collective action, and the reasons for the limited and uneven appeal of unionization for clerks are all discussed. One principal argument of the chapter is that the traditional belief that the supposed individualism of the clerk precluded collective action should be dismissed. It was working conditions themselves that were the principal determinants of whether clerks organized themselves or not. The relative failure of clerical workers to organize is consequently a powerful argument against those who argue for a deterioration in office working conditions.

A Note on Sources

The study has drawn on a wide range of sources. Its originality lies in the fact that not only has it looked at new material, but it has also used evidence not employed before by historians of clerks, namely diaries and oral histories. These sources were invaluable in that they gave access to individual experience. Oral history and diaries acted as a counterweight to the rather didactic tones of more traditional sources such as trade union magazines and company reports which tended to follow certain agendas. While these sources do not offer a transparent view of the past, they do enable clerks to be looked at from different perspectives than has been previously possible.

The more traditional primary sources included company and governmental archives, journals and newspapers, governmental reports, contemporary material written on clerks and offices such as advice books, fiction, memoirs, and records of the National Union of Clerks. Some, such as the clerical journals, had been used before. Others, such as many company and government records had not been examined previously in relation to clerks. Material which had already been used by previous historians has been re-examined.

The focus of this study is male clerks in London. It does not purport to present what was happening nationally, nor does it do so in relation to female clerks, while not denying the historical legitimacy of either. Most of the sources are consequently metropolitan and male in scope. London was chosen because it contained the largest concentration of clerks in Britain. It is also where I am based. Men were chosen because much of the existing literature has personified them as victims which was something I wanted to question and re-examine. This does not mean that women are completely ignored. It does mean, however, that they receive attention only when the subject, such as technology or the feminization of the office, touches on an aspect which affected male clerks.

In sum, the bulk of the material used is oral material from interviews with clerical workers, diaries, and materials traditionally used by historians of clerks such as company archives, journals and government reports.

Finally, in relation to material used from the Royal Bank of Scotland Archives, namely that relating to the London and County Bank, the London and Westminster Bank, and Glyn's Bank, the names of clerks have been made anonymous due to company policy which prevents the names of former employees from being used. Consequently, these will be referred to as 'Clerk A', 'Clerk B', etc. Eight clerks, 'A' to 'H' have been so named.

The Interviews and Diaries

This material consisted of eleven interviews and five diaries. The interviews were with individuals who were either clerical workers for the period 1880–1918 or were children of such individuals, or were both, with some working as clerks after 1918. In total three were clerks, two were children of clerks and six were clerks and children of clerks. All except one individual lived and worked in London. The exception, Mr. Frederick Henry Taylor, was born in 1879 and lived and worked as a clerk in the potteries in Hanley in the North West.[47] He was chosen because of his educational background and because he worked in the manufacturing sector, a significant area of employment in London, but for which no oral/diary evidence was available. Eight of the interviewees were men and three were women.

Out of the interviews seven were from the Paul Thompson and Thea Vigne national series of interviews, *Family Life and Work Experience before 1918*. These were carried out in the early 1970s and concentrated on the home, community and work life of those interviewed. Three came from the *Millennium Memory Bank*, a series of interviews carried out in the late 90s across Britain to celebrate the millennium. These interviews also concentrated on work, family and community experiences. I carried out the final interview in 2001 with Jim Hancock, a former bank manager at the National Westminster Bank.[48] The interview was

concerned with Jim's father who began work at the London County and Westminster Bank in 1913 and remained there all his working life.

The Diarists

George Rose

George Rose's[49] diaries began in 1900 and ended in the 1950s and were highly
detailed. Rose wrote about everything from his love of music and his pursuit
of art to office politics and Regent Street Polytechnic. Rose was born in 1882
and grew up in the Essex Village of Chipping Ongar. His father was a tailor and
the diaries open with him working in his father's shop and doing some clerical
work in the village. In 1901 he began working as a clerk for the Commercial Gas
Company in Stepney, East London, where he was still working in 1914. In 1904
he moved to London and lived in a series of boarding houses in Kilburn and
South Hampstead. In addition to working as a clerk, Rose was an accomplished
amateur artist.

Daniel McEwen

Daniel McEwen[50] was a clerk in the Office of the Official Receivers in Bankruptcy attached to the High Court. His diary begins in 1887, the year of his
marriage to Ellen, when he was forty, and ends in 1910. The diary increasingly
focused on McEwen's accounts and much of its information is cursory. McE-
wen never had any children, worked in the same office throughout the diary
and recorded living in Camberwell at four different addresses. He was heavily
involved in the Co-operative movement, especially housing, and wrote and lectured on several topics including bankruptcy and social issues.

Andrew Carlyle Tait

Andrew Tait[51] lived in Ilford and worked as a clerk in the City from the age of
fifteen in James, Spicer and Sons, wholesale and export stationers. His father
owned a bookshop in the City. Tait was born in 1878. The diary itself covered
1893–4 and dealt predominantly with his move to Ilford, his early life there, his
education at Tyne Hall School in Ilford and his first few months working as a
clerk in Spicers. Though short, it gives an excellent insight into the education he
received, his interview at Spicers and work as a junior clerk in the City.

William Burgess Evans

William Evans[52] was born in 1867 and was the eldest son of Francis Evans, a
carpenter. He lived with his family in Hackney. Evans worked as a Solicitor's
Clerk in the City at Messers Ashurst Morris Crisp and Co. His diaries deal with
the period 1881–4 (his school and early working years) and 1889–1900. Evans

was a devout Christian and much of the content of his writings deals with his religious life, particularly his activities at Clapton Park Congregational Church. They also deal with him meeting his wife and the early years of his marriage. The diaries do, however, cover his professional life and are illuminating in that the deal with the working environment of a small office.

Sydney Moseley

Sydney Moseley[53] was born in 1888 and worked as a clerk at Waterlow & Sons, Accountants in the City between 1902 and 1909. He lived in Hackney, originally with his family and later on his own. On leaving Waterlow's Moseley worked for a short while as a salesman and then as a journalist, a career he followed for the rest of his working life. His diaries are different from the others in that they were published. Editing must therefore be taken into account. Nevertheless they provide important information on Moseley's working life, particularly his relationship with his colleagues and immediate superiors and his ceaseless attempts to gain promotion and at self-improvement. Like the other diaries, important information is also furnished on his family and social life.

A Note on Theory and Class

While the study is not explicitly theoretical, theory does play a part in informing the reading of the sources and in providing coherence for the overall structure of the thesis. The two main theories which are used are discourse analysis and the social stratification theory of Max Weber and Pierre Bourdieu. Each of these will be briefly discussed.

Discourse analysis is the idea that social action is primarily determined by prior ideological structures which express themselves in and determine language, thought, belief, social interaction, identity, knowledge and practice.[54] These structures for all intents and purposes determine reality as it is perceived by historical agents. Put in another way, social and economic factors do not ultimately produce what is perceived, or the cognitive structures which enable us to do so, but rather it is those very structures which perceive, organize, categorize, signify and make sense of our social/economic environment and give it a sense of everyday (ontological) and historical relevance.

Key to discourse analysis is the belief that individuals are only able to make sense of this reality through ideologically constructed filters. Since these filters or cognitive structures are historically constructed and change in relation to time and space the historian is able to analyse them and establish to some extent the basis of cognitive significance and thus understand and explain social action.

Important work has been carried out on discourse analysis by the French philosopher Michel Foucault.[55] One of Foucault's most important contributions was his analysis of the relationship between thought and institutions. Foucault, particularly in his work, *The Archaeology of Knowledge*, argued that many of our ideological structures and disciplines, especially in the modern period, are determined, produced and given legitimacy by institutions such as universities, educational institutes, hospitals, prisons, clinics and governmental bodies.[56] In order to understand discourse one must therefore examine the relationship between thought and the institutional environment wherein that thought is generated and exercised, a nexus usually referred to as Knowledge/Power.

While discourse theory generally informs the whole study there is one area where it is prevalent. This is the argument that an important development in the later half of the nineteenth century that motivated and structured clerks' attitudes and approaches to work was the growth in the belief and support for merit and meritocratic values. Merit, the idea that an individual's social and economic position should reflect the extent of his ability, became an integral part of clerical workers' outlook and ideology and produced a number of discursive practices and strategies which are discussed in this study. This included a belief in self-improvement and individualism, a commitment to education and the development of the self. While changes in the work environment were bound to lead to re-alignments by clerks in relation to work, it was a discourse based on merit and ability which many clerical workers adopted with which to negotiate their changed working environment and which subsequently had important historical consequences.

In relation to social stratification this study is informed by the works of Max Weber and Pierre Bordieu. Weber's basic model for social difference was one based on his three concepts of class, status and party.[57] These in turn reflected the economic, social and political factors which Weber saw as the bedrock of any given society. An individual's class position is essentially his market position. It referred to ownership and non-ownership, income, job security, promotion; in effect the life chances of an individual. Status, by comparison, is the social respect accorded to an individual due to his position in society. Due to the relative values of any given society some individuals, because of their respective functions, are given more social prestige than others. Finally individuals often belong to collective groups which are able to enhance their positions and give them more social leverage. By party Weber was not referring exclusively to a political entity but rather any collective body such as a union, a church or even an organization such as the boy scouts which operated to enhance the collective interests of its members. While class, status and party often coincide, a lawyer, for example, has a high market position, enjoys a prestigious social status and will belong to a number of professional and civil associations, there are many situations where this is not the case. A clerk's status, due to the fact that he performed non-manual work, was in many respects higher than his class position.

In addition, some clerks may have formed professional associations and trade unions in order to reinforce what were felt to be weak class and status positions in the period of this study.

Pierre Bordieu's work on social stratification, particularly his work, *Distinction*, drew on, developed and in many respects synthesized the ideas of Marx and Weber.[58] From the former, Bordieu derived the concept of capital, from the latter the above model of class, status and party. With the two Bordieu developed and established his key concepts of economic, social and cultural/intellectual capital. Any individual in society has a certain amount of these three capitals. It is their respective amounts and the relation between the three which determine social difference. One of Bordieu's most important contributions was that social groups often legitimate power derived from economic dominance by converting economic capital into cultural/intellectual capital. In this way they are able to reinforce their relative, hegemonic position in society and legitimize inequality. Key to this process is education. In addition, within this model, the focus of Bordieu changes from production, the traditional site of social stratification, to consumption. It is not simply what an individual produces that defines his relative social position, but equally important is what he consumes and how he does this.

The work and theory of Weber and Bordieu is highly apposite to this study of London clerks and enables it to produce an argument which is both original and distinctive from other works carried out on clerical workers in Britain. One of the basic contentions of this study is that London clerks between 1880 and 1914 belonged to a broad middle class and were able to reinforce their position within this group over this period. They did not suffer status anxiety nor entertain a false class consciousness. In terms of their market position, status and collective behaviour they were distinct from the broader working class. Their emphasis on education and cultural/intellectual capital and their consumption patterns were similarly singular, which in turn reinforced their social position. Most of these themes will be discussed in the following chapters.

Finally in relation to class, the contention that clerks were a part of the lower-middle class should be discussed.[59] While this study accepts this argument, it does so with two important caveats. The first is that the lower-middle class should be seen as an important and growing sub-section of the middle class rather than a class in its own right. There were far more things which fundamentally united the middle classes – the fact that they did not perform manual work, their relative stable employment, their emphasis on education and cultural/intellectual capital, and their belief in individualism – than divided them. While what distinguished the lower-middle class from other middle-class groups was their relative paucity of economic and to some extent cultural capital, one must emphasize that being middle class was never simply about money.

In addition, it is crucial to stress that throughout the period of this study it is extremely difficult to say what 'lower-middle class' actually meant. The group was undergoing a process of evolution, it was literally coming into social existence. As a result the phrase was rarely used and when it was there was much confusion and a fundamental lack of agreement on what the term actually denoted. This ambiguity was clearly evidenced during the Macdonnell Commission, 1912–13, established by the government to examine recruitment, pay, working conditions and promotion in the Civil Service, in a dispute between Lord MacDonnell, the Chair, and Herbert H. Elvin, General Secretary of the National Union of Clerks. While for Macdonnell professions such as solicitors, physicians, veterinary surgeons and stockbrokers were broadly consumed in the lower-middle class, Elvin insisted that these came from a higher social stratum:

> (MacDonnell) The majority of them [a list of the professions he had just read out] are lower middle class if I may express myself so? – I should not look upon a lawyer as belonging to the lower middle class.
> No. Not a solicitor? – Certainly I should not. I should not look upon a solicitor as belonging to the [lower] middle class.[60]

Due to the ambiguities and pejorative strains associated with it, most clerks preferred to simply call themselves middle class as did most social commentators.[61]

While the term 'lower-middle class' is relevant and was used to some extent, it should be handled with care by historians, with an appreciation that semantics develop and change over time. The degree of clarity and popularity that the term has enjoyed since the Second World War in Britain and elsewhere did not exist in the decades running up to the First World War.

A Final Caveat – Large Companies *versus* Small

One of the weaknesses of this study is its lack of attention to small businesses, and reliance on sources generated by large business. Many clerical workers in London in the period of this study worked in offices of one to ten clerks. As is argued in the first chapter, while middle-to-large scale companies were becoming more common they were still the exception. A study which focuses too much on the latter will consequently somewhat distort the general picture.

This emphasis on large businesses was due, as in often the case in histories which relate to business, to a lack of sources. Large institutions such as the railway companies, banks and the Civil Service left behind records for posterity, small concerns, unfortunately, usually did not. I was consequently able to find very few business archives of small companies.

It is here, however, that the oral sources and diaries are important. Many of the clerks in these sources, such as William Evans, worked in small businesses. They thus provide important insights into the world of the small office. In addition, some of the reports and advice journals referred to smaller operations and clerical work within these. While these sources do not give as complete a picture as might be hoped, they nevertheless provide some information which this study has attempted to utilize. In addition, subjects dealt with, such as education, and shifts in London's economy affected all clerks regardless of where they worked. In sum, the lack of sufficient attention to small businesses should be kept in mind while reading the study, while at the same time it should not detract too much from its overall relevance and significance.

1 CHANGING WORLDS AND CHANGING PEOPLE: A DEFINITION OF THE LATE VICTORIAN AND EDWARDIAN LONDON CLERK

Four Clerks

'Honour to whom honour is due', announced the *Clerk*, journal of the National Union of Clerks, in August 1890, in relation to the death of Mr A. T. Philpott, for some years clerk to the St George's School Board. In this role Philpott was responsible for elementary education in this London borough. Prior to this, he had been headmaster of the Russell Town British School in Bristol, a position in which he was said to have gained wide experience, and won the confidence and esteem of his brother elementary school teachers. He had also been a member of the Educational Council and had been recognized as an authority on elementary educational matters.[1]

In 1900 in the East End of London, A. Wilkinson was working as an Abroad Clerk for Trumans Brewery. He earned in that year a salary of £850 a year and would retire in 1903 on a yearly pension of £600.[2] As can be inferred from his salary, an Abroad Clerk was a position of great prestige and responsibility in the British brewing industry at this time. Contrary to what one would expect, Wilkinson spent most of his time outside the office. Most public houses in this period were tied to a brewery from which they received their beverages. Abroad Clerks acted as the link between the breweries and these premises. They were the eyes and ears of the breweries, inspecting their properties, guarding against adulteration and fraud, making sure orders and payments were collected and negotiating orders and the weekly returns of unsold beer. They were, in effect, the outdoor representatives of the brewing houses and their importance was such, for example, that a proposal was made in Trumans in 1908 to provide each of them with a car and driver.[3]

In 1902, on his way to school, Sydney Moseley, aged fourteen, bumped into an old classmate who had already 'gone out into the world'. Moseley was told by him that there was a vacancy as a clerk at the Counting House of Waterlow & Sons in the City and was advised to give up school and take the job. On that very day he skipped school, had his mother cut down to size for him (from his brother) an impromptu pair of trousers and that very day started working for Waterlows, joining the army of the tens of thousands of City Commercial Clerks. Moseley started on a salary of eight shillings a week and initially was responsible for calling out rows of figures, requisitions for various numbered items, to a fellow clerk who checked them off. Though starting off with high hopes and some commitment, Moseley quickly came to tire of his office work and gradual yearly increments. He resigned from Waterlows in May 1909, and following a brief flirtation with selling life policies for the Equitable Insurance Company went on to a successful lifelong career in journalism.[4]

Finally, in 1915 Lieutenant G. H. Lewis died while fighting on the Western Front in France. He had been given command of a Company on 25 September of that year. Before the outbreak of war in August 1914 Lewis had worked as a clerk in the Titles Department at the Prudential Assurance Company in Holborn Bars, London, having been transferred from 'L' Claim in 1913. He had been working for the company since 1903 and in the year of his transfer was earning £135 a year. Lewis, while working for the Prudential, had gained his LL.B. degree in 1909, taking honours in English Law, Colonial Constitutional Law and Roman Law. In 1913 he joined Middle Temple and commenced studying for the Bar where he took honours in each of his examinations. It was said that if his career had not met with so untimely an end he would have undoubtedly attained his Doctorate.[5]

Four very different men with four very different stories. Yet they shared in common the fact that they were clerks in London between 1880 and 1914. Did, however, the term 'clerk' in these examples, and thousands others like them, refer to the same type of work? Was there some common denominator in this period which bound all clerks together in one occupational field, in the same way as there was for school teachers, for example? Additionally, if this was the case, how close was this signification, and conversely, how elastic should one be in its application?

This chapter aims to answer these questions. It will first argue that there were two very different uses of the term clerk, which though overlapping were mutually exclusive. One referred to a holder of office, the other to an individual who worked in an office. Having looked at this it will examine the later group in more detail. It will argue that increasingly in this period internal and dual labour market came to operate in the clerical market in London. On the one hand were well-paid clerks who carried out responsible and often skilled jobs which offered good prospects for advancement. On the other were much more routine positions, what were referred to as 'mechanical' jobs which carried with them lower salaries, status and chances of promotion. Following this it will look at how the economy and the employment market for clerical labour in London changed, paying particular attention to structural changes in the City of London, local and national government, and amalgamations in the service industries. In the latter half of the nineteenth century the City was transformed into a global centre of trade and finance, the State began to take on larger role in people's lives, and across a swathe of the tertiary sector there were a number of amalgamations which produced an ever increasing number of large scale bureaucratic organizations. In all these areas the work of businesses and government institutions became more complex. As a consequence there was a growing demand for specialized workers, and at the same time, with the increase in volume of work in many of these institutions, a growing demand for routine office labour. It was, therefore, as a result of these structural changes in the economy and the labour market that internal and dual labour market emerged, an understanding of which is crucial to define clerks and clerical work in this period. The chapter will end with an examination of clerical work in the above three areas, paying particular attention to the specialization of clerical labour.

The Clerk Defined

In 1909 Edward A. Cope, a clerk himself, published his book, *Clerks, Their Rights and Obligations*.[6] Noting that 'The clerical career has a great past behind it: it is quite safe to say that it has a great future before it.'[7], Cope, in his first chapter, proceeded to give a comprehensive historical survey of clerks in which he traced the various contemporary uses of the term. Cope discovered clerks as far back as ancient Assyria and Egypt. The term clerk itself originated in the middle ages, all writing and accounting work being carried out by the clergy or clerics of the Church.[8]

Gradually there came to be a differentiation between different classes of clerks. Some were officers of the church who were not required to be priests. Thus there developed a distinction between 'clerks in holy orders' and other kinds of clerks. Over time the position became more secular, progressively separating itself from the church,

> ... It came to be applied as the designation of the 'officer who has charge of the records, correspondence, and accounts of any department, court, corporation, or society, and who superintends the general conduct of its business,' which is one of the definitions given in the 'New English Dictionary.' We use the word extensively in this sense, as for example in the titles 'Clerk of the Household,' 'Clerk of the Kitchen,' 'Clerk of the Crown'; and 'Town Clerk ...'[9]

Finally came the everyday use of the term, summed up in Dr Murray's definition in the *Chambers Dictionary* as, 'One employed in a subordinate position in a public or private office, shop or warehouse, to make written entries, keep accounts, make fair copies of documents, do the mechanical work of correspondence and similar clerky work.'[10] Cope noted that although the final definition in the evolution of the term was by far the most commonly used, the other older definitions had not been ousted. There were still Clerks of Assize, Clerks of the Peace, and also Clerks in Holy Orders.

Clearly in the four clerks who introduced this chapter, Mr A. T. Philpott and A. Wilkinson were clerks in the office holder sense. Both had responsible positions, and would have been in charge of a large number of staff. A good example of this definition was The Clerk of the Peace, an office abolished in 1888 with the creation of County Councils. The Clerk, who can be seen as the link between the Crown and the Quarter Sessions in the counties throughout England and Wales, was the key legal county official before reform. He advised the sessions on issues of law and administration and kept its minutes. Throughout the year his responsibilities included drawing up indictments, lists of deeds and enclosure awards, and keeping records such as lists of poor law commissioners, candidates for posts of county officers and the decisions of arbitrations of corn rents. In addition to this, he was responsible for supplying copies to the public and correspondence in matters relating to the County and the Sessions. For performing these duties to the public he was entitled to a fee according to a fixed scale. With the abolition of the Quarter Sessions and the office his functions in the new County Councils went to the Clerk of the Council. The Clerk maintained his legal, administrative and advisory role and in addition became responsible for the ever growing personnel of the administration. He was by far the most senior officer.[11] In the capital, for example, following the abolition of the London County Council in 1965, he became the Director General of the new G.L.C.

It is with the other definition of clerk, an individual who held a subordinate position in an office, that this study is concerned. The term, however, was, and has remained, problematic. It was felt that it was not elastic enough to cover the panoply of uses to which it was applied. As the magazine, the *Office*, commented in October 1889, '… 'clerk' is a general term admitting of no precise definition'.[12] Having noted that the term had become completely revolutionized in meaning, the article commented that to some the word meant anyone employed in an office in any capacity apart from the manager, while to others the cashier, bookkeeper, stenographer and anyone not doing work of a purely routine nature would also be excluded. It was, in the opinion of the article, this failure to come to a precise definition that made the creation of a general clerical union impossible. To make matters worse, as the term was felt to have a pejorative undertone, many people who were working in a clerical capacity refused to apply the term to themselves.

The *Office* adopted the latter definition given above, and not wishing to upset the sensibilities of its readers preferred to use the phrase 'office workers'. In many respects, however, this definition was too exclusive. The nomenclature 'clerk' continued to be used throughout this period, and indeed up to the Second World War and beyond to refer to office workers encompassing virtually all grades of work both skilled and unskilled. *The New Survey of London Life and Labour* in 1934, for example, stated, 'The term "clerk" is applied to persons engaged in a large number of heterogeneous occupations of very different character and grade, the only common feature being that they work at a desk in an office.'[13] One important caveat that the above work in its chapter on clerical work contributed to a definition was that, ' ... clerical work ... is not an industry in itself, but an occupation or service common to a large number of industries, and generally speaking it may be distinguished from other commercial occupations by the fact that its technique is essentially concerned with methods of recording and accounting rather than with the nature of the transactions to which the records and accounts relate'.[14]

Although it was frequently pointed out that what precluded any precise definition of the term clerk was the numerous industries and services they were spread across, it should be remembered that the work being carried out in all these areas was for many essentially the same; recording, accounting, registering, retrieving and corresponding. The London clerk Arthur Whitlock, for example, during his fifty-one years of clerking applied many of these clerical skills in the Army and Navy stores, marine insurance, the War Office, the Hearts of Oak Benefit Society and the National Insurance Board.[15]

The Dual Labour Market

The Office did, however, have a point. There had been a revolution in clerical work. It was a change which explains the differences between G. H. Lewis and Sydney Moseley. Lewis worked in the Titles Department of the Prudential, a position which required legal training and specialized knowledge. If he had survived the war he would, undoubtedly, have progressed well in the company. Sydney Moseley's work on the other hand was less specialized. Although by the time he left Waterlow's in 1909, after nearly seven years service, he was doing some accountancy work and paying out wages, his work was still of a fairly routine nature. 'Oh! How hard it is to get on!' lamented Moseley in May, 1905, 'Sometimes I feel as if I can stand it no longer and go along recklessly. Piles and piles of Requisitions – dreary, rotten REQUISITIONS; just calling out numbers endlessly – '4–5: 12–250' – and so on.'[16]

By the 1870s, internal labour markets appeared in mid- to large scale employers of clerks in London.[17] These internal markets offered lifelong employment, career structures and welfare benefits in return for loyalty, hard work and commitment. Internal labour markets will be discussed in more detail in the next chapter in the context of company welfare programmes and the evolution of the office career. For the purposes of this chapter it is important to note that in many of these markets a two-tier system emerged in clerical work. On the one hand were clerks whose work tended to be of a more specialized order, who were usually better educated and came from higher social backgrounds. These earned relatively high salaries and had good promotional prospects throughout their careers. On the other hand, there were clerks whose work was much more routine and demanded less specialization and skill. They were accordingly less well paid, had fewer prospects and were recruited usually from a lower social class.[18] Many of these individuals, as in the case of the Great Western Railway (GWR), were youths or 'Junior Clerks'.[19] While this two-tier or dual labour clerical labour market was primarily structured by skill and to a lesser extent age throughout the period of this study and beyond, it increasingly became gendered. This is perhaps one of the key developments in the history of the office. As Samuel Cohn and Ellen Jordan have argued, from the 1870s onwards, women were increasingly used in offices for secondary clerical work. Their higher education, the relatively higher social status of applicants, their cheapness and most importantly, their readiness to work for relatively short periods of time, made them ideal for employers for this type of labour.[20] This will be discussed in greater depth in Chapter 5.

One of the best examples of a dual labour market can be seen in the Civil Service. As far back as 1855 the Northcote-Trevelyan Report had recommended a division of labour in the civil service based on those who carried out intellectual tasks and those concerned with more mechanical work. The Playfair Commission in 1875 also spoke of the need of, '… making a distinction between those classes of clerks who do the higher and more responsible work, and those who do the inferior work.'[21] As a result of its recommendations an Order in Council of 12 February, 1876, established the Lower Division (subsequently the Second Division in 1890) and, perhaps emulating the GWR, a class of boy clerks. Thus four classes were established; Administrative Officers and Higher Division Officers who were responsible for the administration of the Civil Service, and a clerical grade of Lower Division and Boy Clerks who were responsible for the day-to-day running of the Service. By 1914 the situation had become even more complex. In the clerical grades there were now Intermediate and Second Division Clerks, responsible for the higher grade work, and below them Boy Clerks, Assistant Clerks and Women Clerks who carried out more routine tasks. The 1914 Report of the Royal Commission on the Civil Service distinguished between administrative, clerical and routine work.[22] The difference between the latter two are a clear example of the dual labour market that was operating at this time in the clerical grades of the Civil Service. Candidates for the Second Division tended to come from higher clerical or shopkeeper backgrounds, had received some secondary education, had to sit an examination which reflected this, and had a pay scale from £70 to £300 with opportunities for higher staff positions and even entry (though very rare) into the First Division. Assistant

Clerks, on the other hand, sat an easier examination, had a lower standard of education, and had a pay scale of £55 to £150, with access to some superintendent positions within the grade.[23]

Any account of the distinctions between clerical workers must therefore take note of the emergence of this dual labour market. As a saying of the period went, 'There were clerks, and there were CLURKS'.[24] While it is true that something similar to this had emerged in The East India Company before 1812, it is the increase in its application in the later part of the nineteenth century that signals such an important fissure in the clerical profession. Its heralding of women into the offices would for many radically reconfigure the nature of office work. This is not to say of course, that the dual labour market was operating everywhere. Such a system may have developed more slowly in smaller offices. In addition, it was possible for clerks within these offices to work their way up the various grades, from running messages and copying manuscripts, to keeping accounts and writing correspondence, and finally to positions of trust within the office and management.[25] This, in fact, for many was an essential part of clerical work. Dual markets were not always so firmly established as in the Prudential, the GWR or the Civil Service. It was possible, with perseverance, hard work, and some luck to switch from one side to the other. As Moseley, himself, wrote in his diary at the beginning of 1908, '... If I were to settle here in this Counting House, I could easily get somewhere.'[26] Boundaries were still fluid, clerical structures were constantly evolving. What is important in relation to the dual labour market was, however, that it was a growing trend which was incrementally having an important affect on the clerical profession.

Changes in Economic, Company and Governmental Structures

What was producing the emergence of such a clerical market in London? In order to answer this question, analysis will focus on changes in the capital's office economy. In addition, companies and governmental departments should be examined. Changes in clerical work did not take place in a vacuum. They were to a large degree reflections of changes that were taking place both in the economy and in company and government administrative structures.[27] Between 1870 and 1914 seismic changes happened in both areas which were to have far reaching implications for clerical work.

Between 1871 and 1911 the number of people working in the City of London increased from 200,000 to 364,000, while the number of people residing there fell from 75,000 to 20,000.[28] At the same time the actual makeup of the working population was beginning to change. Between 1881 and 1911, for example, the total percentage of people employed in manufacturing in the City dropped from 30 per cent to 18 per cent. Similarly the proportion of individuals involved in the storage and distribution of physical commodities and trading fell from 38 per cent to 27 per cent. In comparison the percentage of workers involved in finance grew from 4 per cent to 9 per cent and those engaged in internal functions who serviced the needs of the City such as retail and transport grew from 10 per cent to 28 per cent.[29]

What is clear from these figures is that the City was never simply a financial or trading centre. Printers had the largest workforce in 1911 with 38,249 workers, followed by the Drapery and Allied Trades with 35,000.[30] It is also clear from the above figures that finance was gradually becoming more important, while manufacturing and commodities were becoming less so, with a large increase in the number of firms catering to the needs of those working in the City across a whole range of services from office fitters to hairdressers and chiropodists.[31] Concurrent with these changes was an increase in world trade. Total world exports at prices in 1981 ($ Million) have been estimated to have grown from 4,747 in 1870 to 18,697 in 1913.[32]

These changes were not unconnected. Nor in fact were the changes in the nature of the work that was being carried out in the City. Studies by Ranald C. Michie and David Kynaston have given a comprehensive portrayal of changes in the way the City operated in the latter half of the nineteenth century.[33] Michie, for example, has shown that over this period the City became less a centre for manually handling goods and more a centre for organizing world trade. In relation to commerce, office trade as opposed to physical trade became more important to the City. Much of this had been due to the communication revolution which had preceded, and continued apace during this period. The development of the telegraph, railways, steam powered refrigerator ships, and later on the telephone and the wireless meant that an increasingly integrated national and more importantly global economy no longer needed intermediate centres for trade. Producers and consumers were more and more able to conduct trade between themselves. As Michie writes, 'Increasingly continental Europe ... drew its supplies of wheat, wool, rubber and copper directly from the producing countries and not via London, thus avoiding the costs and inconvenience of trans-shipment. Ports such as Antwerp, Amsterdam and Hamburg were all major rivals to London in an international competition for handling the world's trade, especially Europe's exports and imports.'[34] Similarly at home competition from Britain's regional ports, some closer to centres of production such as Liverpool, led to a decrease in the share of Britain's trade that London handled. By 1913, London was handling only 19 per cent of British exports and 33 per cent of imports, measured in value.[35]

While London lost out in this area, it gained in others. With the emergence of a globally integrated economy there was a need for a single centre to act, in Kynaston's words as, '... fulcrum and mediator of the whole process'.[36] The very changes in technology which had led to a relative downturn in the importance of London's power to physically direct world trade paradoxically led to an upturn in its ability to control it. As Michie has noted, '... The result of this communications revolution was that it became possible to conduct a global trading business from an office in the City, maintaining constant contact supplemented by rapid visits and the receipt and despatch of samples and catalogues.'[37] Increasingly merchants, brokers and agents from both Britain and abroad gravitated to the city organizing and controlling world trade, most of which never touched Britain's shores. Not only trade itself, but shipping, finance and a whole host of ancillary services fundamental to world trade such as insurance, law and accountancy located themselves in the Square Mile.

While such developments were going on apace in the City, equally rapid changes were taking place in Whitehall, local government in London, and throughout Britain as a whole. From the 1870s the State began increasingly to intervene in the social and economic lives of its citizens. Education, housing, public health, work, children's welfare and other areas increasingly came under its remit. Analogous to world trade, as society became more complex, there was increasingly felt to be a need for it to be centrally regulated and controlled. This was accompanied by a general weakening in the belief in the doctrines of lassiez-faire and the overall consensus that a strictly non-interventionist government was the best answer for society's problems.[38] Such a change in outlook led to a growth in governmental administrative offices. Non-industrial civil service staffs (a large proportion of whom worked in the Post Office) grew from 53,874 to 172,353 from 1871 to 1911, and following the unprecedented spate of pre-war Liberal Government social legislation to 280,900 in 1914.[39] For the civil servants who worked in Whitehall, Somerset House and other central governmental offices, work grew in complexity and scale. At the Home Office, for example, Jill Pellew has shown an increase in the number of registered papers which annually had to be dealt with from 18,659 in 1862 to 71,153 in 1909. This administration was continually having to battle with the Treasury to increase the workforce in order to deal with such growing responsibilities. Papers by the then Home Secretary, Herbert Gladstone, show the achievements of the Home Office between 1906 and 1909 and give an impression of the scale of its activities. The department had been involved in the passage of forty-two bills, including the 1906 Workmen's Compensation Act, the 1907 Factory and Workshops Act, the 1908 Prevention of Crime Act and the 1908 Children Act. It had been involved in three royal commissions, ten select committees, twenty-one departmental committees and three special commissions.[40] Each major piece of legislation naturally resulted in an increased workload for the staff. The number of second division clerks at the Home Office increased from eleven in 1877 to thirty-three in 1914, while the number of more junior assistant clerks rose from nine in 1896 to fifty-four in 1914, and the number of boy clerks from four to thirty-seven.[41]

Yet it was not just central government that experienced growth. Local government increased at an equally rapid pace. In 1888 County Councils were established and with it the London County Council (L.C.C.). For the first time in its history the capital had a popularly representative body. In 1894 under a further local government act urban district councils were also established. For the growing suburbs around London such as Ilford and Acton, home to many of the capital's clerks, this was a major shot in the arm in fostering growth, improved services and local identity.[42] Finally in 1899 the vestries were abolished and replaced by modern borough councils. Within eleven years nothing less than a revolution had taken place in London's local government. Alongside these structural reforms these various councils were given teeth to tackle the pressing social problems of the then largest city in the world. Education, transport, housing, public health, gas, water, lighting, food inspection, libraries, parks and a whole host of other social amenities became the responsibility in one shape or form of these various local bodies and their officials. It was indeed, as Tony Byrne has argued, the beginning of the golden age of local government.[43]

Finally any examination of changes in the economy of London in relation to clerical work must take note of the amalgamation movement which was taking place in many service industries. This is doubly important to emphasize as much of the work that has been done on the amalgamation movement in Britain in this period has concentrated on manufacturing industry. Consequently the picture one often has is that this was a period of lost opportunity for British industry to rationalize itself in preparation for the coming global competition of the next century.[44] While this may be true for some areas of the national economy such as cotton and steel, nothing can be further from the truth in relation to a broad spectrum of service industries such as retail banking, insurance, railways, retail, marketing and distribution which amalgamated and centred themselves in London.

The Growth of Bureaucracy

Between 1870 and 1914 large scale mergers took place in the banking, insurance, railway, transport and utility companies. All of these were major employers of clerical workers. Several factors contributed to the process. One was an increasingly integrated domestic economy, itself the product of the communication revolution mentioned earlier, which enabled economies of scale and scope to be realized.[45] Another was growing competition and a third was legislative changes which facilitated the growth of joint-stock companies. The end result of all of this was the emergence of large-scale bureaucratic companies which almost invariably came to have their headquarters in London.

In no area was the effects of amalgamation so deeply felt as in the joint-stock banks. Between 1870 and 1914 these banks replaced private country and town banks as the predominate form of banking in the UK By 1914 regional banking networks had spread over the whole of the country. As J. F. Davis wrote in 1910,

> The last thirty years had witnessed a vast change in the growth and relative magnitude of the London Joint Stock Banks. At the beginning of the period there were only three Joint Stock Banks with a capital of £1,000,000 each, and with current and deposit accounts of more than £20,000,000 ... There are now nine Banks whose average capital is £3,000,000 each, and whose deposit and current accounts exceed an average of £50,000,000 ... These changes have been brought about almost entirely by amalgamations.[46]

The corollary of such increases in capital was an increase in staff (clerks and senior management). In 1909 Lloyd's Bank had over 2,880 staff, the London County and Westminster 2,032. By 1914 the latter had grown to 3,250 though this was eclipsed by the 5,000 who worked for The Midland Bank.[47] Although most of these worked in the branch networks, a significant proportion worked at head office or had passed through it at one point in their careers. The merger of the London and County and London and Westminster in 1909, for example, produced a joint central administration of over 600 personnel.[48]

The extent of the amalgamation movement in London in relation to office work can be seen in the following examples. In 1902 The Metropolitan Water Act created the Metropolitan Board with 3,463 staff, 556 of whom were officers.[49] The Port of London came into existence by act of parliament in 1909 merging the various ports and staffs of the Metropolis.[50] In 1911 the Prudential's headquarters, Holborn Bars, had a staff of over 2,000.[51] Paddington, the headquarters of the Great Western Railway, employed over 1,300 staff in 1922.[52] Yet the epithet of largest office in London went to the Railway Clearing House located in Seymour Street just off Euston Station, with a workforce of over 2,500 clerks in its central office in 1914.[53] In addition to this the Civil Service, the L.C.C. and some London borough councils were large scale employers of clerical staff.

This is not to argue that by the eve of the First World War London clerks had been transformed into thousands of employees of large scale bureaucracies. The majority of London clerks still worked in small to medium sized offices of no more than twenty or thirty staff. According to the 1911 Day Census of The City of London, for example, 3,811 firms of Agents, Exporters and Importers had a total of 33,002 employers and employees, giving an average of 8.66 per firm.[54] Many City Commercial firms were able to possess small staffs and still enjoy large economies of scale via the existence of London's various exchanges, information and news distribution agencies and a network of agents and specialists. In addition, large numbers of London's commercial clerks worked in thousands of small workshops that predominated in the capital's booming manufacturing sector, yet even here there were major exceptions such as the Woolwich Arsenal.[55] London's commercial, financial and industrial base was too vast to neatly summarise. The fact remains, however, that a substantial number of clerks did work in large scale bureaucracies, and their number continued to grow. Out of the sixteen London clerks looked at in this research from diaries and interviews, for example, seven can be said with some certitude to have been in the latter category.

Clerical Specialization

The emergence of the City as the control centre of world trade, the growth of central and local government, the amalgamation movement in large sectors of Britain's service industries, all combined to produce in the clerical profession a growing demand for specialized clerical labour. In this final section, clerical work in all these sectors will be examined. Particular attention will be paid to how these changes led to an increased demand for skilled clerical labour, with a brief discussion of the emergence of a class of lower skilled clerical workers at the end.

As the City increasingly became a centre of world trade and finance, work became more complex. In relation to the various markets which comprised the City, for example, Michie argues, 'Within the growing complexity of both the national and international economy there developed a need for specialist intermediaries to act between these intermediaries.'[56] In 1909, for example, Antony Gibbs and Sons Ltd, merchants and foreign bankers shut down their Liverpool offices and moved its work and staff to London. One of the members of staff affected by these changes was a clerk named Frederick Hunt. Hunt worked in the Produce Division of the office as a correspondent clerk. In that year he was 55 years old, earned £225 a year and had been with the company since 1880. Hunt was by this period head of the Australian and West Indian Department and was responsible, as his title suggests, for its correspondence. In addition to this he was in charge of part of the correspondence of the West Coast Department. He had also for nearly a year, due to the illness of a colleague, had the selling of 'G & Co.'s', presumably a client company of the firm, produce in his own hands.[57] Arthur Whitlock was also progressing well. Since leaving the Army and Navy Stores he had been working for a Marine Insurance Firm covering cargoes of meat and eggs from countries such as Denmark, Russia and Argentina. By 1914 he was in charge of the Policy Department concerning goods from Argentina.[58]

The growth of specialization in commercial clerks was attested to by the content of a host of advise manuals to clerks who told their readers that a knowledge of the 3 Rs was no longer sufficient to 'get on' in the clerical world. F. B. Crouch, for example, advised young school boys eager for a career in the office that,

> Our commercial relations all over the world at the present day are so extensive, that most firms in this country have business connections, to a greater or less degree,

abroad, and, as French is the foreign tongue most in vogue, German ranking next, the boy who is acquainted with either or both of these languages is not likely to have to wait long for a berth as the boy would who is unfamiliar with them, and has a chance of obtaining a better one.[59]

Hazlehurst Greaves went further. Beginning with the dictum that,

> The clerk of today bears no relation to the individual of thirty years ago, when a knowledge of the 'Three R's' formed the indispensables of success. The present-day clerk who desires to succeed must have knowledge: he must know everything concerning the business in which he is engaged, and must act as consulting library and encyclopaedia to his principal, further, he must be acquainted with all the short cuts to business success.[60]

He went on to list the various skills that a clerk who wanted promotion now needed. These included a knowledge of history, particularly that of wars and the growth of free trade, a knowledge of the commercial relations which then existed between Britain and the Foreign Powers, a grasp of commercial geography, proficiency in shorthand and bookkeeping, and of course a command of modern languages. For Greaves, however, these were just some of the basic skills that the aspiring clerk now needed.[61] While most clerks did not directly conduct business, it was emphasized that specialization was needed to assist efficiently their masters and employers in these increasingly complex transactions. In order to operate effectively, these professions became more and more dependent on a group of specialist clerks who were able to supply them with the expert back-up they required.

Specialization was equally evident amongst civil servants. Increasingly complex legislation to meet the demands of a more multifaceted and sophisticated society resulted in the growing need of specialized staff to administer and execute these enactments. In addition, more and more was being demanded of civil servants. The 1914 Civil Service Commission, for example, noted that,

> In recent years the activity of the legislature (especially in connection with problems arising out of the conditions of social and industrial life) has placed a large number of new Acts upon the Statute Book. These Acts are in some cases of extreme complexity and impose upon the Department administering them obligations of a serious nature, which occasionally go far towards obliterating the distinction hitherto maintained between legislative, executive, and judicial functions.[62]

Giving evidence to the Commission, the Chairman of the Board of Customs and Excise stated,

> The work of a taxing department today is an absolutely different thing from what it was twenty, or even ten, years ago. In those days Parliament, when it fixed a tax, settled every detail, leaving to the department only the administration of the tax on the lines laid down by Parliament. The tendency of Parliament nowadays ... is to lay

down only principles to the discretion of the department. I think it is fair to say that a department like mine nowadays exercises powers which are often judicial and which sometimes get near to being legislative.[63]

These points have been echoed by Pellew in her study of the Home Office. Laws increasingly contained only the fundamental principles from which technical or administrative details were to be worked out and applied by civil servants. 'Officials', Pellew writes, 'were delegated powers to make rules made by a third party (such as managers of mines or prison authorities).'[64] Second Division clerks in their support role were mainly responsible for the organization of incoming and outgoing correspondence, the accounts of the Home Office, the metropolitan police courts, 'special police', and the reformatory and industrial schools, and preparing statistical reports covering all the aspects of the department's work for governmental and public consumption. All of this needed technical and often legal knowledge.[65]

Such growth in responsibility and administrative skill was mirrored among the officials of the L.C.C. Following its establishment in 1889 the L.C.C. embarked on new projects, and applied itself to the existing responsibilities of the former Metropolitan Board of Works with increased vigour. In the 1890s it began an innovative scheme of slum clearance and public housing, in addition to establishing its own Public Works Department. In 1898 it took over London Tramways, and in 1904 it took over the responsibilities of the London School Board. This expansion witnessed a corresponding rise in it labour force. In 1890 there were 3,369 council employees, 12,000 in 1904 and 35,316 in 1905. In 1909 the L.C.C. claimed to be London's largest employer.[66]

Such a volcanic rise in its workforce and responsibilities resulted in a corresponding addition to its central official staff at its headquarters in Spring Gardens, just off Trafalgar Square in Central London. In 1889 164 officials worked at the L.C.C.'s central offices, in 1899 this was 412, and in 1905 stood at 1,188.[67] A corresponding increase was seen in its temporary official staff, responsible for the more routine aspects of office work such as typing and filing and temporary increases in work, who later became part of the Minor Establishment in 1902, a body akin to the Assistant Clerks of the Civil Service. Their numbers in 1895 stood at 120 and rose to 540 in 1905.[68]

The work of the officials of the L.C.C., who would later in 1904 become part of the Major Establishment was no less skilled than that of the Second Division, and in some cases more so as there was no higher grade above them. Similarly though the work of the Minor Division was of a lower clerical grade its work was becoming increasingly technical with more of it being devoted to permanent rather than temporary work. An excellent document which provides a valuable insight into the work of these officials is a detailed report which the Head of the

Statistical Department, Laurence Gomme, sent to the Establishment Committee in 1898. The report dealt with the work of his department and included an outline of its responsibilities, the role and duties of each officer within it, and the work they had been occupied with in the current week. The department dealt with a whole range of responsibilities which included; the compilation of the ongoing volumes of 'London Statistics', work on County Rates, returns for fire insurance companies, the certification of rates and taxes payable by the Council, the accounts and charges of electrical lighting companies, the distribution of representation on vestries and district boards, reports and returns for Council bills in Parliament, and the Council's library.

The department had sixteen established officials, excluding Gomme, and eleven temporary clerks. Of the sixteen permanent staff, all but three juniors had their own specialized areas. A Mr D. B. Roche, for example, worked on water statistics, and dealt with royal commission and Parliamentary matters affecting questions other than County taxation. His colleague Mr A. F. Hoare was responsible for electric lighting companies' accounts, fire invoice returns, and assisted his colleagues Messers J. C. Spenseley and H. H. Beadle in analysing accounts in connection with London statistics, telephones and local taxation matters. Beadle, himself, that week had been working on the Expenditure and Taxation Returns for 1896–7, analysing the accounts of vestries and central bodies, dealing with forms for the analysis of local accounts, working on rates payable by the Council, and dealing with the deficiency of the Poor Rates for Tower Bridge.[69]

In both national and local government in London there is thus evidence of increasing specialization and expertise. With growth in responsibility and scope came an increasing professionalism amongst government officers. In addition, as higher ranking officials took on more responsibilities they downgraded some of their simpler duties to grades below them. There was thus a pull effect whereby a rise in skill in one grade led to a general increase in skill in the grades beneath them.[70]

The railway industry will next be examined as an example of a large scale bureaucratic company produced via a process of amalgamation and the growth of a specialized workforce. Railway companies took a leading role in the amalgamation process in the latter half of the nineteenth century. Following a wave of amalgamation between 1880 and 1910, fifteen companies emerged in 1911, many of them regional monopolies, controlling 84 per cent of total mileage.[71] Peter Yardley, for example, has estimated that while the General Post Office in 1907 was Britain's largest civilian employer, with a staff of 199,178, the next six biggest concerns were railway companies, with the largest, the London & North Western Railway Company, employing 84,377 workers. Out of the sixteen biggest employers, ten were estimated to be railway companies.[72] The Board of Trade estimated that there were 608,750 railway employees in Britain and

Ireland in 1910, among which were included 79,089 railway clerks.[73] London, as the centre of the railway industry, was affected by these changes. All main lines ran to London, and all major railway companies, with the notable exception of the North Eastern, had their main termini there. In addition the head offices of many of the most important railways, including the Great Western, the Great Northern, and the London and North Western were situated in the Metropolis.

The business concerns of the railways were manifold, and as they increased in scale as a result of amalgamation and expansion, their interests naturally grew. Main sources of revenue for railway companies were the transit of people and goods. In relation to the former, railway companies, particularly around London, Manchester, Liverpool and other major cities, were developing suburban lines during this period. Many of the suburbs in metropolitan Essex which grew up in the 1880s and 1890s, for example, owed much of their development to line extension by the Great Eastern. In many cases the company worked in direct conjunction with builders and developers.[74] Another important source of income was shipping. Most of the main railway companies had a fleet of steamers and had developed ports, the North-Eastern at Hull, the GWR at Fishguard, the London and South Western at Southampton, and the Great Eastern at Harwich, for example. These ports and fleets were used as much for travel and leisure as they were for trade. In relation to the latter, railway companies played a major role in developing the holiday industry. They owned hotels, organized excursions, helped develop seaside resorts, and organised holidays and trips abroad. In 1914, for example, one was able to buy a ticket (or rather a series of tickets) to Japan from Liverpool Street Station.[75] For those with less time on their hands and a taste for less exotic locations the company heavily promoted excursions to resorts along the east coast such as Yarmouth and Southend. Finally, railway companies produced much of their own rolling stock. In railway towns such as Crewe, Swindon, Derby and Stratford locomotives and carriages were designed, built and maintained. In addition, many of the companies were self sufficient, producing, for example, their own gas and electricity. The Great Eastern Railway even had it own printing press.[76] In all of these activities clerks were involved.

With the growth of companies through amalgamation, an increase in markets, the introduction of more sophisticated and powerful technologies and the leap in revenues in the entire railway industry from an estimated £45,078,143 in 1870 to over £123,000,000 in 1910,[77] railway clerical work became more complex and specialized. This phenomena was clearly outlined by Mr E. C. Geddes, the chief goods manager of the North Eastern Railway in a speech given at the York Railway Lecture and Debating Society in 1910, which was subsequently printed in the *Railway News*. Taking 'Education and the Advancement of the Railway Clerk' as his theme, Geddes devoted a large part of his speech to the theme of specialization in railway clerical work. He began this section by discussing railway companies in the 40s, 50s, and 60s, '... The railway companies in those days were smaller concerns. The method of working was more primitive. The clerks were far more in touch with the various aspects of railway work than they can possibly be to-day. The posts at the top were not, as a rule, so onerous, and the men looking towards them for promotion had pretty clear ideas about the work demanded in these appointments.'[78] The situation was compared by Geddes to the present situation in the railways which he saw as being typified by specialization and concentration. He argued that the work of the railway clerk had changed in much the same way, and his comments deserve to be quoted in full:

> In early days a clerk at a station saw the reception, loading, despatch, and working of traffic generally, as well as taking part in the clerical work, setting the claims and dealing with the public. To-day at the smaller country station he does get an all-round experience, and we may, I think, call the clerk fortunate who gets a portion of his early training at a small station; but the vast majority of the staff on a large railway cannot possibly obtain that thorough training in every branch, and if they are to acquire a general knowledge it must be by other means than by engaging in each branch of the work themselves... The reorganisation of 1902, with its clear definition of the functions of the train officers, was a great stride towards specialisation, and we can trace the same process within the department. Probably every railway used to dabble in figures, but with the starting of the Traffic Statistics Office, and the systematic circulation of statistical information amongst the Company's officers, a new field was created for the comparatively small numbers of men who are gifted with the particular ability in interpreting statistics. Again, sub-departments have been formed at head quarters to control the supply of wagons, the working of motor vehicles and the cartage of goods traffic. Advertising is the sole concern of a separate office. An inspector has been appointed to supervise the heating and lighting of the Company's premises. The inauguration of the commercial agency emphasised the distinction between the functions of the man who creates and obtains traffic and his operating colleague who is expert at moving traffic economically. Lastly, the development of the Continental business in recent years has led to the creation of an office where a wide knowledge of shipping and general business is indispensable. These examples by no means exhaust the list.[79]

This trend of growing specialization was repeated in the other major railway companies as a detailed survey of the various departments and offices of the Great Eastern Railway in its company magazine between September 1912 and May 1914 showed.[80] All the above departments were listed and a number of others including the Season Tickets Office, the Excursions Office, and The Trains Delay Section were given. The complexity of its internal structure was, perhaps, revealed by the length of time the monthly magazine took to give its readers an adequate impression of the various departments, offices and sections of the company.

The converse of such specialization was the growth in demand for clerks to perform more routine, 'mechanical tasks'. In all the examples given above such staffing was evident. In the City, for example, there was a large increase in female and juvenile labour. Moseley started work in Waterlows aged 14, as did many other boys his age around the turn of the twentieth century.[81] In both national and local government service boy clerks and female typists were introduced.[82] At the same time lower clerical grades were established, the Assistant Clerks in the Civil Service in 1904 and the Minor Establishment in the L.C.C. in 1902. In all these areas the creation of such grades was due to the large increases in routine work, and in all cases the aim was to save money.[83] In addition, with the increase in specialized clerical labour some clerical work became more routine. Train stations increasingly, for example, came to be controlled by head and regional offices, railway clerks there losing some of their autonomy. One important element in the history of railway clerks was the dissatisfaction of this lower clerical grade with their income and general working conditions as was evidenced by the growth and increasing militancy of the Railway Clerks Association.[84]

Conclusion

Two distinct definitions of the word 'clerk' have been presented in this chapter; a holder of office and an individual who worked in an office in an executive rather than administrative sense, an individual who as *The Clerk* neatly put it in 1890, enabled a business to know exactly where it was, what was due, what was owing, what was the cash balance and once knowing this, enabled it to arrange fresh bargains and open new undertakings.[85] It is this second definition that this study will use. As the economy and society became more complex in the latter half of the nineteenth century, as company structures developed and terms of trade changed, clerical work became more manifold, both in terms of the tasks it performed and the responsibilities it undertook. With this development definitions of clerks became more problematic. Some commentators came up with various formulas, others tried to use the term as little as possible, some tried to use it not at all, doubting the continued validity of its usage. The continued use of the term, however, means that some kind of working historical definition must be devised for the term if the group it refers to is to be historically analysed.

The solution to this problem can be found, as this chapter has argued, in the use of dual labour theory. Changes in clerical labour came about due to the growing complexity of the economy and society and with it business and governmental administration. The result of this was in some, but not all cases, the emergence of two types of clerical workers, the specialised and the more mundane, two types of clerks who carried out different but complementary work. If we take the above definition with the qualification that this was a process that was still very much evolving at the time and cannot be applied to all offices in London, especially the smaller ones, and, in addition, that movement was possible from secondary to primary positions, one is provided thereby with a working tool to examine the history of this important group of London workers.

2 THE CLERK, THE OFFICE AND WORK: CHANGING HORIZONS

What was the actual experience of work for the male clerical worker of the late Victorian and Edwardian period? Since the 1970s, when historians and social scientists began to discuss this area there has been an overwhelming tendency to follow the Braverman line of argument.[1] Before 1870 clerks were seen as all-round craftsmen who derived a sense of satisfaction from their work. They were relatively autonomous, skilled, responsible for the execution of important tasks within a company and consequently enjoyed relatively high status. The onset of advanced capitalism, growth in business concerns, and the application of tech-nology and rational procedures to work changed all of this. Division of labour and specialization transformed clerks into a demoralized white-collar proletar-iat. The previously close ties between the clerk and his employer were broken. Clerks became assembly workers in monstrous bureaucratic machines perform-ing repetitive tasks, the end-goal of which they had no idea. The result was alienation and a growing sense of disorientation. As this analysis reflected the commonly held belief that office work is routine, repetitive and essentially bor-ing much of it has remained intact. Paul Attewell's article, *The Clerk Deskilled: A Study in False Nostalgia*, for example, one of the first attacks on the Braverman thesis, simply confirmed this argument by claiming that there was no real break in the nature of clerical duties in the latter half of the nineteenth century.[2] For the vast majority of clerks, before and after 1870, clerical work had always been routine, tedious and mind-numbing.

This chapter will take a closer look at the role of the male clerical worker between 1890 and 1914, and his relationship to his work. It will argue that while Braverman is correct in arguing for structural shifts in the clerks' working envi-ronment and the nature of the work carried out, this did not necessarily imply a deterioration of the work process itself. Working practices simply changed. This did not automatically result in them becoming any worse. There is, in fact, evi-dence that for many the experience of work actually improved.

This chapter is divided into two sections, one examining the relation-ship between the clerk and his employer, the other analysing the relationship between the clerk and his work. In relation to the former, there was for many a fundamental shift from a master–servant relationship to a more impersonal employer–employee one. It is in this context that the emergence of company pensions, provident funds, canteens and sports and social facilities and most importantly career structures should be located. No longer able to maintain personal relationships with their employees, companies turned to providing social welfare and the promise of steady promotion to retain the loyalty of their workers. The role of sport and social clubs in companies will be discussed in detail in this section. It will also be argued that the career and changes in pay structure changed relations. Both created a more depersonalized relationship between clerks and employers as position and remuneration became linked to an objective scale rather than rewards for services rendered between master and servant.

The second part will argue that a growing division of labour in the office should not necessarily be seen as an unfavourable development. Division of labour did not mean that clerks were stuck in one position for their entire working lives. Clerks usually passed through a number of positions during their careers, thus developing their occupational skills. For others it meant specialization, and even semi-professionalism. Such changes resulted in a fundamental change in attitude for many towards their occupation. Work became increasingly seen as a slow but gradual progression up a series of scales. This section will also argue that as there was a loosening of bonds between the clerk and his employer, so there was also a weakening of ties between clerks and their place of employment. Clerical turnover, contrary to widespread belief, was relatively high. Finally, it will look at how the working atmosphere for clerks changed. With an increase in numbers and a more depersonalized relationship between clerks and employers a more disciplined and regimented atmosphere was established in the office. At the same time this should not be exaggerated. There is evidence which suggests that while stricter discipline may have been introduced into the office, the workplace for clerks was still relatively flexible and open.

The Change from Master–Servant to Employer–Employee Relations

In 1953 Roger Fulford published a history of Glyn's Bank to mark its bicentenary. Bought by the Royal Bank of Scotland in 1939, it had remained to that date one of London's foremost private banks and was to be the last of its kind on Lombard Street. Discussing the clerks of the bank and the changes they had experienced in the nineteenth century Fulford wrote,

> … the change in the nineteenth century, so far as the staff is concerned, is not so much in salary as in their relation to the partners, and generally in the House. Mr. Ovington, in Stanley Weyman's novel…once said in reference to his clerks, 'We are all in the same boat though we may not all steer'. As the nineteenth century developed the

clerks became less concerned with the progress of the boat than with the amenities of their own position inside it. The change from the old conception of the clerk as the personal servant of the partner – proud of the good name of the House and sensitive to every whisper which might effect it – to the new conception of the clerks as one of a larger staff – certainly still proud of the House but much concerned with their own conditions and rights – was an inevitable development.[3]

At the beginning of the nineteenth century bank clerks lived-in over the bank with their masters. There was thus a close personal relationship between the two. Clerks were often sons of associates of the partners and had gained their positions via patronage. Despite such close ties, however, masters were free to hire, treat and dismiss clerks as they saw fit. There were no contractual agreements between the two, neither was there much in terms of legal or parliamentary regulation. When the clerk married often depended on the sanction of the partners. Financial aid during periods of illness or when they were able to work depended on their good will. Bank clerks were in effect commercial servants.[4]

By 1900 this situation had changed. Clerks no longer lived with the heads of banks. Only managers in the joint-stock banks lived over branches. While recruitment still depended on recommendation, it was also conditional on passing an entrance examination and/or holding external qualifications. On retirement most bank clerks received pensions. If forced to resign due to illness there were provident funds to protect them and their families. Contracts were now signed between clerks and the bank, agreeing terms of employment, guarantee funds had to be secured by the clerk to insure against possible future loss, a corpus of laws had evolved which partially regulated the relationship between the two.[5] Most partners, directors or senior managers would be hard pressed to name more than a fraction of their clerical workers. Clerks had effectively become employees, rather than servants, of the bank.

This change in relationships was clearly not uniform amongst all clerks. At the Hongkong and Shanghai Bank until as late as the 1970s officials had to obtain permission to 'resign' from work. Throughout this period and beyond they had no formal contract and could not marry until they had been ten years in the service of the bank.[6] In the smaller offices personal relations were still prevalent between owners, partners and clerks. Patronage was still essential for gaining access to many clerical positions, and pensions were unevenly distributed throughout the professions. Despite this, however, relations were clearly altering. Relationships between clerks and the companies they worked for were becoming gradually more formalized. Symptomatic of these changes was a book published in 1909 by Edward A. Cope entitled, *Clerks Their Rights and Obligations*.[7] Cope noted that a body of law had evolved which to some degree regulated the relationship between clerks and employers. Bankruptcy Acts gave clerks certain rights in the event of the insolvency of a company, the Workmen's Compensation Act, 1906 gave them protection from injuries incurred in the workplace, the Prevention of Corruption Act, 1906 made them liable to serious penalties in the event of committing corruption offences. The ability of an employer to dismiss a clerk was curtailed by various judicial precedents. The work, in effect, listed the legal protection that a clerk could receive and the duties he was obliged to perform. Its very appearance was proof of the change that had taken place in the last century between clerks and their masters, and on a broader scale in the employment market in general. It is fitting that the book was published in the midst of important reforms by the Liberal governments of Asquith and later Lloyd George which were, in many respects, statutory acknowledgements of these shifts.

While such changes were beneficial to employers as a result of the greater manoeuvrability it gave them, they were also a liability. The old paternalistic master–servant relationship had earlier guaranteed the loyalty of clerical workers. As clerical workers were often directly responsible for large sums of money and handled confidential information this was vital to the well-being of most companies. With the loosening of bonds between master and servant it was increasingly feared that clerical loyalty to employer and company could not be guaranteed. Stories in the press of embezzlement by clerks in this period were common. An examination of the Clerks Register at Glyn's Bank, for example, shows that between 1890 and 1914 nine clerks were dismissed for embezzlement, robbery and fraud, or suspicion of having perpetrated such acts.[8] In one case in 1905, for example, Clerk G, an employee in the Town Office, was dismissed for serious irregularities, and another three were dismissed for being 'mixed-up' with Clerk G in connection with money lenders.[9]

It is this context which precipitated the emergence of industrial welfare in large-scale British industry and bureaucracies. Industrial welfare consisted of a series of programmes aimed at improving the wellbeing of the employee such as pensions, sick pay, staff-management committees, paid holidays, canteens, company magazines and social and sporting clubs.[10] While some employers had catered to workers' needs since the beginning of the Industrial Revolution, the difference was that industrial welfare was based on employer and employee contributions and rights of entitlement to welfare while the former had been grounded in individual patronage and ex-gratia payments. Robert Fitzgerald has attributed the precipitation of industrial welfare to the growth of internal labour markets which led to the employment of 'core' long-term employees and heavy investment in plant and process flows.[11] For such investments to be profitable, employers had to ensure that they had a loyal group of workers who would not leave the organization. Industrial welfare was thus an attempt by employers to obtain and maintain key workers, and to reduce as far as possible staff turnover, absenteeism and employee dissatisfaction which were seen as detrimental to the long-term viability of enterprise.

The relevance of Fitzgerald's arguments to a study of clerical workers is clear. Bureaucracies such as the railway companies and the banks from the late nineteenth century began to develop internal labour markets based on career structures (which will be discussed later in the chapter) and industrial welfare programmes. Such strategies formed the basis of locking clerks into organizations and constituted a new platform for employer–employee relations which were gradually beginning to emerge. Bureaucracies provided security, welfare and, for those prepared to conform to its ethos and rules, life-long career prospects. In return clerical workers were expected to promise fealty, commitment and service. From the 1870s onwards amongst large-scale bureaucracies in London one can clearly observe the emergence of industrial welfare. Pensions, provident funds, widow and orphan funds, profit sharing, bonuses and life insurance replaced the older system of Christmas boxes, gratuities and 'assistance'. These various benefits helped to maintain loyalty because they clearly linked the well-being of the clerk with that of the company he worked for. In addition, the amount one received depended on the length of time one worked for the organization. Pensions, for example, in many offices were paid at the rate of one sixtieth of a clerk's final salary for every year one had served up to a maximum of two-thirds. Payments were conditional on a minimum period of service, usually ten or twenty years. It was clearly, therefore, in the interest of the clerk to remain loyal to his employer in order to maximize his pension.[12]

Many of these schemes first originated in the Civil Service and then spread to the banks, railway companies, local government and other large organizations. From there they filtered down to other firms. Again the development was neither uniform nor ubiquitous. Some companies persisted in the older methods, others differed in their extent and generosity. Banks, for example, tended to cover the total expenses of pensions, while the railway companies only paid a part. In 1914 in London many clerks who worked in smaller offices were paying into friendly societies and life insurance schemes.[13] Nevertheless that such companies assisted social insurance amongst clerks was a crucial innovation of this period and was a growing trend. They were immensely popular for the security they offered and acted as a major attraction to new recruits. As Jim Hancock has said in relation to his father, for example, it was the promise of a regular income and a pension at the end which made his parents opt for a clerical career first in the civil service, and then in a bank for their son.[14]

The Growing Importance of Sport and Social Clubs

In addition to social insurance, another manifestation of industrial welfare in London bureaucracies was the introduction of subsidized sports and social facilities.[15] The background to this, in addition to the structural changes taking place in business outlined above, can be located in the growth in the interest in sport and in social clubs and voluntary recreational societies, particularly amongst the middle classes.[16] The degree to which these were introduced, encouraged and supported by banks, insurance houses, railway companies, national and local government and other sectors in London cannot be exaggerated. Between November 1899 and February 1904, for example, the Great Western Railway (GWR) spent £2,030 on the GWR Athletic Association.[17] This money was spent on the building of a sporting club and pavilion on a seventeen-acre ground in West Ealing, the equipping of the club and its upkeep. The capital came from several block grants and annual donations from the board. The facilities themselves were exclusively used by the clerks of the GWR, their friends and family and were well patronized by the staff. Football, cricket, tennis, hockey, bowling and other sports were played at the grounds. Members fees were subsidized by a yearly grant of 100 guineas from the board and annual subscriptions and donations from directors and senior management. Writing to the Board of the GWR in 1910, the Secretary of the club, E. E. Davies, noted, 'It is difficult to imagine what would happen to the Athletic Association if the Directors discontinued their annual contribution of 100 guineas'. After listing the activities and benefits of the club he candidly closed by pointing out that,

> The support of the Company is most certainly fully appreciated and is doing good work, not only by helping to keep the Club afloat, but because the average man will always think more kindly of an employer who takes interest in and helps to provide amusement and recreation for his leisure hours; and this is evidently the opinion of many firms such as Messers Lever Bros., Messers Cadbury Ltd., Messers Otto Monsted Ltd., and most of the large West End Business Houses, as well as various other Railway Companies.[18]

Similarly by 1905 both the London and Westminster and the London and County Banks had sports clubs in Norbury, south-west London. In addition to this, the London and County had a rowing club and boat house, all paid for by the bank, and a plethora of other social and sporting organizations. In 1911, for example, *The County and Westminster Magazine*, the staff journal of the now merged London and Westminster and London and County Banks listed the clubs and societies of the bank. These were composed of 30 associations which included nine cricket teams, four football teams, four rugby teams, a rowing club, a swimming team, a tennis club, a boxing club, a rifle club, a chess team, a photographic club, a debating society and an orchestra. In addition, a Cross Country and Athletic Association was in the course of formation, and a Motor Cycle Club was being planned.[19] Not content with this, however, the Magazine added, '... With all these activities ... we still lack a Sword Club, and Mr A. F. Hatten, of Wimbledon Branch, is anxious to know if any member of the Staff is willing to meet him occasionally for a little fencing. We hope this invitation will prove to be the nucleus of yet another Club'.[20]

No organization, however, outdid Holborn Bars, the headquarters of the Prudential, which appears to have been as much a social centre as one which organized life assurance. All of the various clubs of the company, which emerged from around the 1860s were affiliated in 1871 to the Prudential Clerks' Society, which later became known as 'The Ibis'.[21] By 1878 the Society had begun publishing its own journal which reported the activities of the various clubs, as well as providing articles on social, literary, artistic and contemporary subjects. Like the GWR Athletic Association, the society was supported and sponsored by the directors and senior management of the company. In addition to the cricket grounds at Dulwich, its rowing club and rifle range, Holborn Bars itself had a library, a gymnasium, reading rooms, a canteen and a staff hall with stage. The latter regularly hosted concerts, plays, music, and social events including the regular Christmas performances.[22]

A major event for many was the annual sports day in which the staff, their families and friends participated. In addition the clubs themselves organized leagues in which they competed with teams from other companies. From 1908, for example, an annual Inter-Banks' Athletic Championship was held at Stamford Bridge.[23] Inter-bank matches were also played between rowing clubs and cricket and football clubs. Banks had their own London football league which competed yearly for the Banks Challenge Cup.[24] At major matches members of staff would attend in support of their respective teams. In 1913 the Oxford Street Branch faced the Country Managers for The Leaf Cup, the Inter-Departmental tennis trophy of the London County and Westminster Bank. The branch chartered a motor omnibus which brought the team and their supporters to the sports grounds at Norbury.[25] Such support for sporting clubs clearly enhanced staff loyalty. In supporting their team clerks were associating themselves with their branches, departments or companies. In relation to this, staff colours, badges, songs and a whole host of other insignia grew up around these teams, thus ultimately strengthening the bond between clerk, organization and office.[26]

The teams were well patronized, and the clubs well attended. In 1911, for example, the membership of the London and County Sports Club stood at 1,233 out of a possible figure of 2,700.[27] Just under 50 per cent of the staff therefore belonged to its clubs, a high figure if one considers that many of its clerks would have been spread out all over the South-East of England in its various branches. Membership appears to have been common among younger clerks before they married.[28]

In a previous article, I have argued that one reason sport was important in companies was its role in developing and building up organizational cultures, an innovation of the period.[29] Organizational culture is a set of shared assumptions based on a common institutional experience and history, which are learnt and used by members of organizations as normative and cognitive structures.[30] It produces stability by establishing a common corporate identity shared by all members and inculcates uniform values and practices which cover all aspects of the group's activities and outlook. It can be seen as the ontological glue which binds organizations together. Such cultures were important in the attempt to instil in clerical staff's sets of values and practices which facilitated feelings of working together in a common community. They created a sense of belonging in the face of growing bureaucratization and impersonal relations that were affecting many organizations.[31] As Weber argued, the basis of the entry of an individual into a bureaucracy was a pledge of loyalty by the former in return for a commitment of security by the latter.[32] Yet this was a loyalty born not out of personal relations but devoted to an impersonal agency. For such loyalties to be given, organizations would be forced to construct ideologies cemented by cultural values to earn such allegiances from its members. Corporate cultures became the basis of such ideologies.

Sport facilitated the development of corporate cultures, which were germane to bureaucracies because of its practices and values such as teamwork, character building, loyalty, fortitude, strategy and hierarchy. It also built up social spaces within bureaucracies where community and culture could be nurtured and strengthened. It helped to build up, in the words of these clubs and associations, a sense of esprit de corps within organizations. In December, 1904, for example, Mr Blair, an officer in the Education Department of the L.C.C., gave a speech to 300 guests at the Annual Staff Dinner. In it he urged the younger members of the staff to associate themselves in their clubs and institutions, so as to, '... weld and cement together the great body that we represent here tonight'.[33] Viscount Goschen, the chairman of the successor of the London and County Bank, the Westminster Bank, at the annual dinner of the bank's sports club in 1923, explained how when a sports club at the bank was first suggested in 1905 there had been opposition from some directors who thought that it might upset the operations of the bank. 'There were some', he stated, 'who felt the machine might lack efficiency, but I think the greater number thought – and I am glad to think that our hopes have been fulfilled – that if in place of the machine we had a Sports Club we should substitute human beings whose efficiency would be added to by the happiness and bodily well-being that would come from a well-organized Sports Club'.[34] Discussing the importance of instilling feelings of esprit de corps within organizations, the actuary T. E. Young wrote in his work, *Insurance Office Organisation, Management and Accounts*, first published in 1904, that '... [the] integrity of associated work depends upon the harmonious combination of the characters and capacities of the workers, or in other words the promotion is what is customarily termed an esprit de corps'.[35] He later emphasized the need for companies to encourage sport and social facilities at work as a means of realizing this integration.[36]

Finally, sport helped to reinforce power and status distinctions within this community. In many of these company and organizational sporting and social organizations a common trend is seen in their formal structures. At the top was the president of the society, who, particularly in the case of larger clubs such as the athletics society, would normally be the chairman of the company or a senior director. Below him were vice-Presidents who were usually directors and senior management. Below them were the secretary of the club, its treasurer and the members of its governing committee. These men were usually senior members of the staff. Below these were the members of the club itself, made up predominately of the general staff.[37] The power structures of these social organizations therefore replicated similar structures found in the workplace. Lord Goschen at the London County and Westminster Bank may have sincerely enjoyed giving talks at the Sports Club dinners, assisting the Rowing Club, or taking part in the discussions of the Literary and Debating Society in the Bank. Yet while doing this, he was reinforcing and legitimating the entire power matrix of the organization which he directed.

Sport thus played a crucial role in these emerging new bureaucracies. Old forms of personal patronage were replaced by corporate patronage via the assistance corporations gave to their staff via their sporting and social activities. Instead of giving direct personal assistance, a company, such as the Great Western Railway, now contributed money towards a sports ground. Such support integrated the Staff more fully into the newer impersonal relations which were beginning to dominate larger firms. It gave them a sense of a common organizational identity. In the face of such versatility and usefulness it is no wonder that such sporting and social clubs were springing up in offices in London, and why so many directors and senior management were so willing to give so generously to such activities for the 'benefit' of their staff.[38]

The Rise of the Career

At the heart of the new relationship between the clerk and his employer stood the career. Clerical workers increasingly, particularly in large-scale organizations, could expect over the course of their employment to be promoted through a structured path of higher positions, each one successively better paid and with wider responsibilities. Such mobility was not guaranteed but was contingent on performance, attitude and dedication. The creation of the career was in many respects revolutionary for the clerk and redefined his entire orientation to work and employer.[39] Work now became seen as a long-term project, a series of gradual, incremental advances which resulted in the construction of a number of occupational strategies by clerks such as the adoption of a long-term orientation to work, a commitment to education and the improvement and monitoring of the self, the creation of professional societies, and in some cases associational behaviour within work which was hoped would improve career chances.[40] Many of these strategies will be discussed in detail in later chapters of this book.

Various explanations have been given for the development of career by organizations. Weber argued that the experience of promotion and the continuous shifting of jobs and responsibilities meant that employees ceased to see occupational positions as personal possessions (as in the older clerical model of sinecures, nepotism and patronage) and instead saw their jobs as simply successive, temporary steps in a series of upward, career advances. The career thus cemented the concept of executive authority within bureaucracies.[41] It was office and competence rather than personality and association which became the basis of sovereignty within these institutions. For Weber the career also enhanced the division of labour of the bureaucracy which was one of the pillars of its superior speed and efficiency. It encouraged the adoption and development of specialized labour within the organiaztion.[42] It further motivated the employee to work harder to gain superior posts because of the elevated status which such office conferred on him.[43] The theme of enhanced efficiency was taken up by the business historian Alfred Chandler in his seminal work on the rise of the modern corporation and management.[44] Such corporations relied on the development of a professional cadre of career managers to ensure their control, functioning, speed and planning. The development of departments and divisions within these corporate giants also encouraged the development of efficiency, professional specialization and hence careers.

Another explanation for the development of the career is the emergence of internal labour markers within bureaucracies and large-scale organizations. In his work on labour management, Howard Gospel has noted that until the Second World War most British companies were typified by a loose style of labour management which was ad hoc, dependent on external markets for workers, short-term and minimalist in labour relations.[45] Layoffs and temporary employment were common. Yet by the latter half of the nineteenth century a new style of bureaucratic management emerged in certain sectors of the economy which had large, stable and uniform markets and were capital intensive.[46] In these sectors it was vital that a cadre of employees could be engineered who were loyal and committed. This was due to heavy investment in their training and also a result of the need to maintain continuous production which would keep markets supplied and guarantee returns on expenditure in capital investment.[47] This new bureaucratic management developed employment strategies and labour policies based on long-term relations with employees, internal training, steady employment, life-long career structures, company welfare programmes and systematic recruitment. Employment relationships were internalized rather than dependent on external markets. While Gospel focuses on manual workers in railway and utility companies and later on at the new industries in consumer goods and light engineering, large-scale employers of clerks perfectly fitted this model. In organizations such as retail banking and life insurance mass, stable markets emerged which companies responded to by heavily investing in distribution, marketing and retail structures. Employees were carefully selected, invested in, offered the possibility of life-long employment, provided with skills and knowledge which were vital to the long-term vitality of the organization, spent their professional life working their way through internal labour markets, were remunerated accorded to seniority and grade, and enjoyed a series of welfare benefits such as pensions, insurance and paid holidays. The clerical career can thus be seen a result of this new style of management and the internal labour markets which it engendered.

Evidence for the importance of clerical internal labour markets and internal recruitment can be seen in a series of letter from senior managers of the GWR to its Secretary G. W. Mills between 1900 and 1901.[48] The letters were a response to a memorandum sent by Mills on behalf of the chairman of the GWR in November 1900.[49] The memorandum proposed the creation of a special grade of university graduates who would be trained and prepared to take up senior management positions within the GWR. The proposal was clearly based on the recruitment of first division officers in the Civil Service and was already in operation at the North-Eastern Railway company in York. The memorandum provoked a series of lengthy responses by senior management at the GWR, all of which were negative. In all cases, the reasons for the rejection of the proposal were the same; recruitment and entry to management positions at the company was based on internal recruitment and the expectation of such recruitment. Anything which interfered with this system would disturb labour relations amongst clerks at the railway, lead to unrest, a fall in motivation and a rise in the labour turnover. As M. F. Staines, manager of the stores department at Swindon wrote in February, 1901, 'It is of the first importance that all youths entering the service should have before them the prospect of advancement to the higher positions. If the rank and file felt that such positions were reserved for a special class, it would cause discontent amongst them; it would remove the chief inducement to diligence and progress, and would lower the standard of the general staff by leading the best men to seek employment elsewhere'.[50]

The most incisive response to the memorandum came from another senior manager, A. W. Solten. It deserves to be quoted in full as it succinctly set out the principles and rationale of internal recruitment and labour markets at the GWR,

Hitherto the practice has been to draw from the general staff to fill such positions, the men who, by their ability, zeal and assiduity, have singled themselves out for promotion outside the ordinary routine, and to whom the knowledge that the prizes of the service are open to all, has been an incentive to cultivate the good qualities they possess.

The successful management and administration of a Railway depend very largely on the zealous and capable discharge, by a contented staff, of duties, some of mere detail and routine, others involving in a greater or lesser degree the exercise of thought and judgement. To introduce into the service, however delicately, the mere suspicion that the chief positions are likely to be monopolized by a favoured few individuals, thereby arresting the natural flow of promotion throughout the service, would I feel convinced, cause a feeling of discontent which would operate to the detriment of the Company by reason of the removal to excel, which under existing circumstances tends to their benefit; and would also lead to the better men, who might leave the service for appointments outside such as would not otherwise attract them.[51]

Here we clearly see the role of internal recruitment and promotion (and hence the career) as a way of locking individuals into organizations, providing a basis for low labour turnover, motivation and excellence. Faced by such a barrage of opposition the proposed scheme was scrapped and did not reappear until 1914.

A final explanation for the rise of the career, by writers such as Mike Savage and Alan McKinley, has been its role in disciplining employees.[52] These writers focus on the relationship of the career with power relationships in organizations rather than efficiency and functionality as the above authors have done. Careers forced employees to control their behaviour and monitor their performance. Employees began to self-reflexively manage themselves in a manner which was germane to the organization and its senior management. Such practices were reinforced by inspection and the long-term external monitoring of employees using disciplinary technologies such as report cards at banks which evaluated staff and were used as the basis for annual promotions. As Alan McKinley, examining bank clerks in Scotland, has noted, what was monitored was not simply performance, technical skill and behaviour, but also attitude and personality.[53] Even dress and physical appearance such as height and hair colour was controlled and investigated. In this respect the power relations and the career system which it rested on became total. It rewarded clerks for being the right kind of employee and *person* and co-opted the individual into colluding with a disciplinary system which was designed to remove his very agency and capacity for individual thought and action.

The stress upon the career as a disciplinary construct in no way contradicts or invalidates any of the other explanations which have been proposed for its emergence. Weber, for example, argued that the superiority of bureaucracies was based on the career, taut discipline and control.[54] The three were linked. Efficiency was clearly based on authority, regulation and the iron cage of rationality. Internal labour markets, promotion and lifelong employment were only

available to those who could discipline themselves into the routines of bureaucratic life and the organizational cultures which these bureaucracies developed.
McKinley's bank inspectors and report cards were equally active in London and
England. The National Provincial Bank, an institution which would merge with
the Westminster Bank (itself a merger of the London and County and London
and Westminster) in 1968 to form the National Westminster Bank, was assidu-
ous in its monitoring of its employees and its control of their careers. Stacks of
its report cards still remain in its archives, retaining, disclosing and confessing
the minutiae of the careers and everyday lives of its thousands of former employees.[55] Yet the degree to which such control was alienating can be questioned. As
we will see in the next chapter, the success of the career as a disciplining device
rested on its appeal to the intrinsic values of its incumbents. Clerical workers
were an aspirational class who had been nurtured on Smilesean values of self-
improvement, perseverance and duty.[56] In many respects they were a conservative
group who were drawn to the security and predictability of bureaucratic life and
its career structures. The danger of the career was not so much the control and
demand for self-discipline and reflexivity that it imposed upon clerks. Its danger
lay elsewhere, in its potential failure to deliver promotion and social mobility,
thwarting years of hard work and pent up aspirations.

Changes in Pay Structure

An important change in the relationship between the clerk and his employer
was remuneration. Increasingly, pay scales replaced the older system of arbi-
trary pay increases. The newer system meant that a clerk was paid at a certain
rate depending on how long he worked for a company or office. Increases were
strictly regulated according to the scale and affected all clerks.

Such a system of payment first appeared in the Civil Service and can be
linked to the emergence of internal labour markets and career structures. On the
recommendations of The Playfair Commission the Lower Division of the Civil
Service was created by an Order in Council of 12th February, 1876. A salary scale
was established of £80 to £200 rising by triennial increments of £15, or £90
rising by similar increments to £250.[57] Such pay scales quickly spread to other
areas of clerical work. Like company subsidized sporting activities, they tended
to be implemented initially by larger employers such as the railways and banks
and then disseminated down to smaller organizations. At the London and Westminster Bank for example, in 1909, clerical salaries started at £64 and increased
at a rate of £8 per annum for 17 years, and £10 for the subsequent 10 years. In
addition, there were 'class salaries' for those not holding special appointments.
A fourth class clerk could earn up to £20 extra a year, a third class clerk up to
£40 extra, a second class clerk £60 and a first class clerk £100. Again these extra

incomes were subject to incremental increases, an annual increase of £5 for fourth and third class clerks, and £10 for second and first class clerks. A first class clerk at the end of his scale could therefore earn £400 per annum.[58]

While not universal in London, especially amongst smaller firms, such arrangements were becoming increasingly the norm for clerical workers. Firms, such as the Metropolitan Board of Water often adapted Civil Service rates of pay to their own scales.[59] Trumans, the London Brewers, for example, had by 1903, a system of minimum and maximum salaries based on class.[60] Such changes introduced a radical shift in relations between employers and clerks. Pay became based on an objective criteria which had been previously agreed rather than on the goodwill of the employer. Employees now worked their way up scales as salaries became based on a depersonalized system of annual rises .

Such a change had clear implications for how clerks negotiated with their employers. In the older system increases were organized on a individual basis. Employers who personally knew their clerks awarded rises on individual merit and need. This system was widespread in London. William Evans, for example, a legal clerk, was married on 25 September 1897. On 11 December he was given a 5/- a week pay increase. A similar increase came the following December, four months after the birth of his first daughter.[61] In the newer system, in offices where such intimate relations were impossible, attempts to increase the overall level of salaries could only come about if the entire scale was altered. Such changes were facilitated by the whole staff acting in unison to demand such alterations. As a result, as will be seen in Chapter 8, clerks began to discover new advantages in acting together against their employers. Such a development inevitably had radical implications for the whole nexus of employer–employee relations amongst clerical workers. It was in such a change that the seeds of clerical co-operation began to develop. It is no surprise, for example, that clerical trade unions and associations initially appeared in the Civil Service and the railway companies where such pay scales had first been introduced.[62]

Division of Labour

Perhaps the most important change for the clerk in relation to the work he carried out was an increased division of labour and with this specialization which first appeared in the early part of the nineteenth century. There were clerks who kept accounts, wrote correspondence, supervised, etc.[63] The change in this period was one of degree rather than of kind. Its extent, however, caused radical changes in clerical work. The change was due to four factors. The first was because of increases in the size of many organizations. As offices got bigger there was an increased need to assign certain individuals to certain tasks to maintain efficiency. The second was increased competition. Increased market entry and the expansion of existing companies in the latter half of the nineteenth century created a more competitive environment. In 1896, for example. Richard Foster, of the City firm of merchants Knowles and Foster commented that:

> In these days of railways, steamships and telegraphs, merchants have to work more cheaply than they did forty or fifty years ago, and they have to do more work to make an equal, perhaps a smaller amount of money.[64]

In such an environment employers became much more cost conscious. Clerks, among other employees, were put to more efficient use, their labour was divided more rationally. The third factor was the introduction of various technologies and the application of more rational approaches in the workplace.[65] Typewriters, telephones, addessographs, adding machines, copiers, filing systems, etc., to be used most effectively needed to be used by certain groups of clerical workers. More sophisticated systems of accountancy and storing and retrieving information required greater division of workers. The final factor was the growth, as has been seen earlier, of the dual labour market in clerical work. Some clerks specialized in particular areas of work, others were divided between more routine tasks. Clearly the extent to which this happened was partially related to the size of a company, the larger the organization, the greater the division of labour.

The reaction of many commentators to these changes was generally negative. The *Clerk* in February 1908, for example, argued that, the whole trend of modern commerce precluded the advancement of the modern clerk,

> The small office now gives place to the great bureaux of such limited liability companies and trusts, and the two or three clerks of the office of the past are replaced by small armies of men and women for that matter, who, are pretty much like teeth in a great administrative machine. Concentration of this character has led to differentiation of function with the result that each individual tends to become specialized on one operation, and the possibility of getting into his fingers all the operation of the office are remote. Such being the case, that very fact alone suffices to fix the clerk permanently in one particular groove.[66]

The language used here was typical of the critique of the age. Newspapers, clerical unions and writers such as George Bernard Shaw, who had had the misfortune to have previously been clerks, all voiced the sad plight of the black-coated worker.[67] Clerks were increasingly portrayed as becoming dehumanized parts of colossal bureaucratic machines.

Closer examination of the work that clerks carried out, the policies of companies towards their staff, and clerical career histories reveals that much of this criticism was unfounded. There is strong evidence which suggests that clerks throughout their working career within one organization frequently changed jobs. This could either take the form of being transferred to a new section, department, or branch, or being given different responsibilities within their existing units. Very often it involved both. George Dewley, for example, entered the service of the Great Western Railway as a clerk in 1890. Between that date and 1909 his work experience was anything but static. For the first two years of his career he worked on railway passes at Southall, Castle Hill, Ealing, and Bourne End. After this he worked for five years in the Receiving Office at 193 Oxford Road. For the next four years he worked in the same office at Minories. In 1905 he was promoted to Agent at 124 Holborn, W.C., a position analogous to Station Master on the goods side of the railways.[68] Though Dewley was not typical of the hundreds of clerks found in the Staff Register of the GWR who joined between 1890 and 1910, not all clerks became agents or station masters, he was in no way an exception. It was change rather than continuity which was the rule in the GWR, a company which at the time had one of the most finely divided systems of clerical labour.

This tendency was found to be case in the various potted career histories of clerks who had retired or died in the clerical and company journals consulted.[69] The diaries and interviews repeat this trend. All five diaries revealed changes at least once in the clerical work carried out by their writers. Andrew Carlyle Tait, for example, started working as a boy clerk in September 1894 for the City stationery manufacturers James Spicer and Co. Tait's work included writing and copying letters, invoice work, and collecting samples. As he himself wrote, 'My duties are too numerous to suit me. I attend to all the letters in the evening, order as well for out department'.[70] Tait's diary, unfortunately, only dealt with a few days of his working experience, from 4 September to 13 September 1894. After this was an entry for 4 November of the same year stating that he has been transferred to the Counting Department and one for 5 November which chiefly described his firework display at home in Ilford. Following this there is a final undated entry which had clearly been written some time after. In this section Tait described the subsequent changes which had taken place at work, including those of people he had earlier worked with and described,

> ... I looked into its [the diary's] pages and thought how things had changed. I am still at Spicers, but the drudgery of the Boards dept. is far behind. I got set down a peg or two after a months muddling of the work and have since risen till I am now Junior Clerk o' the Manchester Dept. under the same Wells aforementioned with Mr Cayser as Manager. Aylott has left, Mr. Marshall is dead, and only the Managers stick to the same tasks as when I came.[71]

Tait's initial experience seems to be fairly typical. Office boys were regularly transferred between different departments. What is most interesting, however, is his late comment indicating the extent of change of the clerical duties carried out at Spicers.

There were several important reasons for the relative frequency in changes in the duties which clerks carried out. The first was the preferred system of internal promotion, discussed earlier, which virtually all organizations implemented. Companies often shifted clerks, particularly promising ones, around the various departments and branches of a company in order to prepare them for promotion to higher positions.[72] A railway clerk, for example, might be shifted between different stations, then moved back to head office where he was moved between different sections and departments, and then transferred to a more senior position in another station or regional office. Banks often did the same. Clerk H, for example, began working for the London and County Bank in 1898 at Midhurst. From 1899 to 1901 he was at Chichester, 1902 to 1906 at Worthing, 1907 to 1909 at Brighton, 1910 at Lombard Street, 1911 in the Birbeck branch, 1912 to 1914 at Knightsbridge and 1915 at Hanover Square. From 1915 to 1919 he joined up and was a Second Lieutenant commanding No. 6 Railway Supply Detachment in the First Army of the British Expeditionary Force in France. In 1919 he was promoted to Inspector's Clerk, in 1921 he was made the manager of the Yarmouth Branch and in 1925 was promoted to Inspector of Branches.[73] The experience which Clerk H gained at Head Office and all these different branches would have been crucial to his promotion. In addition, with the bank expanding in this period, experienced clerks were often transferred to new branches.

Such a policy of transfer was also partially due to the fact that British offices in commerce, industry and government had no formal system of training. Britain distinguished itself from its competitors by the amount clerks were expected to 'learn on the job'.[74] This came from a combination of learning one's duties whilst actually doing them and gaining knowledge from existing experienced members of staff. The fact that clerks tended to work in small groups, even in large bureaucracies, facilitated this process. David King has described this process at the Hongkong and Shanghai Bank,

> ... their [clerks] qualification for promotion depended on what insight they gained from their clerical assignments and/or what informal instruction, what hints at implications were given them by their immediate supervisors. A junior who showed interest might be told quietly of the secrets of exchange rate calculations, a junior on current accounts asking whether an overdraft should be permitted might be subjected to a barrage of questions relative to his knowledge on the account, questions designed to instruct him in the principles of personal credit.[75]

As clerical work was often part of a larger whole, rather than atomized units of autonomous production. Experience of the different processes that items of office work went through was thus crucial before an individual could actually be promoted to a position of responsibility. As a result, clerks would be regularly transferred to different sections and departments, once they had become proficient in their existing work. Again the process was by no means uniform for all clerks. More promising individuals would be transferred more often, less capable clerks less so. Despite this, however, to perform all but the most mechanical clerical activities it was necessary, particularly in a clerk's early years, to move him around the office.

A good example of this was bookkeeping. Account books, especially in larger companies, often related to other books. Depositing or withdrawing money from a bank account, for example, required entries being made by the cashier in his books, by another clerk in the waste book, by another in the current account register, or in the sectional check ledgers, and by another in the 'Current Accounts' of the general ledger. Checks would be entered into the clearing book, bills of exchange would have their separate ledger.[76] In order to be promoted to Inspector, as was H. P. G. Archer, one would need years of experience on all these separate ledgers, in order to detect, for example, any irregularities in the entries. To understand fully how the accounts of an organization worked, one therefore required experience working on the various ledgers which made up the greater whole. Transferring clerks to different ledgers was part and parcel of the effective running of a bureaucracy and the smooth operation of promotion and filling senior positions.

It was because of this that seniority was so important to clerks. The longer a clerk worked for an office the more knowledge and insight he gained into how its different parts worked. This fact was reflected in the incremental pay structure of a clerk's salary. As a clerk became more experienced the value of his work increased.[77] Work for many clerks had long learning curves. It is in this respect, rather than the actual tasks that were carried out, which made office work skilled work. This was a fact which eluded many contemporaries who saw in clerical work mindless repetitive tasks which could be performed by anybody who could read, write and add up. John Stuart Mill, for example, observed in the 1860s, to the chagrin of many clerks, 'A clerk from whom nothing is required but the mechanical labour of copying gains more than an equivalent for his mere exertion if he receives the wage of a bricklayer's labourer. His work is not a tenth part as hard, it is quite easy to learn, and his condition is less precarious, a clerk's place being generally a place for life'.[78] Such remarks made John Francis Davis in his work on banking which appeared in 1910 ponder how so able a man as Mill could come out which such remarks, which displayed in his own words, '... a remarkable want of insight into the nature of the clerk's work'.[79] Copying was just one part of a modern clerk's qualifications, clerical work was quite as fatiguing as that of a brick layer, writing and spelling correctly were themselves relatively scarce skills. Finally if one took Mill's arguments to their logical conclusion, Davis argued, a navvy ought to receive more than a prime minister. A qualified clerk at 18, was, in his opinion worth in the open market twice if not three times the wages of a first-rate bricklayer.[80]

Clerical Turnover

Clerks were not, however, always prepared to patiently work their way up, 'waiting for dead men's shoes', as the saying went. Despite corporate patronage, some clerks moved around between companies. Ties between clerks and the workplace appear to have weakened during this period. An examination of the Clerks Register at Glyn's Bank, for example, belies the generally held belief that clerks stayed with one employer for life. Out of the 235 clerks taken on by Glyn's between 1890 and 1914, 67 had left by the end of 1914. None of these were due to enlisting in the armed forces for the hostilities which started in this year. Reasons given were death, resignation (no reason given), resignation due to ill health, resignation to change to a different job, or dismissal. One clerk even absconded with £113. Only thirteen resigned on account of ill health. Another resigned due to lunacy, one died while still working, and one individual shot himself accidentally in the head![81]

Most resignations at Glyn's took place within the first two years of a clerk joining the bank, or around five years later in order to join another bank. It the case of the former it is highly likely that clerks were forced to resign – effectively they were dismissed. Clerk I, for example, left the bank on 9 February, 1891, only having joined on 2 June, 1890. The Registrar reads, '... Found him unequal to the work and got him appointed to North British Insurance Co'.[82] Many, especially those who left after five years did so to move to a better position. For them this was real upward mobility. A number had, in fact, previously worked for other companies. In this respect, those who did leave were simply following an established precedent. Clerk J, for example, born in 1861, entered the bank in 1880 after having worked for four years at The Railway Clearing House. He resigned on 14 December, 1892, to take up a position in the Bank of Montreal.[83] Many clerks left their positions, like Clerk J, to work abroad. In countries with developing economies from Canada to Australia, and Japan to Argentina, there was strong demand for men with clerical skills and experience of business. The result for some was elevation to positions which they would have had to have waited years to achieve at home. Clerk K, for example, left Glyn's in February 1896 to become the Registrar of the Government of South Australia, a position he received at the relatively early age of thirty-six.[84]

Yet it was not just to go abroad that clerks gave up positions. Clerks were also increasingly able to move to different companies. Evidence of such a change can be seen in the growth of Radius Agreements between employers and clerks which began to appear around the turn of the twentieth century. These prohibited clerks from accepting similar employment within a specified distance or 'radius' of the place of business at which they were engaged.[85] The principal aim of such an agreement was to prevent clerks working for neighbouring competitors, taking with them important and potentially damaging information from their previous employers. These agreements were by no means universal. In 1909, for example, they were said by Edward Cope to be 'very far from being general, but it is obviously growing'.[86] Their very existence and growth, however, is a clear indication of the increased manoeuvrability of clerks by 1900.

The Working Atmosphere of the Office

Frank H. H. King has argued in relation to the Hongkong and Shanghai Bank that as the organization grew larger discipline became more important in the office. It was a discipline King argued, 'coming not from self-motivation of the ambitious, mature clerk, in close contact with an inspired leader, but a discipline enforced downwards by a Sub-Manager on a group of youngsters'.[87] Growth in organizations usually resulted in an influx of large numbers of adolescent boys, often fresh from school. Congregated together in close contact in offices all day with work to carry out and agendas to keep to, discipline clearly became an issue. In such an environment, regulations and rules, enforced by senior clerks, quickly began to multiply. A host of such standing orders has been illustrated by King. One on 13 July 1893 ordered that, 'The practice of throwing pellets of paper about the office must be discontinued'. Others related to late arrival, smoking during office hours, taking longer over tea breaks, lurking in the corridors and sitting in the basement. One was issued against putting pins in the mouth for fear of contracting blood poisoning.[88]

Strict hierarchies imposing chains of command, impersonal regulations and rules all contributed to imposing increased discipline in the office, matching the internal control which was vital to the career. In many respects these bureaucratic structures imitated the public schools which two or three generations earlier had been faced with similar problems of control.[89] The hierarchies of masters, senior boys and juniors was replaced by managers, special officers, senior and junior clerks. House loyalty was replaced by allegiance to department and branch. Attendance registers replaced school registers, manager and inspector's reports those of school reports.

The Establishment Committee Reports of the London and Westminster Bank for 21st April, 1904, provide an excellent example of the above comments, and how, in general, discipline was imposed by the bank. They read as follows,

> The Committee proceeded to consider the Manager's Special reports upon the Staff, as on the 1st of March last.
>
> Clerk L, 4th Class, Assistant Clearer, City Office appeared before the Committee, the report stating that he is a very slow clerk, not able to do his appointed duties, and not recommended for promotion, and it was resolved that Mr. Hill's salary be fixed at the present amount, £188 per annum and that he endeavour to find other employment within a reasonable time.

Clerk M, 4th Class Crediting Clerk, City Office, who is reported as a troublesome clerk, frequently absent, and frequently late was also told that he must endeavour to find other employment within a reasonable time and in the mean time his salary to be fixed at the present amount viz, £148 a year.

Clerk N, City Office (Teller) said to have ability, but cannot be recommended for 4th Class at present, was reprimanded, and warned to be more careful in his work and manner in future.

Clerk O, 3rd Class, Inscribed Stock Clerk, Country Office, 'A capable clerk but not always reliable' was warned to be more careful.

Clerk P, 4th Class, Inscribed Stock Clerk, Country Office, 'Has ability but is wanting in industry and requires constant supervision' was cautioned and warned that better report will be expected at the 2nd of six months.[90]

Discipline was clearly tight at the bank. Dismissal for failing to obey the rules was an option. Yet the transfer for many of these juniors from school to office was relatively smooth. Both had hierarchy, discipline, deskwork and plenty of sport. King even notes that the food served at the subsidized Luncheon Club of the Hongkong and Shanghai Bank was reminiscent of school meals.[91]

Despite the introduction of such discipline, however, one must not exaggerate the restrictions which were imposed on clerical workers in their office. Clerks for a significant part of their working life were not chained to their desks. At the Prudential, for example, when a shareholder complained to Henry Harben, the Secretary of the company, about the conduct of his clerks at the Annual General Meeting in 1872 he replied, 'I fully admit that our clerks do read the papers and chatter; but I have yet to learn that human nature can go on all day long without some little relaxation'.[92] Such a liberal attitude was certainly evident forty years latter. At the Hongkong and Shanghai Bank, despite all its regulations, H. E. Muriel noted, 'I entered London office in Lombard Street in 1905 from Westminster Bank; the change from a formal ordered strict regime to the undergraduate atmosphere of the Hong Kong Bank was very pleasant though rather startling...about half of us were reasonably serious over our work'.[93] The degree of discipline was clearly relative to the institution. At the Commercial Gas Company in East London around the Christmas period, clerks regularly returned to work after extended lunch breaks worse the wear for a few drinks. On 28 December 1902, for example, George Rose wrote,

> The work comes as a very unwelcome change. And indeed there's very little of it done in our office. In the afternoon four choice spirits go out and drink, (Harry [chief clerk] is ill and away). They come into the office at about 4.30 and more or less drunk and kick up a wicked row, and we are supposed to be working till seven tonight! S. Jones is upstairs so there'll be trouble tomorrow.[94]

Despite Rose's predictions nothing was done about it, and several more similar incidents appeared in his diaries.

Discipline also depended on the individual concerned. Asked whether the workplace was strict, Arthur Whitlock, after fifty-one years' clerical experience, cryptically answered, 'Well, that was left to our own discretion to a certain extent, really'.[95] In the myriad and often highly political relations of clerks and seniors at work in London in this period what else could one expect? Friction between clerks and seniors could, however, boil over into open confrontation. Sydney Moseley's relations with his immediate superior Mr Almond seemed to oscillate between paternal affection and open warfare. On 5 July 1904, Moseley wrote,

> Went to the office full of determination to 'be a man' – but Fate opposed! My boss Almond kicked up a row, I joined in, and then – behold – a big Row – lost his temper. He shouted: 'If Mr Smythe [Senior Manager] were here you wouldn't be working another five minutes'. I answered him back and he said that tomorrow when Mr. Smythe returns he would tell him and see that I left without getting any pay and without a character. Fine eh? Just see what that means...Here I am alone in the world – no Father – No Mother – No Employment and no 'good Character' certificate. Still I don't care!! My strong-willed nature would have the better of me; so I sneered at his remarks.
>   At 7 o'clock I was in the washroom when he came in (of course I arranged to be there!) We had a talk. He gave me some good advice and we are friends again.[96]

Indiscipline and resistance to authority could take other, more subtle forms. In 1882, for example, the widely disliked manager of Glyn's Bank, William New-march, said to be a rough, uncouth Yorkshireman with a grating accent, suffered a stroke at work. It was whispered that the clerks who carried him out were care-ful to bump his head on each of the steps so that he would not return. In this, Roger Fulford assures us, they were successful.[97]

Finally, it should not be assumed that clerks were kept behind their desks, writing continuously until allowed to go home. Offices were at times relatively relaxed and flexible. At Glyn's if a clerk wanted an afternoon at Lord's he could usually manage it by paying someone else to do his work for him.[98] Offices were tolerant about giving leave to clerks who felt ill. George Rose's office went through periods of seemingly total inactivity. On 25 May 1910, for example, he wrote,

> Arriving at Stepney at about 9 a.m. the next hour is consumed in newspaper reading and toilet operations, and from ten, I give desultory attention to the collection of Gas Revenue; until twelve o'clock lunch. This hour allows me 30 minutes in which to rush off indigestively to the Dock Sketch [a picture he was working on] and the next hour I am allowed to do what I like, it is winked at, in fact the head clerk goes to sleep next to my desk. After two the office fills again and I retire on some small pretext to an empty room upstairs where I doze, only interrupted by a telephone which asks me to go to a concert with it. The next noticeable thing is a cup of tea after which I furtively write rubbish in this book till 4.30 when I prepare to leave my clerkly labours.[99]

Such periods, however, were sandwiched between others, such as quarterly accounts, when clerks worked continuously till late in the evening.[100] Despite this, office work for many did not seem to be as strenuous as one would think.

We are thus faced with an almost paradoxical situation in relation to discipline in the office. On the one hand, there existed a strict regimen, a tight hierarchy, and ever-expanding rules. On the other, there was flexibility, leniency and, on occasions, an almost complete disregard for working practices. Much of this, however, was dependent on context and situation. Juniors were subjected to much stronger discipline than seniors. Individuals like Sydney Moseley were 'punished' later on by being refused promotion.[101] Acts of theft, dishonesty and character lapses were treated with the most severe punishments. Clerks at Glyn's, for example, were dismissed for 'insobriety', impecuniosity or marrying too early. Clerk Q was dismissed in February 1913 for pilfering stamps.[102] Employers were lenient to clerks during lax phases in return for obedience and hard work during heavy periods of work when most clerks did not leave their desks. In many respects, the working atmosphere of the office was probably not all that different from how it is today.

Conclusion

Between 1880 and 1914 a revolution took place in most offices in London. Though uneven in their extent, discernable trends took place – the introduction of technology, the emergence of the career, specialization, growth of internal labour markets, for many growth in companies, and perhaps most importantly, changes in markets relating to labour, capital and products. These changes had an important impact on clerical work.

These affected two specific areas, the clerk's relation to his office, and his relation to his work. In relation to the former, relations became more impersonal. Clerks changed from commercial servants to office workers, employees of companies and government offices. As this happened formal pay structures, fringe benefits and social welfare appeared. Much of this was done in an attempt to reintegrate clerks back into their workplace. Work for many clerks changed. Structured career paths and specialization became increasingly the norm for the clerk. Pay became more incremental. The result of all of this was that clerks took a more long term perspective towards their work. Finally, as work became more specialized and complex, the office became more formalized. Discipline became more rigorous. These changes should not, however, be overemphasized. Discipline was only enforced when the work demanded it. At other times the atmosphere of many offices was relaxed and flexible.

In all these changes, one should not see inauspicious developments. Changes in relations with employers may have resulted in a more depersonalized set of immediate working relations, yet they also resulted in more formalized benefits for the clerk which were not dependent on human caprice. For a group of individuals who valued security, such changes must not have appeared to have been completely unfavourable. Nor, in fact, would have been the growth in sporting and social facilities supplied by the workplace, which appear to have been genuinely appreciated by clerical workers. Similar arguments can be applied to work. Why would increased specialization, for example, over a life-long working period have been so bad? If one was forced to remain in one position, there are certainly grounds to believe this. Evidence shows, however, that this was not the case. Increased division of labour, in the context of the London office with its lack of formal training, only worked if one was transferred around the office and between departments. In addition, such specialization gradually increased the worth of the clerk which became reflected in his salary and sense of security.

Finally, these changes made the clerk more independent. The corpus of laws which emerged in this period created increasingly established parameters which he was able to operate in on a more even and steady basis. Increased specialization and a growing market resulted in his skills becoming more marketable. An increase in security, ensured by his growing skill and formal pay structure, gave him more freedom to transfer between employers or, as was more often the case, to develop career paths within organizations. While in some respects clerks were becoming more integrated into their work, in others they were becoming more autonomous and detached from it. In such an emerging environment, developments do not appear to have been particularly pernicious.

3 ATTITUDES OF THE CLERK TOWARDS WORK

What did the clerk think about his work? What values did he invest in it? Security and a regular income have already been discussed. For most clerks, in an insecure age, these were clearly the most important aspects of their work. Yet beyond this there were other values attached to clerical work. Values which gave clerical work significance despite some of its more monotonous characteristics.

These values will be looked at in this chapter. They can be seen as the non-manual, interpretive character of clerical work, professionalism, service, character, esprit de corps, the importance of working in London and, the reward for all of these, promotion and career. Clerks did not carry out manual labour. This was something they were aware of. An essential element of their job was service. Clerks did not produce tangible goods but rather provided services which were beneficial to those they served. It will be argued that this concept of service changed towards the end of the nineteenth century from services rendered to an individual to those rendered to the company or for the community at large. In addition, there were a number of qualities which were felt to be essential. One was the need to be conscientious, to take pride in work, to be accurate, efficient, pay attention to detail and furthermore to try and improve ones clerical skills. This was expressed in the idea of professionalism. Moreover, to be able to carry out work proficiently, it was felt that one needed to have character. This was felt to be vital to clerical work in terms of an individual's honesty, sobriety, willingness to improve oneself, and ultimately for promotion.

Esprit de corps was another important factor for clerks. It meant the ability to see oneself as part of a larger group, a working community rather than an anonymous unit of production. In addition, working in London was felt to add value to a clerk's work. There is evidence of a widespread feeling of pride amongst clerical workers at working in what was considered by many of them as the greatest city in the world. Finally, promotion and career advancement was regarded by clerks with great esteem. Next to security, this was probably the most important factor in a clerk's working life. It was often seen as the sum factor of all the other qualities needed for clerical work, the reward for the work one did and for the qualities which enabled one to do it. In this respect, promotion was often as important ideologically as it was practically. This chapter will look at all these elements in turn.

In the final part of this chapter, the question of whether clerks were satisfied with their work will be posed. Clerks have been depicted by commentators as being vocationally dissatisfied.[1] The bases of these remarks will be questioned. Sources which have sustained these views, it will be suggested, have been looked at uncritically. Many were not written by clerks, others were written by individuals who had worked in offices for only short periods, some by clerks writing in journals whose sole aim was to criticize clerical work. While no doubt not all clerical workers were satisfied, the question which needs to be asked is how representative of clerks were this group? Evidence from the diaries and interviews, for example, shows approval or at least a lack of dissatisfaction from clerical workers. This chapter will conclude by arguing that the value system outlined above created in clerks a coherent sense of occupational masculinity based around the value system depicted in this chapter. As a result of material security and the lack of stasis between such a system and the environments which clerks worked in, there are serious grounds to question what has previously been written on clerical workers in relation to their attitudes towards work.

The Non-Manual Aspect of Clerical Work

Jose Harris, in her work on the social history of Britain between 1870 and 1914, has noted how manual work was tainted with, '... inferiority, bondage and lack of access to culture, status, and power'. A study in 1895, example, was said to have, '... deplored the persistence of the 'old stigma attaching to the workman or the factory hand'.[2] While clerical work was certainly subject to critique and a certain degree of condescension, it was never quite looked down upon by society in this way. In addition to enjoying a secure salary, and a higher income, the clerk enjoyed a higher status because he did not perform manual labour.[3] He got, for the most part, neither his hands nor his clothes dirty. This was something which clerks were well aware of. 'The office is to the business, profession or trade, what the head is to the body', wrote the *Office* in October 1888, in an article entitled 'Qualifications for Office Work'. 'The brain', it continued, 'is the directing force of all the power exercised by the limbs of the body; so the power put forth in any department of a great business is directed from the office, where the principal or his trusted agent may be said to be the brain of the whole working body of subordinates. If the brain and body are not both in a healthy condition the human machine does its work imperfectly ...'[4] Clerks often referred to themselves as 'brain workers'.[5] As the analogy located them in the upper reaches of the human torso, so they distinguished themselves from the 'inferior' manual workers.

This belief also actualized itself in practices at the work place. In his study of railway workers between 1840 and 1979 Frank Mckenna has written,

> Although many of the clerical officers, even after long service, still earned less than a main-line fireman, the confidence born of superior education combined with the collar and the status gave them an air of superiority when they paraded for lunch, or met the uncomfortable oil-stained artisan across a shiny-topped desk. In the presence of a clerical officer on duty, the practice of removing hats was always demanded.[6]

In organizations that employed both large numbers of clerks and manual workers such as the railways, the brewing industry and larger units of industrial production, clerks were associated with the management. They were members of 'The Staff', a term which then referred exclusively to the management and their administrative and executive officers rather than the whole of the workforce. T. R. Gourvish and R. G. Wilson, for example, have noted the strong distinction in the brewing industry between the brewersmen engaged in the production of beer and those employed as clerks, travellers and agents. The 1907 Census of Production distinguished between the 64,953 wage earners and 14,727 salaried people, many of the latter being made up of clerical workers in addition to management and senior officials. The distinction was important as the former were charged to manufacturing expenses, while the salaries of managers, travellers and clerks were included in distribution costs.[7]

This distinction from manual workers, and association with management was clearly seen in the dress of the clerk, his suit, collar, tie and hat. To argue, as Geoffrey Crossick has done, that clerks dressed in this manner due to pretence and a need for display is crude to say the least.[8] Clerks dressed differently from manual workers to emphasize, as Crossick admits, that the work they carried out was essentially different.[9] They also did so because many were or would become management. They were often referred to, for example, as officers or officials of an organization, whether this be in the banking, insurance, local government, utilities or railway sectors.[10] Finally clerks dressed in this way to represent social position. Non-manual clerical work conferred on its holders in the late-Victorian and Edwardian period middle-class status. Their dress code was a simple sartorial reflection of this.[11]

Service

Clerks worked in the service sector. Most did not physically produce goods but either furnished services which facilitated the production of goods, via the provision of finance, trade, transport, costing, purchasing, distribution and increasingly marketing and advertising, or provided services directly to the public, as in transport or local government.

Ideas of service amongst clerks gradually changed in the latter half of the nineteenth century. A clerk's sense of service had earlier derived from his relatively close relationship with his employers. Clerks as commercial servants faithfully served their masters. Satisfaction was derived from providing personal, loyal service. The interests of the master and the business house were tightly related in the clerk's mind to his own interests and the service which he provided.[12]

With the closer integration of the national economy in the latter half of the nineteenth century, with the increasing dependency of industry on services such as the railways or the financial and commercial houses and exchanges of London, ideas of service became more associated with the work clerks provided for the well being of the general public, nation and Empire rather than any one individual or company. Herein lies part of the reason for the deep patriotism that clerks were noted for.[13] Clerks readily identified themselves with the Mother Country and Empire because they felt that their labours were tied up with its interests.[14] This process was further assisted by the growth in the scale of offices and break down in personal ties between employer and clerk. Similarly with the growth of national and local government, public officials gradually became more involved with the community at large in the services which they provided for it.[15]

Such a sense of public service can be seen in two quotes from staff magazines. The first comes from the *London County Council Staff Gazette*, a journal written by the clerks of the L.C.C.,

> ... every young officer during the first year of service, should be given facilities for visiting all the Council's works. He should see the mighty engines of our pumping station; he should be brought face to face with the practical working out of the gigantic drainage problem, he should see the fleet of steamers that day and night toil to and from the sea that London may maintain her reputation as the healthiest city of the world's great cities, he should see the great ferry and burrowing tunnel which unite the populations on either side of the Lower Thames. He should see the Chemists in their laboratory, the examiners at the gas-testing stations, the workshops of the Works Departments, the blocks of artisan's dwellings that have displaced reeking slums, the wonderful organization for dealing with fires, for it is only when he has seen all these that the young official can realize the greatness and the importance of the vast organization in which he is to become a factor.[16]

The second comes from the *Great Eastern Railway Magazine*, and describes the functions of the Bishopsgate Goods Station, located in Shoreditch, on the parameters of the City of London,

> Situated in busy Shoreditch, its proximity to the docks, wharves, markets and great City warehouses, places Bishopsgate in an exceptional position for dealing with no inconsiderable proportion of the carrying trade of London.
>
> ... As London is the great distributing centre of the world, so Bishopsgate in its outward traffic reflects the nature of the business of the capital of the Empire. The

goods despatched are cosmopolitan in character and go not only to the Company's own line, but to the Midlands, the North, and the Continent.[17]

Both these quotes illustrate the pride that was felt in working for these concerns, and in the services they provided. In the first, the very health of London was guaranteed by the work of the L.C.C., in the second it was the trade and welfare of not only the capital, but of the Empire itself. In both examples the service aspects of these organizations was emphasized.

Professionalism

Many clerks took active pride in their work. The *Office*, for example, in 1889 wrote, 'An office occupied by highly qualified, active, intelligent men is as certain to be the centre of a progressive and successful business, as one occupied by incompetent men will assuredly prove the reverse ...'[18] The success of an office was thus dependent on the degree of professionalism that individuals applied to their work.[19] This in turn was a reflection of the competency of the men selected to work in the office. The *L.C.C. Staff Gazette*, for example, often referred to the officials of the L.C.C. as 'men of intelligence and ability', qualities which were seen as essential for the effective execution of the duties of the officials of the Council.[20]

When asked if his father had felt dissatisfied or bored with his work at the London County and Westminster Bank, Jim Hancock answered, 'No, I don't think so at all, I think he had a great interest in detail, in accuracy, and I think he would always have been very conscientious about whatever task, or whatever position he was in during his career'.[21] These qualities which Jim listed, attention to detail, accuracy and conscientiousness were seen as the essential qualities which a clerk needed.[22] In addition, in an age when most clerical tasks were still done by hand and brain, these were required characteristics of his work. In many respects, the craft of the clerical worker, the ability to write in a legible script, to compose letters and documents that were grammatically accurate, to rapidly add up rows of figures and perform complex mathematical calculations, was no different in terms of its exclusivity and status from the skill of an artisan.[23] Clerks, like skilled workers, took great pride in the accuracy and tidiness of what they produced. These were qualities which were often commented on when a clerk left the employment of an office or passed away. When Rodney C. Baker, for example, retired from The Prudential in 1918 after 44 years he was applauded for not being absent at any time during his duties, nor having infringed any of the regulations of the Company. Baker had been a member of the staff of L-Claim, a department whose motto was 'Nothing Second Rate'.[24]

One important aspect of commitment was attending evening courses to improve ones clerical skills and further ones education. Laurence Gomme, for example, Clerk of the London County Council wrote in 1900 that officers of the L.C.C. should look at themselves as much as students as officials. 'A clerk', he argued, 'is a better clerk if he copies a report or letter not only correctly and neatly, but with a full knowledge of the subject matter, and a professional officer is doubly important if, besides being a specialist in his own profession, he knows some of the influences which have produced his work and which his work is in turn likely to produce'.[25]

Shorthand, bookkeeping, and foreign languages were just three of the many subjects that clerks studied after office hours. In August, 1903, for example, Sydney Moseley began to attend night school. In March of the following year he entered for the Chamber of Commerce Shorthand examination, and for the National Union of Teachers Book-keeping qualification.[26] Much of this was due to the strong self-help and self-improvement ethics found amongst clerks. Attending such courses improved ones chances of promotion. For many, they were essential skills for the duties of the modern clerk. Yet all of these factors need to be seen in the light of the clerk's professional commitment to his work. As 'brain-workers' clerks were expected to improve their education. In addition to evening courses, such commitment could take other forms outside working hours. The article referred to earlier on 'The Education of a Goods Clerk', encouraged its readers to read newspapers, magazines, even the advertising columns of trade journals. Exhibitions were seen as sound sources of education, as were visits to factories or simply the intelligent scanning of a shop window. On 1 December 1904, for example, George Rose, went to a Gas Exhibition where he saw, '... a good many of my fellow clerks'.[27] The London civil servant Daniel McEwen, wrote a book on bankruptcy accounts which was subsequently published in 1889. He was quick, on its publication, to send a copy to his most senior superior, the Inspector General.[28]

Character

In February, 1900, an article in the *L.C.C. Staff Gazette*, entitled, 'Advice written by one with thirty years official experience to Juniors', stated, '... it is important to bear in mind that in most branches of the Council's work character is at least as important, and is as much looked for as ability'.[29] The argument was a well rehearsed one. T. E. Young, ex-President of the Institute of Actuaries and ex-Chairman of the Life Office's Association, argued in 1904, in slightly more convoluted terms,

> ... High character, especially in those occupying the more responsible posts, is worth much intellectual adroitness, since by the tone and temper with which it pervades an assembly of boys and men of different dispositions, varied accessibility to diverse temptations, and inequalities of moral strength, it exercises a purifying influence and adds conspicuously to the order, discipline, and effectiveness of the entire staff.[30]

Speaking nearly a hundred years later Jim Hancock, retired, but still working in the archives of the Royal Bank of Scotland, noted,

> Doing my work at the archives at the moment, transferring historical information of the Staff Magazines of the various constituency banks to the computer data base, I've come across this impression that you were dealing with men, and later women, of course, coming into the bank, of the highest integrity. I can't emphasize that enough. They were quite remarkable men and women.[31]

The importance of character had much to do with Victorian values of manliness, which had been so assiduously cultivated in the Public Schools, and had been extolled by public figures from William Gladstone to Samuel Smiles.[32] A man's true value lay in his inner worth, in his integrity, his honesty, his assiduity, his desire for self-improvement and his sense of loyalty and duty.[33] The sum product of this was seen as his character. Asked, for example, what he meant by 'integrity', Jim answered, 'Total honesty, trustworthy, the way they conducted themselves. People whom you had the highest respect for'.[34] Success in one's work and by extension in worldly terms lay in applying one's character to one's labour and one's dealing with other men.[35]

Character was seen as important to a clerk's success for several reasons. One was the support it gave in one's drive for self-improvement, for the getting of knowledge which was regarded as so important for a clerk's success. In addition to this was the whole question of honesty and trustworthiness. Clerical workers were often responsible for handling large amounts of money and dealing with confidential information. It was therefore vital that they could be trusted.[36] A clerk's promotion, for example, and annual salary increment was often seen as an indication of his employer's trust in him, and was thus the source of great pride. George Rose, for instance, wrote of his 'public disgrace in the office' in January, 1902, at only having been given a £5 pay increase.[37] With the increase in size in many offices, and the break down in personal relations which this entailed, this need for trust, and men of high character, became correspondingly greater.

Character was felt to be important for promotion and career advancement in other respects. There was seen to be a relationship between the depth of one's character and the amount of work that one could be responsible for. This was felt to be especially important when clerks began to become responsible for other clerks. T. E. Young, for example, argued,

> ... in every promotion the element of moral character should be assigned a dominating place. No ability can atone in the fulfilment of duty and trust for deficiency of high principles. Both in the selection of candidates, and particularly in their appointment to higher ranks where their influence will be materially widened and more pervasive, this consideration is of primal consequence.[38]

Mr W. A. Webb, for example, a second-class assistant in the General Construction Section of the Architects Department of the L.C.C was passed over twice for promotion in 1897 and 1898. In a memorandum stating his reasons, The Architect, the head of Webb's department wrote, '... he is well conducted and well intended but has not so far shown the ability to take entire responsibility, and to supervise others as in the case of other officials'.[39]

Finally, in such a highly individualistic era, it was felt that the character of each individual member of a company represented the total character of the organization itself. This belief has been seen in the *Office*'s argument in which a successful company could only emerge if it were filled with competent men. 'The character of the employees in an office', the article argued, 'is in fact one of the most prominent indications of the nature of the business in which they are engaged'.[40] In anatomical terms T. E. Young argued, '... the character or nature of the units or parts of which the organism is composed determines the character or nature of the aggregate when the units are associated for any specific end'.[41] The equation was simple. The more character your staff had, the more successful your organization. The emphasis, therefore, became to attract as many men of high character as possible.

It was in this context that the importance attached to sport at the workplace can partially be located. Since the mid-nineteenth century sport had been seen as character building.[42] It built up strength, induced discipline, developed teamwork and increased ones endurance. The more sport one did, it was assumed, the more character and manliness one developed. This in turn was seen to result in the office and wider organization one worked for becoming more successful. T. E. Young argued regarding this, 'It need scarcely be remarked that the institution of athletic sports among the staff serves as a most helpful agency of union and stimulus. No more accredited aid to the promotion of moral character ... can be devised than innocent, healthful relaxations ...'[43]

Esprit de Corps

As offices and departments became larger and more impersonalized, management became increasingly faced with the problem of how to weld all their personnel together into one unified working group. It has already been seen in the previous chapter how in terms of practical working conditions this was attempted by introducing a more rigorous discipline in the office, particularly among the younger members of staff. In addition, management were faced by the further problem of creating in their members of staff the feeling that they were members of a company, individuals who shared something in common, and were not simply cogs in the wheel of some lumbering bureaucracy.

This sense of belonging, of being part of a greater family, was created as has been argued earlier, by means of corporate patronage and introducing ideas of company loyalty. Clerks increasingly associated themselves not with the person they worked for, but rather with the organization. A sense of corporate identity developed, especially for those in larger offices. The evidence suggests that there were strong associations between clerks and their places of work, reinforced by the long periods that clerks often stayed with a company or office. George Rose, for example, hated being a clerk and dreamed of being an artist.[44] Despite this, however, Rose's diary is full of reference to the office he worked in at the Commercial Gas Company, of the politics of the office, of his position within it and of the colleagues he worked with. Such sentiments also did not prevent him from attending the social activities of his office.[45]

Frank H. H. King has also noted, in relation to the Hongkong and Shanghai Bank, that as the organization grew larger, in addition to the establishment of a more rigid system of discipline, a vertical familiarity was replaced by a greater knowledge of ones peers.[46] Put more simply, as companies grew larger there were increased opportunities to form friendships with individuals of a similar age. Such friendships with colleagues from work seem to have been strong amongst clerks, many reinforced by the existence of sporting clubs and other social activities associated with work, and appear to have been an important element of their professional life. When he began work for the Civil Service at Somerset House in 1910, Alfred Henry Pyle was able to meet men of his own age with whom he lunched and socialized in London. Friendships were also formed with individuals he met on his daily commute up to London.[47] Jim Hancock believed that the most valued thing his father had derived from working at the Westminster Bank for over forty years was the colleagues whom he had met there and formed lifelong friendships with.[48] Esprit de corps was therefore seen not only as the degree to which one associated with one's company, but also the extent to which one was able to get on with one's colleagues, both during and after office hours. Being part of a team was clearly an important element in a clerk's working life.

London

The clerks of this study not only worked for companies, individuals and government. They also worked in London, then the largest city in the world, Imperial Capital of Britain and its Empire, and hub of the world's trading and financial system. This was something all clerks knew and regarded with pride. Such a feeling was articulated by W. Howarth in 1900 in his work on Britain's banking system,

> Without a doubt, London is the greatest centre of industry in the world. In it one can see trades and professions of every kind, manufactories, institutions, industries, &c., in fact, everything ... can be procured in that monstrous overgrowth of warehouses,

offices, shops and buildings of all sorts ... London with its population of nearly six millions; London with its stupendous public buildings, with its magnificent cathedral, with its numerous and excellent institutions; London, the capital of one of the greatest Powers of modern times; and most assuredly the capital of a country whose dominion extends from pole to pole; London, with its perfection of organization, its unequalled civic law without a question does business of a gigantic character and of dimensions unknown to any but itself. Its financial institutions, its banking art and science – for banking unites the taste of one with the dignity of the other – are now unrivalled in the civilized world.[49]

Size clearly did matter. Despite the hyperbole of much of Howarth's language, there was also some truth in what he wrote. In 1914 no city rivalled London in terms of its commercial and financial strength. In addition, it was a major centre of industry, the professions, and retailing, besides being the national seat of government. Clerks were very much a part of all of this. As the *County Magazine* stated in 1909, for example, the London Banks were, '... a representative of the most important business community in the greatest city in the world'.[50]

Nowhere can the sense of pride be seen better than in the term 'City Man'. The term applied to those who carried out office work in the City of London, from the Head of the Bank of England to the lowliest clerk.[51] Widely used in this period, it can be found in newspapers, journals, novels, speeches and even diaries and was clearly a term which carried much kudos and status. For the *Ilford Guardian*, the local newspaper of a growing London suburb, mainly populated by office workers and their families, the City Men were the cream of the town. At a celebratory meal for the opening of the new Town Hall at Ilford the paper reported Councillor Henry Weeden's speech in which he stated, '... Their townsmen were nearly all City men. They had to work extremely hard during the day and would like to see more social life in the town without having to go to the West End of London for it'.[52] In fact, less than half of Ilford's male inhabitants would probably have commuted to the City at that point, but of course Weeden was talking about the men who mattered, and in this he was not contradicted by the local paper. In 1911 the official promotional brochure of Ilford, written by its local council, repeated Weeden's sentiments, '... Ilford was created by the city worker for the city worker, and it is a model of what a residential locality should be for the professional and commercial class.'[53]

By 1914 City workers had created a particularly strong occupational and regional sense of identity. On 28 February 1913, for example, George Rose moved yet again to another set of rooms in South Hampstead. His diary entry for that day read,

I left the office at Midday today to get on with the moving. We had interviewed four or five women for to choose a house keeper last night, much to the amusement of the trades people in Kings College Road through which we are becoming notorious in the immediate neighbourhood. They tell the servants and the servants tell their mistresses of the two bachelors (Citymen) about to set up housekeeping in a flat. But we are thinking that the girls will not stand the devil of a chance now we are getting so independent and I have observed recently one living opposite showing a very interested face at the windows.[54]

When Rose used the term 'Citymen' to refer to himself and his flatmate Duncan (a stockbroker's clerk), he was identifying himself with a larger collective. While most clerks would have had some form of occupational identity in this period, identifying themselves to some degree with their place of work, those who worked in the City shared a supra-corporate identity. The dress codes of the City, the obligatory wearing of straw hats in the summer, for example, expressed this.[55] It was one which its holders appear to have adopted with pride, dignity and satisfaction.

Promotion and Career

Next to security, promotion (including salary increases) and career were the most important aspect of a clerk's job. Its centrality cannot be exaggerated. Clerks wrote memorials about it, they sent petitions to superiors and letters to newspapers about it.[56] They composed poems over it, mused about it in their diaries, wrote short stories and even novels on it.[57] The work *69 Birnam Road*, for example, written by William Pett Ridge, a former clerk, and widely read by clerical workers and their families, revolves around the career of Fred, the husband of the main character Ella, from railway clerk to Superintendent of the Line.[58] In writing such a novel Ridge was articulating the dreams and aspirations of many of his readers.

Promotion and career were important for several reasons. Firstly, it meant more money for the clerks and increased security. For married officials with families this was crucial. The poem 'On Salary', for example, written by 'Piper', clerical official and poet of the *L.C.C. Staff Gazette*, comically showed the importance of promotion and salary increases to the married clerk, his offspring and his home. In the poem the author addressed a letter to his manager asking for promotion and a salary rise, a yearly ritual for most clerks. In the first three stanzas he wrote,

> I sent a letter to the chief
>   And said 'It passes all belief
>   How many noble things I do
>   For such a mediocre screw.
>   Enclosed are portraits of my twins
>   (how sleek and pink their baby skins)
>   'Two bring the tear drops to your eyes
>   To hear them lisp, 'Where's puppa's rise?
>   I told them what it cost for coals

How little socks contracted holes
What Hannah spent in frocks and frill
And what we paid in Butchers Bills.[59]

As can be seen in these stanzas, a higher income was not only of economic significance for officials, but was also of social value, particularly for a group who were as socially competitive as clerical workers.[60] Higher-paid clerks could live in larger houses, in 'better' areas, go on more luxurious holidays, join more affluent social and sporting clubs, dress their children better, keep them in school for longer, and at more prestigious institutions. For fathers among the staff, usually as sole breadwinners in the household, this led to a reinforcing of their prestige and position within the household.[61]

Promotion also meant increased status. Clerical work was extremely hierarchical. Clerks were often divided into classes with juniors and office boys below them, and special officers, chief clerks and managers above this. Everything in the office, from one's salary, to the work one was responsible for, to very often, one's position in the sporting and social clubs was a reflection of this. Offices in this period appear to have been every bit as political as they are today. George Rose's diary, for example, is full of the machinations of power within the office where he worked. On 18 December 1905, for instance, he wrote, 'Heard from Edwin that Freeman is deposed. H. Parr is to be head of the office and Edwin to go upstairs and assist Bradfield the head accountant. So there is "boulversement". Of course I do not expect any advancement. I believe when they look my way the thought which arises is of Art (Art as a plaything they mean) and certainly not of a responsible business man.'[62] On 3 January 1906, his diary entry concluded the saga of the hapless Freeman, 'Small groups cluster at intervals about the office today, gleeful on two subjects: the rises and G. Freeman's dismissal. He came up today and was 'sacked'. It must be like a nightmare to him after the amount of influence he had at the office.'[63]

Finally, promotion and career were an indication of the degree of attainment of the other qualities listed above. How professional one was, how devout one was in serving the company and its broader clientele, how well one worked with one's colleagues and associated oneself with the organization one worked for and, most importantly, the depth of one's character, were all reflected in the extent of an individual's ability to climb up the office ladder. Promotion was seen as the reward for merit and ability. It was the ultimate mark of success. As a result of this, the disappointment that some clerks displayed at failing to obtain promotion was profound and deeply personal. George Rose's public humiliation in the office at failing to achieve a large pay increase has already been seen. W. A. Webb, the second class Assistant in the General Construction Section of the Architects department was so incensed at being passed over twice for promotion that he wrote to the newspaper, the *Echo*, about it which resulted in a large article being written in 1898 on staff grievances at the L.C.C.[64] At Glyn's Bank in October, 1902, Clerk R was 'allowed to resign' because he had been passed over in favour of another clerk.[65]

The weight that was given by clerks to promotion and career can be illustrated by the reaction of the officials of the Major Establishment at the L.C.C. when changes were made to the classification system of the grade by the Council between 1908 and 1909. Before these dates officers at the L.C.C. had been divided into four classes. It had been assumed that any officer of average or above ability would be able to proceed through his career through all four classes, arriving at a final salary of £300. A Standing Order of 1909 changed all of this. Promotion to the first class, would now only take place if a vacancy became available, or if the extension of work merited such a promotion. Promotion to the senior grades was now fixed. What became known as the £200 barrier, the highest salary one could reach as a second-class official, had been created.[66]

The news of this proposal in December 1908 was said to have sent a shock wave through the staff. As C. D. Andrews and G. C. Burge wrote fifty years later in the half-centenary anniversary of the L.C.C. Staff Association, 'To most of the Staff this was the grossest betrayal'.[67] The Council was felt to have reneged on its promises to the staff. More importantly, the act contested the hallowed belief that merit should be the principle criteria for promotion. By creating the barrier, it was argued, artificial obstacles were being erected to impede progression. Spontaneous agitation against the proposals quickly took place. On 18 December 1908, 600 Staff assembled in Birkbeck College. By 1909, the L.C.C. Staff Association had been formed to protect the interests of the officials of the Council and to protest as a group against the imposition of the £200 barrier. Though strictly speaking not a formal trade union, the Association marked a turning point in the history of the officials of the L.C.C. For the first time officials negotiated collectively rather than individually with the Council in relation to their terms of employment. Staff relations would never be the same again.

An important article on the subject appeared in the *L.C.C. Staff Gazette* in February 1914. This was the month that promotion and pay increases were announced, and thus awakened a sense of grievance in the staff to the changes of five years earlier. The staff's sense of outrage and disappointment was as acute as it had been in 1909. Starting from the argument that it was wrong for the Council to fix men's salaries at £200 during a period of rising prices, the article went on to depict the Staff's sense of betrayal at the Council's actions, and its implications for their professional lives. '... human nature', the article argued, '... can understand that financial considerations may prevent a capable and deserving officer from receiving an increase of salary. It is more difficult, however, to appreciate the point of view which denies an outlet to a man's ability because having devoted himself to his duties from an early age he is compelled ever more to be classified in a certain way'.[68] Citing the examples of 'distinguished administrators such as Sir Laurence Gomme, the Clerk of the Council, and Sir M. E. Haward, its Comptroller, both of whom had risen through the ranks, the article went on to argue, '... The Staff is inspired by such examples and naturally is anxious that the great field of achievement that lay before the servants of the Council years ago, shall be open to the men of today, provided they in turn prove their worth'.[69]

This article, and the entire debate at the L.C.C. between 1909 and 1914 concerning the '£200 Barrier' was instructive in relation to the clerk's attitude to promotion. While financial concerns were always paramount in a clerk's mind, there were also important ideological considerations. Promotion was the reward for a man's ability and faithful duty at work. It was a direct reflection of his inner character and merit. The basis of its legitimacy was guaranteed by the precedents of the Senior members of Staff. There was a belief that its working was almost natural. The sense of betrayal thus expressed came not only from a breach of trust, but also from a feeling that the whole working of the professional nexus of a clerk's life, the virtuous circle of merit, work, promotion was being grievously broken. It was an argument which was often repeated in disputes between clerks and employees, and illustrates the centrality of promotion, both in terms of material reward and ideology, to a clerk's working life.[70]

Work and Satisfaction

To what extent did clerks in London derive job satisfaction from the duties they carried out? For a group of individuals who would devote up to forty-five years of their life to clerical work the question is clearly pertinent. No attempt here will be given to provide a definitive answer. The numbers of individuals concerned were too large, their tasks too varied. Nevertheless, the question can be discussed and suggestions offered. The degree of satisfaction of clerks with their work would obviously have had an impact on the actions and attitudes of these individuals, both at work and outside of it.

The general agreement in the literature is that clerks were anything but satisfied. Braverman's depiction of the clerk's increasing anomie has already been seen. Anderson's portrayal is of a group of men hopelessly fighting the tide of history, swamped by the vicissitudes of unemployment, falling incomes, women, foreigners, technology and youths, and generally not content with their professional lives.[71] Paul Attewell begins his article on clerks by arguing that not only were clerks dissatisfied with their work after 1870, but that they had never been satisfied! An extensive barrage of quotes is directed at the reader to force through this point from individuals such as Charles Lamb to anonymous contributors to contemporary journals.[72]

Many of these arguments were reflected in, and based on, the contemporary literature of the day referred to earlier. Newspaper articles, poems, novels and even songs depicted clerks who were thoroughly disillusioned with their work and life in general. 'The daily paper', the *County Magazine* wrote in 1907, 'is becoming a terror to us, for fear it may contain yet another article by a self-appointed champion of our cause'.[73]

This last quote reveals the weaknesses of many of the arguments made above. Much of the case has been made on the basis of a selective and uncritical reading of sources. Many of these articles and poems were written by individuals who were not clerks and were writing more with an eye to their readership than to a desire to depict with objective accuracy what was actually taking place. This can be seen in the case of W. A. Webb, the official at the L.C.C. who had been passed over for promotion. As a result of writing a letter to the *Echo*, stating his own personal grievances, the newspaper produced an article which depicted the entire Staff of the L.C.C. in a state of near anarchy and revolution. Here was a classic example of the grievances of an individual being inflated by an unscrupulous journalist to represent the feelings of the majority.[74]

How representative such criticisms were must also be treated with a degree of scepticism. This is for several reasons. The first is that while some of these writers were former clerks, they had been so for only relatively short periods. There was a strong tendency to depict in extremely hostile terms the agonies which they went through when they had been chained to the desk of some godforsaken office. 'The extreme of active misery' wrote George Rose in 1909, a man who clearly associated himself with these literary greats, 'I suffer from contact with my fellow clerks seems insupportable. Imagine the bulk of a man made up of and consisting of vile, gangrenous putrefying concretions of slugs, worms, eels and rats and you will realize a little of what some of these men are to me'.[75]

The author George Bernard Shaw wrote a series of articles about his own experience as a clerk for the *Clerk*, at the beginning of 1909. Shaw had been a clerk in Dublin for four and a half years, and left the field before he was twenty. Writing in March 1908, he stated, concerning the clerical worker:

> ... I have sometimes wondered whether clerks perform any useful function in the general scheme of the universe ... his work is either a hopeless routine which he does not understand , he too often knows it to be work that had better not be done at all. He is more than any worker, the instrument of greed, chicanery, and parasitism ... The clerk too often produces nothing but the incidental cheating.[76]

This quote was typical of attacks by writers who had been former clerks. Taken at face value, they are a damning condemnation of the entire clerical profession and put to flight any suggestion that clerks were satisfied with their professional lot in life. Though emphasizing his experience as a clerk, however, there were clearly limits on the insights that even a man as gifted as Shaw, and others like him, could have gained into the entire clerical profession as a teenager working in an office in Dublin for such a brief period. This argument is repeated in David King's critique of P. G. Wodehouse who had lampooned the Hongkong and Shaghai Bank and the workings of the City in his satirical novel *Psmith in the City*. Wodehouse, like Shaw, had worked as a clerk. Like Shaw, however, he had only done so as a teenager for several years. 'Wodehouse', King argues, '– and others like him – neither understanding its [the work they carried out] purpose at the time nor willing to wait until much had become clear, was not in a position to evaluate the consequences of the routine jobs he and his colleagues were required to perform'.[77] Individuals like Shaw and Wodehouse often criticized clerical workers for carrying out work, the purpose of which they had no idea. Such writers' criticisms, while providing amusing and sometimes original insights, should consequently be treated with caution when historically discussing clerical workers.

In addition to newspapers and writers, historians have often turned to clerical journals to demonstrate clerical worker's dissatisfaction. Again, there are serious grounds to question the general applicability of these sources. Many journals, such as the *Clerk* and the *Railway Clerk*, were the magazines of clerical trade unions and associations whose very purpose was to articulate the misery of the black coated worker. the *Clerk*, for example, wrote in its first edition in 1908, 'Our Journal and our Union will grow together. The experience of the past eighteen months has proved what possibilities open up as soon as time, energy and esprit de corps are given to propaganda and organization in the whole-hearted manner which we have seen lately'.[78] One could hardly expect anything other than general criticism from a press whose purpose was to criticizer. One could equally, for example, turn to company journals, such as the *County Magazine*, to prove how wonderfully happy and contented clerks were. There are clearly limitations in the use of both forms of literature when attempting to evaluate a clerk's satisfaction with their work.

A final source of criticism which historians have looked at are the petitions and memorials which clerical workers periodically sent to superiors. If clerks had a grievance at work they would petition their employers, asking for the situation to be ameliorated. As the nineteenth century progressed, it became increasingly typical for clerks, especially in larger offices, to send joint petitions. In the case of an organization such as the Great Western Railway, for example, such petitions could be signed by several thousand clerks. Such petitions could be seen as proof of clerical dissatisfaction with work.[79] There are, however, two problems with this. The first is that they were a traditional method of employer–employee relations. Rather than negotiate directly with their superiors, clerks were forced to write down problems which they felt needed to be resolved. The result was a particularly negative system of arbitration, which on the surface made it appear that clerks were constantly racked with dissent and antagonism towards their employers. The reluctance of the latter group, up until 1914, to discuss regularly issues which concerned clerks at work exacerbated this. The second problem is that the petition tended to exaggerate grievances. If the situation was felt to be serious enough, clerks would be granted a meeting to discuss the issue, or even have some of their demands met. It was therefore in the clerk's interest to amplify their complaint(s) as much as possible. The Whitley Council, set up after the First World War, went some way to resolve these problems by encouraging more negotiation between Staff and employers. Before 1914, for example, clerical trade unions and associations in the Civil Service had argued, 'that a formal negotiating procedure should be established together with the facilities for conciliation and arbitration'.[80] It was the lack of such a negotiating procedure amongst clerical workers, and the exaggerated claims that this encouraged, that should make the historian extra careful when looking at such material.

There are therefore strong grounds to question the traditional belief that clerks were dissatisfied with their work. This is not to argue that all clerks were blissfully happy or to argue that there did not exist any who were not. The evidence shows a wide variety of responses to work. It is only to question how representative these criticisms were and to what extent they accurately depicted clerical grievances. Perhaps the most effective and simple argument against such claims is that one usually complains when one has a grievance but remains quiet when one is content. Detecting evidence of clerical dissatisfaction is not the same thing as saying that all clerks were dissatisfied.

Evidence from the diaries and interviews supports these arguments. George Rose and Sydney Moseley were certainly not content with their professional lot in life. Yet the latter left the clerical profession to become a journalist and the former considered himself to be an artist who used clerical work, which he felt to be below him, to support his art work. Rose, indeed, was typical of that class of clerk who Haslehurst Greaves, a lifetime clerk, described as not being adapted to their calling, '... they have missed their vocation in life'. Greaves commented, 'Their hearts and minds are elsewhere, they should have been engineers or actors, doctors or lawyers, but force of circumstances has chained them to a desk ...'[81] Both clerks, while typical of a certain class of clerical worker, were not typical of the majority who remained in offices for their working lives. Diarists such as William Evans or Daniel McEwen, never raved nor complained about their work. It was a subject they never touched in their diaries. Similarly the majority of clerks interviewed expressed either satisfaction with their work or a lack of frustration with it. The same tendency was repeated when they spoke of their parents who had been clerks. Only one former clerk, Geoffrey Rogers, stated he wished he had had a different kind of occupation.[82] Rogers had had no say in the type of labour he would perform. This decision had been taken by his parents, and he himself, years later, stated he would have preferred to have done a more manual job, such as carpenting for example.

Clearly this is not to say that all clerks were satisfied with their work. There were clerks who were not suited to clerical work and left the profession. There were others who remained silent and simply put up with the work. It would be wrong, however, to use these as representative examples. Clerical registers show the overwhelming majority of clerks as remaining with their organizations or moving to join other offices as clerical workers.[83] Most clerks remained as clerks. Evidence from diaries and oral sources indicates that there was some degree of satisfaction. What should one expect otherwise from a position which in an age of insecurity and widespread poverty provided for many security, a relatively high and rising income, paid holidays, sick pay, opportunities for promotion and for an increasing number pensions and subsidized sporting and social facilities?

Conclusion

This chapter has attempted to argue that in addition to providing security there were other factors in office work that were valued by office workers. Some, such as performing non-manual work or working in London, were extrinsic. Others, such as the importance of service, character and esprit de corps were values which were specific to clerks and the work environments they operated in. All, however, contributed to forming a value system which sustained and directed the actions of these workers. London Clerks regarded themselves as men who possessed character, who provided services, who associated themselves with the companies they worked in and colleagues they worked with. They saw themselves as being different from many other men in that they did not perform manual work and worked in the great metropolis. The value of their labour became enhanced not only by their attitudes to their work but also by the place that they performed it in.

These values became very much the corpus of their occupational masculinity.[84] It was the value that clerks attached to their work that established the professional worth of a man. Promotion, in particular, as a way of measuring many of these values, was seen as the hallmark of a clerk's occupational masculinity. It acted as an important signifier in the matrix of a clerk's discursive framework. It revealed distinctions between himself and different clerical workers. The extent of a clerk's commitment to these ideals and his belief in promotion as a sign of distinction has been seen in the reaction of the L.C.C.'s officials to the Council's imposition of the £200 barrier. Their outrage, as much ideological as it was practical, can be seen as a clear indication of their attachment to the values outlined in this chapter.

Finally, this chapter has argued that the grounds for which many commentators have located strong dissatisfaction amongst clerical workers with their work can be strongly contested. Many of the sources used have been too readily and uncritically accepted. Evidence based on sensationalist newspaper articles, disgruntled clerks or clerical journals needs to be placed in its historical context.[85] Oral evidence from clerks, and from their diaries and memoirs presents a very different picture. Many clerks appear to have been satisfied with the work they carried out, and/or offered no serious grounds for complaint. Such attitudes can be seen to be a result of both the financial rewards which this work offered and the cognitive and ideological ones which were sustained by the value system outlined above. There are thus serious grounds to question the claim that the clerical literature of complaint was representative of this professional group as a whole, which much of the previous historiography has readily accepted and embedded in its discourse.

4 WORK, INCOME, PROMOTION AND STABILITY: THE LATE VICTORIAN AND EDWARDIAN LONDON CLERK REVISITED

Between 1870 and 1914 clerks in Victorian and Edwardian Britain have been portrayed as being increasingly under strain. Following 1870, it has been argued, with the widespread availability of education and the large increase in clerical numbers, clerks came to suffer serious status anxiety. Their literary and numerical skills suddenly became available to a much wider group, and with growth in numbers the clerical dream of working one's way up into a partnership was becoming increasingly impossible. In addition, because so many individuals were entering the clerical profession the market was argued to be overstocked with the result that salaries were stagnating or falling, and unemployment was becoming more and more prevalent. Growth in the size of companies is claimed to have led to a breakdown in relations with employers and the deskilling of clerical work by the introduction of a rigid division of labour. Finally clerks were said to be assailed throughout the period by the introduction of women, youths, foreigners and technology in the office. The clerk, however, shackled by his beliefs in his respectability, loyalty to his employer and distaste of anything that smacked of the working classes, refused to unionize to protect himself. The whole tragedy of the black-coated worker was that his conceit and 'false consciousness' precluded him from taking action against his steadily worsening market situation.[1]

The origins of the above lay in arguments that were being presented at the time by a number of clerical trade unions that were beginning to appear. These unions, via their journals, portrayed a golden past when clerks were given a fair wage by their employers with whom they enjoyed close relations.[2] Work was engaging, provided satisfaction and offered the aspiring young man with talent an opportunity to become his own master. All this was to change, however, with the coming of the latter stages of capitalism in Britain. With the increase in competition and scale of economic activity, relations between clerks and employers broke down. The spread of education made his skills less exclusive. Masters increasingly attempted to drive down wages, foreigners, youths, women and technology were brought into the office in increasing numbers in an effort to do so and work became progressively more disenchanting.[3]

As has been argued in the Introduction, this account was faithfully passed on to future generations by the work of successive commentators. Klingender represented it in the 1930s, Braverman and Anderson in the 1970s.[4] Its most recent appearance came in 1998 via R. Guerriero Wilson's account of Glaswegian clerks, 1880–1914.[5] What was originally an argument put forward by a group of small but very vocal and ideologically driven trade unions has become today historical dogma.

This chapter aims to examine the veracity of these claims. Did clerks suffer status anxiety and even crisis? Were their salaries being hammered down, their positions threatened by the 'invasion of new recruits' into the office? Did their prospects weaken while their jobs themselves become ominously less secure? The question of income will be first discussed. If the clerical market was overstocked one would therefore expect to see a downturn in salaries. Examination of clerical salaries in London from a selected group of companies in fact does not suggest that this was the case; salaries were rising not falling. While this may not be conclusive proof for income rises in all clerical sectors, particularly in secondary clerical labour markets, it is nevertheless evidence that clerical salaries were not as volatile as has been suggested. Following this, the question of clerical work will be analysed. How far are the claims true that changes in the economy and company structure affected clerks. Were the doors of promotion and independence closing in their faces? Again the answer appears to be in the negative. The promotional policies of the London County Council, the railway companies, in particular the Great Western, and the London County and Westminster Bank will be examined. It will be argued that all three organizations had a strong commitment to internal promotion for all positions, and that their practices conformed to this. This policy was reflected in most organizations. Companies and government offices preferred to recruit internally because they realized that the prospects of promotion would attract strong applicants to the company and once appointed they would be motivated to work hard with the goal of promotion in mind. Such a policy was therefore beneficial to both employer and employee.

In addition, it will be argued that the belief that opportunities for promotion decreased rapidly as a result of the large influx of clerks is questionable because it does not take into account the fact that as organizations became bigger the number of responsible positions within them grew with the increase in their personnel, thereby maintaining an equilibrium for promotional opportunities. Side by side with this, the argument that it was relatively common for clerks to become masters before 1870 appears to be extremely dubious. There is not much evidence of this, and those clerks that did were usually men from relatively prosperous backgrounds who could bring capital into the company with them. In addition, there is little evidence to suggest that the possibility for London clerks to set up their own businesses was diminishing. The argument, therefore, that career prospects for clerks in this period were deteriorating should be questioned.

Finally, the security of clerks' positions will be looked at. Were clerks increasingly falling victim to unemployment? Clerks did suffer from unemployment, but there is no strong evidence to indicate a deterioration in job security. The limited evidence there is suggests that clerks suffered far less from unemployment than other groups such as skilled manual workers. There did exist, however, a group of older unemployed clerks who, due to the nature of clerical unemployment, once out of a job found it extremely difficult to find a new one. The general picture, however, appears to be that the extent of clerical unemployment has been much exaggerated. Furthermore this section will argue that a far more serious problem of the period was underemployment, the lack of consistent full-time work, rather than unemployment. It was this phenomenon, rather than unemployment itself which encouraged many parents, from skilled working-class and small-business-owning backgrounds, as well as clerks, to place their sons into clerical positions. It was, in fact, the stability of the clerks position which attracted so many to it. Overall, it will be argued that there are serious grounds to question the idea that there was any serious crisis in clerking in the late Victorian and Edwardian period. This is not to argue, however, that status crisis, the fear of losing social respect, was never far from the back of the minds of many clerical workers.

Clerical Incomes

In 1908 in the first edition of the rejuvenated journal, the *Clerk*, the President of the National Union of Clerks, wrote:

> A generation back, clerks as a rule were recognized as persons of some importance to the world, and no inconsiderable number of them received payment commensurate with that importance. With the wider spread of rudimentary commercial and professional education, the clerk has lost, not in real importance, but in the power of impressing his importance upon those who utilize his services. The law of supply and demand is temporarily against him.[6]

The writer argued that the consequences of this was an overstocked clerical market and falling incomes. An article in the magazine the following month argued that the market was saturated and those seeking work would do well to look outside the clerical sector.[7] These arguments were being perpetuated eighty years later. Geoffrey Crossick, for example, argued in 1977 in his introductory essay in a collection of essays on the Lower Middle Class that, 'Female labour was almost certainly less of a threat to clerks than oversupply in their own ranks'.[8]

The question of whether there is any evidence that salaries were falling will be first examined (See Table 4.1). Five organizations were located which had extant continuous series of salaries available for the period. In all cases the averages were calculated from figures in salary books. The entire populations of the selected areas of the organizations were sampled with the exception of the Prudential Assurance Company. Here the Industrial Branch was selected for 1871 and 1880. This held 75 per cent of all male clerks employed in the company for 1871 and 85.5 per cent in 1880.[9] The organizations selected were the Prudential Life Assurance Company, The London and County Bank Head Office, Heseltine Powell and Co. Stockbrokers, The Lambeth Water Works Company and the Comptrollers Department of the L.C.C. all had an incremental system whereby most employees' salaries increased by around £10 a year to a maximum figure of between £200 and £300. In terms of recruitment, recommendations from individuals connected with the firm were required for both the Prudential and the London and County Bank. In relation to the latter an entrance examination also had to be passed.[10] Similarly at the L.C.C. a series of examinations had to be taken.[11] No information is available for the other two companies, but, based on standard procedure in office work, it is likely that recommendations were required.[12] The lifetime clerk George Rose, for instance, required one from his former employer to gain employment at the Commercial Gas Company.[13] There is no reason to assume that this was not the case for The Lambeth Water Works Company, nor for a City firm such as Heseltine Powell and Co.[14] It must also be emphasized that in all companies level of income did not depend on age but rather on length of service. Similarly, length of tenure was an important factor when promotion was considered.

Tables: Clerical Average Salaries (£) to the Nearest Decimal Point

Third column is the income adjusted for inflation based on Bowley's figures – see p. 12

Table 4.1: Average Salaries at the Prudential Assurance Company.

Date	Salary	Adjusted Salary By Inflation
1871	66.1	66.1
1880	89	87.2
1894	175.4	196.4
1900	199	216.9
1910	227	229.3

(Note that the years 1871 and 1880 are for the Industrial Branch, the largest branch of the company. 1894 to 1910 are for the whole company.)
(Source: Archives of the Prudential Plc, MS-1264, 'Register of Clerks, 1858–79', MS-1271, 'Register of Clerks, Managers Office' MS-1278, 'Register of Clerks, 1885–1909', MS-1279, 'Register of Clerks, Managers Office'.)

Table 4.2: Average Salaries at the London and County Bank Head Office.

Date	Salary	Adjusted Salary By Inflation
1870	128.2	128.2
1880	162.8	159.5
1890	184.1	206.2
1900	190.7	207.9
1909	182.4	195.2

(Note that the eight highest salaries in the salary ledgers were not included as these were those of the senior offices such as the managers, secretary and accountant and would have distorted the results.)
(Source: RSBGA, GB 1502/WES/1²⁵⁄₁–11, 'London and County Banks Clerks Registers, 1870–1909'.)

Table 4.3: Average Salaries at Heseltine Powell and Co., Stockbrokers.

Date	Salary	Adjusted Salary By Inflation
1874	171.5	171.5
1880	198.6	194.6
1890	242.2	271.3
1900	235.8	257
1905	238.9	256.6

(Source: London Guildhall Archives, MS-23,260, 'Heseltine, Powell & Co, Salary and Bonus Payments, 1876–1929'.)

Table 4.4: Average Salaries at the Lambeth Water Works Company.

Date	Salary	Adjusted Salary By Inflation
1872	105	105
1880	103.3	101.2
1890	138.1	154.7
1900	155	168.9

(Source: London Metropolitan Archives, ACC/2558/LA/03, 'Lambeth Waterworks Company, salary records, 1872–1904'.)

Table 4.5: Average Salaries at the Comptrollers Department, London County Council.

Date	Salary	Adjusted Salary By Inflation
1890	207.9	232.8
1909	201.6	215.7
1914	238.9	241.3

(Note that the Comptroller's Salary has been omitted for each year. In addition, Minor Establishment Clerk salaries for 1909 and 1914 were not included as data for temporary clerks in 1890 was not available.)
(Sources: London Metropolitan Archives, L.C.C./CO/GEN/7⁄₃, 'Comptroller Department, wages and salary records 1889–1903', London County Council, *London County Council Services and Staff For the Year 1909–10*, 82–91, London County Council, *London County Council Services and Staff For the Year 1914–15*, 88–99.)

Only two of these organizations, the London and County Bank and the London County Council, had pay scales. Neither of these scales changed during the period of analysis and consequently had no effect on actual levels of salary paid. The London County Council did make promotion from Class 2 to Class 1 (when income rose from £200 to £300 p.a. in £15 and £20 yearly increments) more difficult in 1909 by basing this on entry into vacant positions rather than automatic promotion.[15] This appears, however, to have had no impact on salary rises as presumably growth in the Council maintained a steady flow of advancements. It is important to note that only a minority of male clerks in London over this period, particularly in the private sector, would have been on an official scale. Even when this was the case these were nominal rather than real income grades. Incremental increases were not automatic, were seen as a form of promotion and could be withheld. A report at the London and County Bank in 1909, for example, noted that while according to its scale a clerk was expected to reach £230 p.a. in his eighteenth year, the actual average salary at the bank was a little over £200.[16] A understanding of trends in clerical income levels is thus dependent on an examination of existing salary data rather than a survey of existing scales.

It should be emphasized that the companies were chosen simply because they had retained existing runs of salary figures, something which is highly difficult to find amongst company archives. These figures are not meant to be seen as representative of clerical salaries in London. Bank and Insurance clerks were among the highest paid groups in the clerical profession, as were Stock Brokers' clerks in the City.[17] They are, nonetheless, important because if the clerical labour market were overstocked there would have been a general fall in salaries. The figures, consequently, say something about what is happening to clerical salaries in London over this period. The L.C.C. salaries are also important as they reflected civil service salaries which were used by many large-scale organizations as a benchmark for levels of white-collar pay. Finally, the income figures for The Lambeth Water Works Company were by no means untypical of contemporary estimated averages for London clerical income, and here too one sees a distinctive rise.

The next question is how statistically representative were these averages. Were they distorted by an unequal distribution of incomes throughout the company? The statistical breakdown of these figures in the tables below suggests that these averages are to some degree meaningful and thus demonstrative. Average and median levels of income in Tables 4.6–4.10, are constantly similar in all five organizations. In relation to distribution of incomes, calculations for Standard Deviation show that while deviation, and thus distribution, do increase in most cases, this is closely correlated to increases in the size of the samples. As levels of income in these samples are symmetrical, i.e. they are roughly equal either side of the average, this would indicate that income was becoming more distributed in the companies as they grew due to an increase in employees and thus salary levels, but not more unequal in terms of distribution. The fact that Standard Deviation tends to stabilize as overall increases in employee numbers became less dramatic further suggests this.

Tables: Statistical Analysis of Salary Figures Given

Table 4.6: Statistical Breakdown of Salaries at the London and County Bank.

Year	1870	1880	1890	1900	1909
Size of Sample:	137	164	186	219	242
Average:	128.175	162.805	184.086	190.708	182.377
Median:	110.000	145.000	160.000	170.000	160.000
Standard Deviation:	61.102	73.959	101.203	98.389	87.899
Skew:	1.780	0.990	1.937	1.603	1.048
Increase in Average (%):	n/a	27.018	13.071	3.597	-4.368
Increase in Standard Deviation (%):	n/a	21.042	36.837	-2.780	-10.662
Range:	60-380	60-400	50-675	70-700	70-500

Table 4.7: Statistical Breakdown of Salaries at the Prudential Life Assurance.

Year:	1871	1880	1894	1900	1910
Size of Sample:	65	367	806	1043	1314
Average:	66.154	89.251	175.413	199.228	226.994
Median:	60.000	70.000	165.000	180.000	220.000
Standard Deviation:	38.179	60.112	115.190	139.897	141.326
Skew:	1.458	2.093	0.782	0.910	0.395
Increase in Average (%):	n/a	34.914	96.541	13.576	13.937
Increase in Standard Deviation (%):	n/a	57.448	91.626	21.449	1.021
Range:	15-223	30-525	20-630	20-800	20-660

Table 4.8: Statistical Breakdown of Salaries at Heseltine Powell and Co.

Year:	1874	1880	1890	1900	1905
Size of Sample:	11	16	22	25	22
Average:	171.500	198.562	242.182	235.800	238.867
Median:	150.000	150.000	210.000	210.000	210.000
Standard Deviation:	127.733	154.929	149.609	143.096	154.488
Skew:	1.793	2.464	1.746	1.121	1.521
Increase in Average (%):	n/a	15.780	21.968	-2.365	1.301
Increase in Standard Deviation (%):	n/a	21.291	-3.434	-4.353	7.961
Range:	30-500	50-700	78-700	60-600	60-700

Table 4.9: Statistical Breakdown of Salaries at the Lambeth Water Works Company.

Year:	1872	1880	1890	1900
Size of Sample:	6	9	13	18
Average:	105.000	103.333	138.077	155.000
Median:	110.000	110.000	120.000	155.000
Standard Deviation:	49.598	44.441	67.254	90.440
Skew:	0.018	0.452	0.324	0.681
Increase in Average (%):	n/a	-1.588	33.623	12.256
Increase in Standard Deviation (%):	n/a	-10.398	51.333	34.475
Range:	40-175	40-190	50-250	40-360

Table 4.10: Statistical Breakdown of Salaries at the Comptroller's Department, The London County Council.

Year:	1890	1909	1914
Size of Sample:	33	221	234
Average:	207.9	201.6	238.9
Median:	169	163	200
Standard Deviation:	125.053	119.812	133.657
Skew:	0.657	2.209	2.062
Increase in Average (%):	n/a	-3.03	15.613
Increase in Standard Deviation (%):	n/a	-4.191	10.359
Range:	80-450	80-600	80-700

In addition, there was no change in terms of real earnings over the whole period. Britain experienced deflation between the 1870s and mid-1890s, and from 1896 onwards underwent a period of inflation. The statistician and economist A. L. Bowley, for example, estimated that at 1914 prices the cost of living index was 102 for 1880–4, 89 for 1885–9, 88 for 1890–4, 85 for 1895–9, 91 for 1900–4, 93 for 1905–9 and 99 for 1910–14.[18] Of course the argument was relative; for a clerk who began earning after 1900 the price rises were real, for one in work before this date they were not so serious. This point will be examined in more detail later.

Another question is the relationship between tenure and salary. Clerical income, particularly in larger offices and organizations, was heavily tenured. Salaries increased over time, sometimes, as has been demonstrated, along structured pay scales. This could mean, however, that while average income may have been rising because of an overall increase in tenure, individual income could still have been falling. To test this the salaries of clerks at the branches of the London County and Westminster Bank were examined for the years 1880, 1890, 1900 and 1913 (see Table 4.11). Over this period the number of branches increased from 118 to 248, and the number of branch clerks from 769 to 2092. As can be seen from the table, salary trends in the branches were basically the same as at the head offices, though with branch clerks earning around £20 a year more. Salaries at branches increased by 27 per cent between 1880 and 1890, maintained this increase between 1890 and 1900, and then fell slightly by 5 per cent between 1900 and 1913. What is interesting, however, is that on examining clerical workers who had been employed for five, ten and fifteen years, salaries remained broadly the same over the period, adjusting for inflation. Salaries were not falling, but neither were they increasing. How can one, consequentially, explain the overall increase in salary averages which were relatively substantial? This can be done by examining the average tenure of clerks at the branches which jumps from 11.39 years in 1880 and then jumps to 14.65 years in 1890 and then only increases slightly to 16 years in 1900 and 1913. It is thus an increase in tenure rather than an increase in actual individual salaries that explains overall rises in average income.

Table 4.11: Average Salaries at London County and Westminster Bank Branches, 1880–1913, Also Showing Average Tenure and Average Salaries After Five, Ten and Fifteen Years Service.

	Average Tenure	Average Salary (£)	Five Years Average (£)	Ten Years Average (£)	Fifteen Years Average (£)
1880	11.4	183.5	102.8	165.5	250
		(179.8)	(100.7)	(162.2)	(245)
1890	14.7	203.6	103.8	148.8	230
		(228)	(116.3)	(166.6)	(257.6)
1900	16	203.1	101	148.1	214.8
		(221.4)	(110.1)	(161.4)	(234.1)
1913	16	207.9	104.4	154	246.1
		(210)	(105.4)	(155.5)	(248.6)

(Note that bracketed averages have been adjusted for inflation)
(Source: RSBGA, GB 1502/WES/125/3, GB 1502/WES/125/6, GB 1502/WES/125/8, GB 1502/WES/125/13, 'London and County Banks Clerks Registers, 1880, 1890, 1900, 1913'.)

What implications does this have for the argument of this chapter and indeed that of the whole book? On the one hand it could point to a period of stagnation for clerical workers in an era when income and the standard of living for other groups was increasing. Yet this would discount the growth and importance of internal labour markets for clerical workers, which transformed the structure of their experience, expectations and outcomes of working life. Overall income levels for clerical workers rose over the entirety of their working lives because of the creation of internal labour markets which offered clerical workers incremental incomes, established career-paths and increased job security, which enabled them in turn to realize rises in salary. This was clearly beneficial for clerks and demonstrates that the strategy of internal labour markets was successful for those organizations which implemented them, as it resulted in increased tenure and an assumed increase in loyalty from their employees. It should also remind one that when examining clerical incomes one should take a longue durée perspective rather than taking periodic analysis only at certain points. Clerical incomes during this period only make sense when applied over the entirety of their careers, which it would appear were becoming increasingly more stable and enjoying increased longevity.

A final question is what do these figures tell us about clerical incomes as a whole in London? With the exception of the Lambeth Water Works Company, these salaries are taken from the better-paid segments of the clerical profession and so can be argued to be non-representative. In relation to this, it can be argued that these figures do tell us something about incomes in the clerical sector. Those factors which were supposed to have such egregious consequences for clerical work such as mass education, oversupply, departmentalization, feminization and technology were equally applicable to the organizations selected and therefore should have had a negative impact. In addition, they support data from Samuel Cohn's study of clerical work in the Great Western Railway and Post Office which shows a doubling in income for the former between 1870 and 1930 and an overall trend of increases in the latter.[19] This is important since according to statistics published in the *Journal of the Royal Statistical Society* in 1901, which showed the percentage of individuals by profession who earned over £160 p.a. and paid income tax, railway workers were the lowest paid sector amongst clerical working containing only 10 per cent who paid direct taxation.[20] While post office clerks were classified as civil servants their salaries were lower than employees working at Whitehall and would have been more akin to commercial clerks of whom 23 per cent paid income tax. A combination of clerical incomes demonstrated in this article with Cohn's figures thus shows strong rises in incomes across *all* sectors of the clerical profession. While the range of clerical incomes were broad, thus making it difficult to generalize about such a diverse profession, the evidence suggests that there was no overall decrease in clerical incomes over the entire period and certainly no crisis.

A possible argument against rising clerical incomes is the development of dual-labour markets in clerical work, which was discussed in Chapters 2 and 3. While primary clerical work was well paid, skilled and offered opportunities for promotion, secondary work was, by contrast, poorly paid, routine, insecure and offered few prospects. Whereas there may have been increases in the level of primary clerical income this was not reflected in the secondary sector.[21] The problem with this argument is that the while clerical work certainly developed primary and secondary sectors between 1870 and 1914, this was increasingly by gender.[22] For the majority of male clerks office work was performed up until 1914 in unified clerical grades. Only the civil service (including the post office) had dual labour markets over the whole period.[23] The banks, insurance houses, railways, utility companies, legal and accountancy firms, and most of London's commercial houses had single male clerical grades. An examination of records of firms held by the London Metropolitan Archives and the London Guildhall, for example, only showed one firm, the confectionary chain Lyons, using secondary male clerical labour at its head office Cadby Hall near Hammersmith in West London.[24] Further investigation also showed male, dual-markets at the Port of London Authority.[25] However, four out of the five organizations whose salary levels were examined had unified clerical grades (with the L.C.C.'s implemented only in 1907), as did the vast majority of the organizations who employed the clerks examined in the diaries and interviews used in this study. Out of the latter sixteen clerks examined, only two worked in organizations with dual male clerical grades. The existence of dual clerical male labour markets in London between 1870 and 1914 is conspicuous by its near absence.

The lack of dual labour markets amongst male clerks is also importance in relation to the employment of women during this period. Using dual-labour market theory, Samuel Cohn's study of the Great Western Railway and General Post Office, and Ellen Jordan's study of the Prudential Assurance Company have shown that the employment of female clerks did not detrimentally impact on male clerks.[26] Office work required a great deal of routine work such as entries into ledgers, addressing letters and making copies of correspondence.[27] Much of this work was not done by clerks but by copyists. Before the 1870s the work had been performed by male adolescents who were taken on as apprentices but were then dismissed after two or three years. By the end of the nineteenth century, due partially to public criticism and also to changes in social attitudes, this practice was gradually wound down. Employers replaced male adolescents with young females and a new class of secondary labour was created.

The use of women as a secondary clerical workforce buffered labour costs and enabled employers to reserve primary positions for men and enhance their promotional opportunities. As Jordan noted at the Prudential, it enabled the company to maintain a policy of patronage for recruitment but meritocracy for promotion amongst its male clerks.[28] Without the employment of women this would have been impossible. Due to the imposition of marriage bars, which insisted on female clerks forfeiting their positions upon marriage, employers were able to impose a system of 'synthetic labour turnover'. Since clerical income was based on a system of tenure, with clerks enjoying yearly salary increments, this kept salary costs down and secured a flow of employees who were prepared to accept remaining in entry level jobs. It is this which mostly explains why the influx of large numbers of women into clerical work failed to have a negative effect on clerical male income.

If there was no crisis in male clerical work, how does one explain such vocal complaints amongst clerical unions and in some sections of the press? One explanation, based on the salary figures, is that while there was a rise over the overall period, the rate of increase appeared to have peaked by 1890 with some slight falls by the end of the period. In addition, inflation at the turn of the century would have accentuated this trend as is shown in the adjusted salary figures. Since office salaries were yearly, clerical income lacked flexibility and was less able to react to increases in prices. Clerical unions were sensitive to price rises and protested strongly at the failure of employers to increase salaries.[29] For clerks entering the labour market following 1900 inflation was more pernicious as they had not benefited from the fall in prices twenty years earlier. It is no coincidence that the principle clerical journals that so lambasted the fall in clerical incomes such as the *Clerk*, the *Railway Clerk* and at the Civil Service, *Red Tape*, all appeared after 1900.[30] In the 1920s, for example, the Bank Officers Guild, the trade union of bank clerks, argued that while the inflation of the First World War and the post-war period was unprecedented, it was something which had been adversely affecting bank clerks, and by association other clerical workers, since 1900.[31]

The evidence, therefore, suggests a more complex picture in London than has been previously portrayed. Inflation following 1900 put stress on clerical workers. Younger male clerks would have been particularly under strain. It should also be noted that London's clerical workforce was becoming so diverse that it would be impossible to provide unequivocal trends for the entire sector. Yet the salary tables as a whole do show increases in income. This has already been noted by other commentators. While some sectors in the clerical workforce in London were under financial strain, particularly after 1900, overall, male clerical salaries were increasing. This failure to find strong evidence of uniform falls in clerical incomes consequently undermines the argument that the clerical sector was overstocked. If the latter were the case, this would be reflected in trends in office pay.

Career Opportunities

The argument that the clerical market was saturated found another outlet in the claim that an increase in clerical numbers was stifling promotional opportunities. An article in the *Clerk*, for example, in February 1908 argued that:

> The small office now gives place to the great bureaux of such limited liability companies and trusts, and the two or three clerks of the office of the past are replaced by small armies of men and women for the matter, who, are pretty much like teeth in a great administrative machine. Concentration of this character has led to differentiation of function with the result that each individual clerk tends to become specialized on one operation, and the possibility of getting into his fingers all the operations of the office are remote. Such being the case, that very fact alone suffices to fix the clerk permanently in one particular groove.[32]

The 'Charybdis to the 'Scylla' of a downturn in salaries was thus a drying-up of promotional opportunities. It was argued that there were too many clerks scrambling for too few places.[33] Overstocking was doubly pernicious for the unfortunate clerical worker. Not only did he suffer financially, but his dream of advancement and independence was steadily coming to nought.

Again the evidence suggests a more complex situation. In relation to promotion there is little to suggest that talented clerks were not being promoted to higher positions. As has been argued and demonstrated in earlier chapters, with the establishment of internal labour markets, companies recruited in-house rather than look outside for individuals to fill vacant positions. In addition, this argument overlooks the fact that with the increase in scale came an increase in positions of responsibility, and opportunities for specialization and profession-alization. There were more sections to supervise, more ledgers to be responsible for, more departments to control, more branches to manage, more knowledge to acquire. This development, for example, is overlooked in a recent article by Timothy Alborn, which argues that promotion amongst British insurance clerks in the nineteenth century was impeded because of a growth in branch managers amongst the expanding networks of life assurance companies, a rise in departmental heads and the executive powers of actuaries.[34] The fault in Alborn's arguments lies in the fact that due to the growth of internal labour markets and increasing specialization, these very branch managers, heads of departments and actuaries had emerged from the clerical ranks of insurance companies. They represent the apex, the highest peaks of clerical internal markets, serving to dem-onstrate the success of clerical promotional ladders, rather than their failure as Alborn would lead us to believe.

Evidence for the growth of internal labour markets and the promotional opportunities they facilitated has already been shown in the case of the Great Western Railway in Chapter 2. A further example will be given for the L.C.C. As the council took on more powers, more responsible positions became available for its officers.[35] *The L.C.C. Staff Gazette*, comparing the council in 1906 to forty years earlier, for example, stated:

> ... In the days to which I have referred, the opportunities of showing one's gist were very few, the work being so limited; now, however, with the duties conferred upon the council ever widening, the astute man, with a little good fortune, may hope to reach a position not dreamed of by those who were my early confreres.[36]

Officials in the council were graded into four classes. Graduation from grade 4 to 2 was usually automatic, with graduation to the first dependent on a posi-tion being available. Following 1909, the system was reduced to a second class divided into sections, and a first class. Entrance to the latter was based again on availability of position. Above the first class and below the heads of department were a number of unclassified positions which carried higher salaries and more responsibilities. These posts were filled internally. A report by the General Pur-pose Committee clearly outlined the L.C.C.'s promotional procedure to these positions in 1908: 'The scheme provided that a vacancy in the lower section of the superior posts should, in the absence of special circumstances, be filled by the promotion of the most deserving official in the first class on the recommenda-tion of the head of the department, through the Clerk of the Council, through to the Establishment Committee'.[37] The system was recommended as, '... it is noted that in order to attract and maintain in the council's service ... men fitted ... to the higher positions in the service ... it is necessary to hold to entrants ... a prospect of rising to such positions'.[38]

This system was also used to fill the most senior positions of heads of department. Vacancies, apart from those of a technical character, were filled internally. Sir Harry Howard, former Comptroller of the council for forty years, wrote in his recollections of the council:

> ... The London County Council, on the whole, favoured the principle of appointment by promotion from its staff, e.g., two-thirds of the present chief officers were so appointed, but not necessarily without prior advertisement of the vacancy. Broadly every junior, outside those in certain strictly professional departments, who entered the service of the council, might be said to 'carry in his knapsack the field-marshal's baton. It was certainly so in my own case, though I never dreamed of it.[39]

Howard was offered the position of Comptroller to the council when it became vacant in 1893, despite being, in his own words, only a junior officer, twelfth down on the list, and earning £260 a year.[40] The process also accelerated with time. Earlier in its history, as the former Comptroller of the L.C.C. noted, the council was forced to fill certain posts from the outside as it lacked the experienced staff. Gradually, however, staff were encouraged to apply, with ultimately many posts being filled from inside. 'No rule was laid down', Howard observed, 'but there was a judicious blending of the two methods [internal and external appointments] according to the circumstances of each case. The effect upon the staff was most encouraging and salutary'.[41] By 1902, for example, *The L.C.C. Staff Gazette* noted that nine out of the sixteen chief officers of the L.C.C. were under fifty years of age, and of these five had entered the service as juniors. With evident satisfaction the article noted: 'It looks as if ability rather than seniority wins the prizes at Spring Gardens'.[42]

It has often been assumed that increase in size of organizations lessened the chances of promotion as there was a larger number of individuals to compete against, and longer staff lines. Anderson, for example, noted in one essay that in 1840 there were only forty-eight staff at a selected London-based insurance company and six departments, while in 1914 there were 314 staff in eight departments. He then calculated that the chances of promotion for these staff had correspondingly plummeted.[43] Such arguments, while having intuitive appeal, can be misleading. With an increase in staff came growth not only in departments but also in sections in these departments. In accordance with the internal principle, these would have generated senior positions available to clerks from the ranks. At the Prudential, for example, the Claim Department was split up into four divisions on 1 January 1879. These were the A.B.C. division under G. Hooper, the D.E.F. division under A. Marshall, the G.H.I. division under M. Smith, and the J.K.L.M. Division under W.E. Craig. The J.K.L.M. division was subsequently split into two divisions on 1 January 1885, the I.K. division under W. E. Martin, and the L.M. division under W. E. Craig. This was further split into the L division under W.E. Craig and the M division under R. L. Baker on the 26 February, 1894. As the Claim Department divided and subdivided, clerks were able to move up into posts of authority within these sections. With growth in business came a growth in promotion opportunities for its employees.

Chandler noted more than thirty years ago that with an increase in scale of organizations came an enlargement of scope.[44] As companies and bureaucracies became bigger they did more things and thus generated more positions of responsibility. In relation to the L.C.C., following its establishment in 1889, the organization rapidly expanded its field of work. In the 1890s it began an innovative scheme of slum clearance and public housing. In 1898 it became responsible for London's tramways and in 1904 took control of the London School Board. Council employees expanded from 3,369 in 1890 to 33,516 in 1905, making it the largest single employer in the capital.[45] As the scope of the Council grew much of its clerical work became more specialized. The report from the head of the Statistical department, Laurence Gomme, in 1898, seen in chapter one, provides an excellent illustration of this.[46] The department dealt with a wide range of responsibilities which included the compilation of the published volumes, 'London Statistics', work on County Rates, returns for fire insurance companies, the certification of rates and taxes payable by the Council and reports and returns for Council Bills in Parliament. Of the sixteen established officials of the department, all but three had specialized areas. One worked on water statistics and dealt with royal commissions and Parliamentary matters. Another was responsible for electric lighting companies' accounts, fire invoice returns and assisted two other colleagues in analysing accounts in connection with London statistics, telephones and local taxation matters. E. C. Geddes's article, also discussed in Chapter 1, is further evidence of this process of specialization in the railway sector.[47]

Promotion for Clerical Work in the Banking Sector

Evidence of clerical promotional opportunities is difficult to obtain as organization's kept scant staff records and little has survived. Cohn's study of the GWR and Post Office has shown a significant increase in the number of clerks doing non-entry level jobs (and thus promotion) at the former between 1870 and 1933, and a more mixed picture at the Post Office, with gains in some departments being offset by losses in others.[48] Jordan has also argued that promotional opportunities for men at the Prudential were sustained by the employment of women.[49] The historical evidence collected thus provides little support for falling male promotional opportunities in clerical work over the period.

One exception to this is Michael Savage's study of career opportunities at Lloyd's Bank between 1880 and 1930.[50] Savage argues that clerks at the bank faced increasing career blockage due to a rise in staff numbers and a slowdown in new branches. This created disquiet amongst employees and was not resolved until the 1920s when women were employed. This created a dual-labour market whereby women were employed in routine, entry-level work and a more specialized and professional grade was reserved for men which restored career opportunities. Savage's argument is thus broadly similar to Cohn and Jordan. While this chapter is in broad agreement with Savage, what is problematic is his lack of strong evidence for a contraction in career opportunities before 1914. His data only describes the period from 1902 onwards and shows no significant reduction in promotional opportunities until the interwar period.[51] It says nothing about increases in promotional opportunities before this due to the extension of the branch network. Secondly Savage argues that clerical work at the bank was divided between accountants who kept the books and cashiers who served the customers. Promotion is defined by Savage as a move from one of these two groups to branch manager.[52] Such an outline is inaccurate and misleading. Accountants and cashiers were senior clerical positions of high responsibility which became open to clerks after more than ten years' service. They were prerequisites for promotion to branch manager, the clerk first becoming a cashier (who was responsible for current funds in the branch) and then accountant (who was responsible for overall bookkeeping and the daily running of the branch).[53] Such promotion simply does not register in Savage's analysis. Nor indeed do many of the opportunities that would have opened up in the bank's head and other main London offices. In addition to promotional opportunities at sectional levels, positions in areas such as securities, brokerage, foreign exchange, trusteeships, fiscal advice and dividend payments became increasingly available in joint-stock bank head and central offices.[54]

Of equal concern is Savage's insistence on wide-scale unionization of bank clerks before the First World War, citing the formation of the Bank Clerks' Association in 1906 and its successor the Bank Officers Guild (B.O.G.) in 1914.[55] Such combination is seen as evidence of bank clerks' dissatisfaction and as providing support for Savage's data and his depiction of decline. In reality, the Bank Clerks' Association was formed in 1914 and was a complete failure, it attracted very few members and was effectively killed off by the outbreak of hostilities in August of that year.[56] The B.O.G. was founded in 1918, had no connections with the Bank Clerks' Association and was the result of the sharp inflation of the First World War which the banks failed to address, rather than any fall in promotional opportunities.[57] A failure to provide historically accurate evidence of combination of bank employees before 1914 or any qualitative evidence of dissatisfaction thus further undermines Savage's argument for career decline before 1914.

Evidence collected from the National Provincial Bank between 1875 and 1914 draws a very different picture to that provided by Savage. The figures are based on detailed staff cards kept by the bank on the career histories of its employees and offer a rich source of career data for this period.[58] Following an apprenticeship at the National Provincial, employees could expect to be moved frequently around the branch's national network in England and Wales over their careers, with stints for many at the bank's central offices in London. After a period clerks could then be promoted to cashier, following this to accountant, and finally to branch manager. Further promotion for some entailed managing larger branches or senior positions at head office. Another possibility was promotion to inspector rather than branch manager, though inspectors often became branch managers later on. Finally some clerks remained at head office for their entire careers where they tended to specialize in areas such as securities and investments. It is also important to note that there were intermediate positions before cashier and accountant which were termed 'pro-cashier' and 'pro-accountant'. These positions gave their holders power of signature in the absence of senior staff though did not contain full responsibilities. It was common for clerks to hold these posts prior to obtaining the full position.

The evidence provided in Table 4.12 shows the average time it took a bank employee to be promoted to a senior position above clerk. Rather than defining promotion as elevation to branch manager, it sees it as an advancement in position beyond entry-level clerkship. The table provides no information on subsequent career development. Here it is important to note that an overwhelming majority of clerks continued to be promoted. Many became branch managers, though other stopped at cashier or accountant. The table shows that promotional opportunities improved quite dramatically at the bank between 1875 and 1914. While it took on average 19.5 years for a clerk entering the bank between 1875–1879 to be promoted to a senior position, this had fallen to 11.1 years for the cohort entering between 1910–14. While the First World War had a destabilizing effect on the development of this trend, many clerks were killed or disabled thus reducing competition in the ranks, the overall trend of an acceleration in the pace of promotion is clear. In addition, with the exception of a skew for the cohort 1900–4, one also sees a reduction in the number of employees who remained clerks and received no promotion throughout their careers.

Table 4.12: Average Time Taken to Receive First Promotion at the National Provincial Bank 1875–1914.

Date	1875–79	1880–84	1885–90	1890–94	1895–99	1900–04	1905–10	1910–14
Sample Size	35	35	35	35	50	50	35	35
Range of Years for Promotions	13–44	11–39	12–36	5–28	9–30	7–28	8–26	4–19
% of non promotions	11.4%	11.4%	5.7%	0%	2%	10%	0	2.8%
Average Years For 1st Promotion	19.5	20.2	18.3	16.4	17.1	14.5	13	11.1

(Source: RBSGA GB 1502/NAT/17⅓–34).

It was not only in these large-scale institutions that evidence of promotion can be detected. Oral and diary sources provide evidence of career opportunities in smaller concerns. Arthur Whitlock worked his way up to being in charge of the Policy Department covering goods from Argentina in the marine insurance company he worked for, and probably would have gone further if he had not left for the War Office in 1914.[59] Sydney Moseley was confident of getting somewhere in Waterlows the accountants, and had in fact already been promoted in 1906.[60] By 1908, he was working solely on accountancy work. Similarly George Rose, who had worked for the Commercial Gas Company in Stepney since 1901, had by 1913 been promoted to Assistant Cashier. His friend Edwin had done even better, in 1906 he was made assistant to one of the Heads.[61] On 19 October 1891, William Evans, who worked for the City Lawyers Ashurst Morris Smith & Co., was transferred to the Cashiers Department where he was to assist its head.[62] In all cases these were individuals who were moving up the company, and as with the larger firms the basic criterion was the same; it attracted good staff, motivated them, and encouraged company loyalty.

It consequently appears that the argument that promotional opportunities were diminishing over this period is unfounded. Company policy, whether large or small, was internal promotion from the ranks. Evidence from the L.C.C and the GWR supports this. In addition, as companies grew in scale the number of responsible positions within these firms showed a corresponding increase which offered expanded career opportunities. The data collected from the National Provincial Bank combined with Cohn's research provides clear evidence of this. This is important as it shows no evidence of career decline across several clerical sectors. In contrast, evidence provided by those who argue for a decline in clerical promotional opportunities is weak. The only solid evidence provided by Savage is questionable for the period before 1914. In addition, Savage himself acknowledges that clerical mobility remained high throughout the late nineteenth and twentieth centuries.[63]

The Dream of Independence

What of the argument that with the growth of large-scale complex companies, and the influx in large numbers of new recruits, clerks were no longer able to realize the cherished goal of being made a partner? In many respects the argument is a highly dubious one, and should be treated as such for several reasons. There is no real evidence that in the 'golden age of clerkdom' before capitalism took a spiteful turn, there was a realistic chance of a clerk being made a partner. As Anderson, who has argued on this point, admits himself, it was only those clerks from prosperous backgrounds who were ever made partners.[64] One should here, for example, not forget the term 'career clerk'. This denoted a professional clerk, one who would spend his working life in a clerical capacity. Such men were very different from those who were working as clerks to learn the ropes of a business, after which they would go onto higher positions, or those who were working temporarily as clerks before they went onto other things. The chances of the former type of clerk being made a partner were small. It should also be remembered that in terms of company structure the partnership model was not devised to reward, but rather to bring capital into companies.[65] It was only those who had sufficient material means who would be made partners in all but the smallest of companies, and it is unlikely that any clerk, unless they were from an affluent background, would be able to do so.

Secondly, for many London clerks, especially in the City, companies remained small. While as Anderson argues many of the middlemen of the pre-1870 world were cut out by the technological revolutions of the later period, these were simply replaced by new individuals who fostered this technology.[66] Why should, therefore, one of the five clerks who worked for the private City firm of Messers Gillett Brothers, bill brokers and money dealers, have had any less chance of being made a partner in 1910 than he would have had fifty years earlier?[67] Finally, in relation to the argument that as companies grew bigger doors were increasingly shut to clerks, it was precisely in those firms that were becoming joint-stock companies and growing in scale, such as banks and breweries, that clerks earlier stood less chance of becoming a partner because of their great need for capital which no employee would have been able to furnish.

One other means of becoming independent for a clerk was setting up on their own. There is no sign that entry threshold levels were being made more difficult in the period of this study than earlier. In fact the opposite could be the case, with more and more businesses being attracted, for example, to the City, both from around Britain and from abroad. With a more developed finance system and with many companies remaining small, one would have imagined that opportunities for openings were becoming greater, not smaller. After building up experience, contacts and capital, many City clerks, who were prepared to take the risk, did try and set up on their own as agents, dealers or brokers. In November 1904, for example, new rules were introduced to restrict membership of the Stock Exchange. A fortnight before the rules were actually implemented some 664 clerks took advantage of the breathing space to become members under the old, less expensive system.[68] It was furthermore not only in commerce or finance that clerks were able to set up. Elsie Barralet's husband, for example, worked as a clerk for the City piano manufacturers, Murdock's, but refused to return to the company after the First World War because they would only pay him the wages that he was on before he signed up. Instead he went to work as a manager, doing clerical work, for his uncle who had a builders' merchants along the Lea Bridge Road. After a while he branched off and set up his own business manufacturing fireplaces.[69]

Job Security and Clerical Unemployment

Finally, in relation to job security, there is little evidence for the claim that clerks' positions were becoming more insecure.[70] Anderson is right to look at employment exchanges to investigate the extent of clerical unemployment. His pointing, however, to a report in the *Daily News*, that in excess of 13,000 clerks and others had looked for work at the employment bureau at Exeter Hall in 1891, the headquarters of the London YMCA, was evidence of widespread unemployment, is a little naïve. Newspaper statistics and figures must be treated with the greatest suspicion.[71] This point was clearly made in an article in 1911 in the *Railway Clerk*, concerning the fantastical salaries and terms and conditions of railway employment which bore no relation to the true state of affairs that had been reported in daily newspapers.[72] Furthermore, the figure refers to clerks *and others*. The YMCA was not in this period an organization comprised of clerical workers, it was an association made up of young Christian men, a large proportion of whom were clerks, but not all. Finally, enquiring about employment, and registering as being unemployed, as 617 individuals did in that year, were evidently two different things. Evidence shows that young clerks, while in employment, were continually looking out for other positions. Alfred Moseley wrote off for a job in the US, and went for an interview as a chief clerk at a meat merchants where he was creative with the truth about the extent of his responsibilities at Waterlow's.[73] George Rose went to enquire in 1906 about a position as a clerk in a music shop,[74] and Arthur Whitlock was considering working for another Marine Insurance firm in 1914 before he went to work for the War Office.[75] The clerical labour market in this period was not static, particularly for young clerks who were ever on the look out for better-paid positions or those with more opportunities for promotion. One grievance of some London clerks, for example, was that those who worked for companies who were members of the London Chamber of Commerce could not put their names down on the roll of its employment bureau without first asking for the permission of their employers.[76] Clerks were clearly looking for work while they were still in employment.

Working out the level of unemployment of clerks in London is difficult, and no more than a rough impression can be expected. Because clerks did not resort to the traditional bodies of relief during periods of unemployment and deprivation such as the Poor Laws, charities, and trade union bodies, one of the best areas to look at are the unemployment exchanges that were springing up around London.[77] In October 1904 the London Unemployed Fund was established to alleviate the effects of unemployment. In 1905 the Central Unemployment Body for London was established under the Unemployed Workmen Act of 1905. Neither body, however, tells us anything about clerical unemployment. One group of statistics that do provide some information are figures provided by the labour exchange in the London Vestry/Borough of Battersea between 1894 and 1900. Battersea itself contained a relatively large number of clerks. The 1901 census returns for the borough for example state that out of 52,313 men engaged in occupations 3,492 were commercial clerks, 503 were law clerks and 568 worked in money and insurance (e.g. bank and insurance clerks).[78] If one adds an extra 1,000 government, post office and railway clerks (which is a conservative estimate), one arrives at around 5,500 clerks, around 10.5 per cent of the total male working population, which is about the average for London. The extent of clerical unemployment can be seen below.[79]

Tables: Rates of Unemployment Amongst London Clerks.

Table 4.13: Number of Clerks Registered as Unemployed in Battersea, 1894–1900.

Year	1894	1895	1896	1897	1898	1899	1900
No. of Clerks Registered as unemployed	48	54	30	22	27	55	38
Total Registered as Unemployed	2,361	3,200	2,525	1,340	1,739	1,383	1,075

Table 4.14: Percentage of Various Occupations Living in Battersea Registered as Unemployed at Battersea Labour Exchange 1898 (Based on 1901 Census Returns).

Occupation	Number Registered as Unemployed	Percentage of Total Registered Living in Battersea
Carpenters and Joiners	25	1.3
Bricklayers	3	0.2
Painters and Paper Hangers	80	4.4
Plumbers	11	1.8
Gas and Hot Water Fitters	7	1
General Labourers	1,206	42
Carmen	128	7
Gardeners	4	2.1
Porters	135	8.5
Clerks	27	0.5
Compositors	1	0.1

Though not aiming to reflect the real extent of clerical unemployment in Battersea, these figures give us some insight into clerical unemployment. They show that the number of clerks registered as unemployed was low, its highest point in 1899 being 1 per cent. Clerks also appear to compare favourably with other groups, with only Bricklayers and Compositors with lower percentages registered. These figures are also reflected elsewhere. Between 1893–4, for example, St Pancras had sixty-six registered clerks and warehousemen, sixty-four were registered in Chelsea, fifty-three in Camberwell, 18 in Westminster and 1 in St. Giles and George.[80] This is hardly convincing evidence of mounting unemployment amongst clerks.

One clerical group that did suffer in this period, however, was older clerical workers. An article in *The Railway Clerk* in 1904, for example, spoke of, '... the out of work clerk, who is said to be too old at forty'.[81] Companies preferred to obtain their clerical workers relatively young. At this age they were felt to be more malleable workers who could be trained into the workings of the company. It was felt that this was more difficult to do with older men. Although older men had more experience than younger this had been gained in a different work environment, where, for example, different accounting systems were used. If a clerk was unfortunate enough, therefore, to loose his job in his late thirties or forties he had a difficult time in front of him. In October 1910, for example, a thirty-eight-year-old clerk was found dead in St Pancras. He had been out of work since June and had died from starvation. In his room there was said to be neither food, money nor anything of value.[82] An article in the *Ilford Guardian* in 1900 on the Darkest England Social Scheme of the Salvation Army, a labour bureau which mostly found unskilled work such as wood chopping or paper sorting for its applicants, spoke of the clerks who came to the scheme, 'by the dozen'.[83]

There were certainly clerks in London in distress. Constituting one of the largest occupational groups in the city one could hardly have expected otherwise. In particular it should be remembered that many clerks in London had migrated into the city and so had no family to support them if they fell on hard times. This point was made in the above article on the Salvation Army. Out of 169 men who had been found work sorting paper, only sixty-nine were London born.[84] Older clerks suffered, so did those who were dismissed from their jobs as happened to Geoffrey Rogers's father during the First World War. Caught 'cooking the wages' at his employer Ashburt, the Bond street jewellers, he was prosecuted and received a four-month sentence. Following this he never worked as a clerk again and thereafter did intermittent casual labouring work such as working on the roads for the council.[85]

There is, however, no strong evidence to support the view that clerks were increasingly vulnerable to unemployment. In the interviews and diaries, among not only the diarists and interviewees, but also among their friends and family members who were clerks, there are only two examples throughout the period of a clerk actually being unemployed. The first was the father of Frank David Charles Lee, who had lost his job while his son was still a baby and remained out of work, living in Dalston, for six years. His father had married young and against the wishes of his and his wife's parents. He was only nineteen when his son was born. Such inauspicious circumstances would certainly have mitigated against him finding work in a period when a clerk's character and credentials were equally as important as his office skills. It was only through the help of a friend at his church that he was able to get back on his feet again, being introduced to Badger & Co., the confectioners.[86] The second example was the close friend and flatmate of George Rose, Duncan. On 9 October 1913, he was told by his Stock Exchange employer that his services were required no longer.[87] This reference was passed off in a relatively nonchalant manner and there appeared to be no indication of disquiet or panic. Despite these two examples, however, the atmosphere that one gathers from these sources is an environment where jobs were stable and clerks were confident enough to leave their work to look for better positions. It is also in many cases one of rising affluence, an image that, in regards to stability of employment, dovetails with the above statistics on labour exchanges in Battersea and other London boroughs.

Perhaps, however, the most telling point which contradicts the argument that clerical work was increasingly becoming vulnerable to the vicissitudes of unemployment in this period is the fact that individuals were attracted to clerical work because it offered stable employment. W. J. Brown's father's advice to his son on leaving Margate to look for work in London was to get whatever jobs he could until he was old enough to enter for a Civil Service examination and then to try for it. 'If you get into the Service', he told his son, 'you're made for life – a permanent job all your life and a pension at the end of it'.[88] 'That to my father', commented Brown on his father's advice, 'represented the Mecca of all earthly hopes, and indeed, I myself had seen enough of the effects of unemployment in our home to put a high value on economic security'.[89] It was, indeed, underemployment, having irregular employment, rather than unemployment, that was one of the greatest problems facing working people in London in the Victorian and Edwardian period. Many jobs, such as in the clothing and building trades were seasonal or highly vulnerable to swings in the market. Many individuals found themselves in the dire situation of having no work for weeks and months on end, often without any assistance. This can be seen, for example, in the labour exchange returns for Battersea. Commenting on the tailoring trade in the East End of London in 1888, one of the biggest employers in the area, Beatrice Potter estimated that, 'it would be fair to state the average work per week throughout the year as four to four and a half days in the shops of the large contractors and for the most competent and skilled hands throughout the trade; three days for medium shops and average labour; and two and a half days and under for the great majority of permanently unskilled or imperfectly trained workers'.[90] In 1911 one commentator wrote in relation to Jewish tailors, who at the time were among the most skilled in London, working at the bespoke end of the trade, i.e. made to order, rather than the mass produced sector,

> The Jewish tailor works on an average no more than six or seven months out of the twelve months. Often he has to be in the workshop for three days to make one and a half days ... when he works at full steam, his average earnings for the year are from 25s to 30s per week, for best tailors, and from 18s to 20s for second class tailors.[91]

The situation did not appear to improve with time. Simon Blumenfeld's novel, *Jew Boy*, for example, written in the 1930s depicts a young Jewish tailor, Alex, in the East End, afflicted by periodic bouts of overwork and long periods of unemployment.[92] Yet even here, Alex and others like him were lucky to have a trade, for the unskilled the situation was even worse.

Uncertainty concerning work was clearly evident in the interviews used in this research. Percival Chambers, for example, was born in 1894, moved to West Norwood in south-east London when he was eleven or twelve and went to work for Pearl Insurance when he was fourteen and a half. Concerning this move he commented, '... it was a clean job and a pensionable job.'[93] From the experience of his father he could also have said that it was a steady job. Chambers's father was a stone mason, a highly skilled and relatively well-paid occupation but subject to periodic bouts of unemployment. Asked whether he ever remembered his father being out of work, he answered,

> Oh yes, quite a lot, quite a lot. In the days when times were very very bad, I've known him walk to London with coppers in his pocket and rather than spend them he used to walk there and walk back. And then come back without a job probably.[94]

There was no attempt by his father to apprentice him into his trade. Chamber's clerical position at Pearl was actually obtained for him via a friend of his fathers.

Chambers was like many boys in this period, the son of a skilled worker who wanted a more stable life for his son. New entrants into the clerical profession did not only come from clerking backgrounds but also from the sons of the petit bourgeois and from artisans. This of course raises a serious question. Why would Chamber's father want his son to be a clerk if the conditions were so bad and the work was so unsteady? Why would George Rose's father, an affluent tailor in Chipping Ongar, or Andrew Carlyle Tait's father, an individual who owned a bookshop in the City,[95] go out of their way to procure clerical positions for their sons if they did not think they were conferring an advantage on them? The answer here is clear. It is the same as that given by W. J. Brown's father to his son. In an age of instability, when unemployment, illness, or death could strike at any time, the importance placed on security in a job was hard to imagine. Clerical work offered in its own small way such a secure existence. Jim Hancock's father, for example, started working as a clerk at the headquarters of the London County and Westminster Bank at Lothbury in the City in 1913. He had earlier tried for the Civil Service but had failed the entrance examination The decision for both his application to the Civil Service and the London County and Westminster had been taken by his father, a relatively well-off commercial traveller living in Stoke Newington. Asked what were the motivating factors for this choice of careers by his grandfather, Jim, a clerk and latter branch manager himself at the same bank answered,

I think ... security was regarded as very important. Don't forget this was in the days when the welfare state such as we know it now simply didn't exist ... generally each person was expected to look after their own fortune. My grandparents would have known that with the Civil Service and with the bank there was a pension at the end of the time, there was the respectability of the job, there was the chance of promotion and a steady job providing you didn't 'blot your copy-book', as the saying went, you would be there for life until you retired.[96]

Conclusion

In the late Victorian and Edwardian period, the argument that clerical work was overstocked, was falling victim to declining salaries, reduced opportunities and growing unemployment in London needs to be questioned. The overall numbers do not add up. Neither does the oral evidence, nor diaries written by clerks at the time, nor the records of companies, nor the fact that so many families, many from relatively comfortable backgrounds, were so eager to obtain clerical positions for their children. In fact the only thing that does appear to support this theory are the records of the National Union of Clerks. An organization, one should hasten to add, whose membership stood at 163 in 1906, and in 1914, at 12,508, represented less than 2 per cent of all the clerks in Great Britain.[97] Clerks did not enter the N.U.C. because they suffered from false consciousness, but because they were too proud to accept the realities of their dire economic and social situation. The N.U.C. failed to attract such recruits because their image of the 'Social Economy of Late- indeed Victorian Clerks' did not reflect the reality of what, for a large majority of clerks, was actually happening.

While there were certainly poor clerks living in London, the extent to which their working conditions deteriorated is open to debate. It is, however, important to note that some in this sector may have experienced falls in salaries, particularly in the inflationary period following 1900, and many, particularly those from the expanding elementary and secondary schools, may have felt they were not earning as much as they were entitled to or had hoped. Despite this, however, for many clerks in London, the period was one of modest progress. Most were earning more, had steady jobs, and were realizing, in most cases, moderate levels of promotion. Part of this was due to the development and growth of internal labour markets in clerical work. Yet in a period of economic expansion, and in a city which was gaining from the growth in international trade and the benefits that this brought, such an analysis is not surprising. The image of the 'poor, suffering clerk' should, perhaps, remain where it originated, in the discourses of trade unionism and the realms of literary fiction.[98]

5 THE MECHANIZATION AND FEMINIZATION OF THE OFFICE, 1870–1914: THREATS OR OPPORTUNITIES?

Between 1870 and 1914 many offices were transformed by the increased use of female clerks and technology. While the 1871 Census for England and Wales, for example, listed only 1,446 female clerks, there were 124,843 in 1911.[1] In relation to technology, a whole array of equipment from typewriters to addressographs, adding machines to filing cabinets, began to be increasingly available and used by clerks. The increased use of women and technology, along with the application of rational procedures to office work, revolutionized the working environment of many clerical workers. It created what was in effect the modern office. Whether these were auspicious developments or the converse, however, has been a widely contested subject. It is this question that this chapter aims to answer.

The majority of commentators have tended to view these changes as an ominous development for male clerks. Paul Attewell in his article, 'The Clerk Deskilled: A Study in False Nostalgia', has listed a whole host of writers from 1912 to 1987, writing on the United States, Germany and Britain who see such changes as precipitating the decline and fall of the male clerk.[2] The most widely quoted of these, Harry Braverman, saw these developments as changing the clerk from the autonomous, skilled worker of the mid-nineteenth century to the automated, assembly line office proletariat of the twentieth.[3] Summarizing the general arguments of these writers, Attewell has written,

> The story begins in the nineteenth century, with the clerk as craftsman or artisan – a skilled generalist, knowledgeable, well-rounded, waiting his turn to step up into a partnership. This is followed by the onslaught of Taylorism, feminization, and office machinery, three forces which reduce the clerk to a narrow machine minder in a clerical factory. The historical coup de grace is left for the present period, when computer automisation removes the last vestiges of skill from a once-cherished occupation.[4]

Gregory Anderson, who faithfully follows this argument, presents women as one of the major culprits in his chapter, 'The Clerk Under Pressure' in his work on Victorian clerks.[5]

The introduction of women into the office was treated in a similar manner by feminist historians in the 1980s.[6] Their tendency was to link the rapid increase in the numbers of female clerks in the latter half of the nineteenth century with the spread of technology in the office in the same period. As women are argued to have handled much of this new equipment, feminization and mechanization are seen to have been inextricably linked. This group also tended to display a zero-sum game approach to the entire subject; the more women clerks and technology in the office, the greater the pain of the male clerk. Jane E. Lewis, for example, has argued, '… To all intents and purposes, clerical work became increasingly feminized and deskilled during the twentieth century. Furthermore, as this happened the wages of male clerks suffered considerable decline, while those of female clerks, whose wages were less than half those of men before the First World War, showed a marginal increase'.[7] In more direct terms, Meta Zimmeck has commented, '… If clerical work was passing out of the men's sphere, it was passing into the women's. If men were losing, women were gaining. If there were fewer jobs for the boys, there were more for the girls'.[8]

These arguments have been the main orthodoxies on the subject for most of the twentieth century. However, more recently two writers have argued against the malign influences of these two factors on the male clerical worker. Paul Attewell has argued against the deskilling and demise of the male clerk. The skilled clerk of the mid-nineteenth century was a myth, clerical work was always subjected to some degree of division of labour, and technology obviated the need for performing mechanical, unskilled work.[9] Samuel Cohn, meanwhile, has argued that rather than undermining male clerks, the introduction of female clerks reinforced their position by introducing a cheap source of labour. The result was an upgrading of male clerical work and better promotional and salary opportunities. Cohn sees technology as having little damaging effect on clerks. While some items of technology such as adding machines may have deskilled clerks, others such as typewriters added to their repertoire of skills. The effect of technology was thus largely neutral.[10] Cohn's argument about the beneficial effects for male clerks of introducing women into the workforce has been echoed by Ellen Jordan's work on female clerks at the Prudential.[11]

This chapter will first deal with the question of technology. It will examine the application of new mechanical devices in the office, paying particular attention to the re-organization of bureaucratic procedures in this period which formed an integral part of the introduction of this new technology. Following this it will discuss the impact of office mechanization. Finally, attitudes of clerks towards this technology will be examined. It will follow the arguments presented by Attewell and Cohn, and argue that the increasing mechanization of the office had no damaging impact on the majority of male clerical workers. Clerks acquired important new skills in the latter half of the nineteenth century via the introduction of such technology. Machinery also upgraded clerical work by getting rid of many repetitive and mechanical jobs. In addition, it will argue that the whole emphasis of the debate has been in many respects misdirected. What was taking place in the office in the decades running up to the First World War was a process not of deskilling, but rather of re-skilling. Much of the technology simply changed the way clerks performed their office work. Old skills had to be jettisoned and new skills learnt. Too much emphasis has been put on technology *per se*. The stench of technological determinism, the belief that technology transforms everything in its path, hangs too heavily over the whole discussion. Technology in the office was simply a tool. It facilitated the work that had to be done. To argue that technology deskilled office work is thus to make a claim from a false premise as it ignores what was actually happening to the work itself. Finally, in relation to clerks' attitudes to this technology, it will be argued that while there is a literature of complaint, there is also one of support and applause for these innovations. In no sense can this technology be said to have been imposed in blind opposition to all clerks.

In relation to the dramatic increase in the use of female clerks, this chapter will question the assumptions that have dominated the debate. These can be seen as follows; the introduction of female clerks was antithetical to the economic and professional interests of male clerks, female clerks were replacing male clerks, the introduction of women into the office was tied up with the inauguration of new technologies, and thus symptomatic of the deskilling of the male clerk, and finally, the growing use of women in the office offended the male clerk's moral outlook by breaking the taboo against women working outside of the home and thus broke gender boundaries. These assumptions are unfounded. The introduction of female clerks did not upset the economic position of male clerks. Their salaries rose and, as has been argued earlier, their promotional opportunities carried on apace. Echoing Cohn, it will argue that it was the very introduction of women clerks as a secondary labour force which reinforced the relatively buoyant position of male clerks in London between 1890 and 1914. In relation to gender stereotypes, it will question the view that the entry of women offended male clerks. While it is true that the employment of married females would have been unacceptable to late Victorian and Edwardian male clerks, there is no real evidence that this also applied to single females. Since the existence of marriage bars, a clause which obliged female clerks to resign their positions on marrying, existed in many offices, the threat of the employment of married women happening was effectively precluded. This in fact is borne out by census statistics which show an overwhelmingly single, young, female work force. In 1911, for example, of the 32,893 female commercial clerks living in London, 31,939 were single.[12] In addition, the vast majority of female clerks concurred in this gendering of the workplace. Gender stereotypes were shared, not opposed, by both men and women in the office. As a result of this, it is difficult to see how male clerks could have been offended by the increasing use of members of the opposite sex in the office. This can be seen in the fact that so many female clerks came from clerical households.

Technology and New Office Procedures: The Evolution of the Modern Office

In February, 1910, an article appeared in the *Clerk*, entitled, 'The Machine Monster and the Clerk', by Murray Fernie. The author, a clerk and member of the N.U.C., had recently visited an exhibition by the *Organizer* magazine, and in the article described the various examples of new office technology which he had seen on show. The article illustrated the advances that had been made in office technology in the years before the First World War. As Fernie wrote, 'The most prominent example to-day of the introduction of the machine into the clerical sphere is of course, the typewriter, but a walk through this exhibition soon convinced one that the typewriter was only a step to a very much larger application of mechanical devices to all branches of clerical work'. Calculating machines, billing machines, addressograph and copiers were among the many pieces of machinery that were on show.[13]

There were two principal reasons for the increased application of office mechanization from the 1880s onwards. The first was the increased scale of bureaucracies and operations. As markets grew and offices became larger more data had to be processed. In insurance houses there were more policies to process, at banks more cheques to clear, in commercial offices more customers to serve. More traditional, labour-intensive processes found it increasingly difficult to keep up. An advert for the Burrough's Adding Machine, for example, promised, '... A speed of from 1,500 to 1,800 items per hour may be obtained by an ordinary operator with a few hours practice, but an expert readily lists from 2,500 to 3,000 items per hour, and some as high as 3,500'.[14] For a large scale bureaucracy such as the Post Office where, for instance, postal orders (first introduced in 1881) increased in value from £3,451,284 in 1882–3 to £57,206,000 in 1913–14 and in numbers from 7,980,328 to 159,242,000 respectively,[15] technology which guaranteed speed and accuracy was a clear solution to a rapidly growing volume of work.[16]

The second reason was that such machinery was quintessentially seen as a labour-saving device. As some organizations grew in scale and turnover there was a need to increase staff. The number of employees, for example, at the Post Office increased from 46,956 in 1880 to 212,310 in 1910 and 249,696 in 1913–14 after the nationalization of the private telephone companies.[17] The railways, banks, insurance companies, national and local government, and other large-scale commercial and industrial organizations, particularly following the mergers of the 1890s, experienced similar proportional growth. Such expansion (alongside an increase in competition) led to an emphasis on the need to minimize as far as possible such increases in staff numbers. Office mechanization and rationalization were a means of doing this. At the Post Office the term 'Labour Saving Appliances' was used to refer to office machinery. Justification for the acquisition of such items to the Treasury was done on the basis of savings in clerical costs. A return to the Treasury from the Money Order Department for 1907, for example, showed an estimated saving 'on clerical labour in connection with Banking Orders' of £78 a year by the use of five Burroughs Adding Machines.[18]

The introduction of technology into the office went hand in hand with a more rational re-organization of office procedures. A good example of this was information storage, retrieval and dissemination. Up until around 1870 the way offices processed information appears to have been extremely haphazard. Business transactions were often recorded in bound ledgers, with loose leaf documents tied together in bundles.[19] Space was allotted to certain areas, and if this proved insufficient new pages had to be found elsewhere in the ledger, or the additional information was recorded in new bound volumes. Information thus tended to be recorded in an unrelated manner in bulky ledgers. Elsewhere they were tied together in bundles of paper. The result was the frequent loss of important documentation, and of office time in the search for relevant documents.[20]

In addition, until the latter half of the nineteenth century offices lacked systems whereby information could be easily located and retrieved. Jill Pellew, for example, notes that at the Home Office certain clerks, who had worked in the office for years, had built up a store of information of where certain documents, such as legal precedents were, and how these documents related to other relevant material.[21] Some even stored information which had not been properly recorded. They were, in effect, human data banks whose jealous guarding of such information made their positions in the office indispensable.

Such a system had immense drawbacks. Only so much information could be provided by one individual at any one moment, the system depended on that individual being constantly in the office. On his death or retirement major disruptions were created in the daily office routine, and of course there was the human element to be taken into account. Information could be as much withheld as given.

The introduction of filing systems from the 1870s transformed the way information was processed in offices along more rational and efficient lines. Looseleaf files, folders and cabinets began to replace and supplement the older, bulkier bound ledgers and bundles of paper. Information was arranged according to topic, subject or company rather than, in many cases, the date of arrival. The Stolzenberg System, for example, was a cabinet comprised of a number of compartments which housed files according to alphabetical letter or subject. Card indexing systems also meant that information could be easily located, retrieved and even summarized.[22] Such systems were capable of holding far greater volumes of information and distributing it far more efficiently than any individual, however experienced.

While the mechanization of the office and its rationalization may have begun in the large bureaucracies such as the Post Office and the Home Office there is evidence that by the turn of the century this had filtered down to medium- and even small-scale offices in London. Applications to the London County Council (L.C.C.) from 1905 to 1914, for instance, for female typists, reveal a large number of applicants who had experience as shorthand typists and operating copying machines in small and medium offices.[23] Despite this, the spread of mechanization and rationalization was almost certainly uneven and it is highly likely that 1914 London would have evidenced a wide diversity of offices, some little altered since Dickens's writings, others boasting the most up-to-date technologies and procedures. Nevertheless, it is clear that for a large number the impact of these new technologies and procedures on the office were immense. As Cohn has argued, the modernization of the office lay not only in the introduction of the typewriter and the adding machine, but in the creation of virtually every piece of office equipment, from paper clips, carbon paper and filing cabinets to looseleaf note books, many of which entailed the initiation of new office procedures which transformed the office.[24] How did these changes impact on clerks and what were their reactions to them?

Machine Monster or Deliverer? The Impact of Technology in the Office

Murray Fernie's view of the new technology he described was overwhelmingly negative. Such innovations represented a direct threat to the job security and financial interests of the clerical worker. The National Union of Clerks's aim to establish a minimum wage would, he predicted, be confounded by the introduction of such technology. In his article he forecasted that, '… while the N.U.C. will be engaged in the much needed increasing in the cost of clerical labour to the employer, the cost of mechanical clerical appliances, at present pretty high, will inevitably be rapidly coming down until their cheapness will lead to their installation, largely to take the place of N.U.C. minimum wage labour'.[25] Technology would thus obviate the need for much clerical labour. In addition, Fernie linked it to a dehumanization of clerical work and the introduction of women and youths into the office.

In the following edition of the magazine, a rejoinder to Fernie was written by R. G. Acock.[26] Acock took a diametrically opposite view to the whole question of machinery and office work. For him technology was beneficial. While it made some clerical work redundant, overall, it actually increased clerical employment by facilitating and creating more business, and thus opening up new fields for clerical labour. In addition, machinery elevated office work by making clerical labour more specialized, which Acock saw as the distinguishing feature of modern office work. 'Present-day office methods tend more and more', he argued, 'towards retaining the clerk who uses his brains, whether it be in typing a letter or keeping books'.[27] For Acock there simply was no option. Offices and clerks had to wholeheartedly accept the new technology or else face bankruptcy and unemployment.

Who was right? Did technology produce unemployment, a decrease in salaries, deskilling and an inhuman working environment, or rather the opposite, an overall elevation of clerical work? From the evidence it would appear that Acock's analysis rather than Fernie's lay somewhat closer to what was actually taking place. The rapid increase in clerical workers of both sexes coincided with the introduction and increased application of these new technologies. Overall, salaries increased rather than decreased. The dystopian nightmare of the dehumanized office machine operator failed to appear. The 1951 UK census, for example, showed that only 3 per cent of clerks were specialized machine operators.[28]

In relation to the question of deskilling, there is convincing evidence that this simply did not take place.[29] Typewriting, shorthand, telegraphy, filing, indexing, even using the telephone, were all new skills which had to be learnt. Felix Owen, for example, who worked for a year in the City as a Junior Insurance Broker at the Royal Exchange in 1918 before going away to sea, listed the skills that one needed before entering the office, '... When I left school, and I was thinking about going for a job, I mean, I used to look at advertisements for jobs, and one of the conditions put down was good at figures, handwriting, able to use the telephone. I mean that was one of the things you had to do before you could get a job'.[30] Florence Johnson studied at a typewriting bureau from 1908 for around two years before she obtained a clerical position at the Metropolitan Board of Water.[31] Similarly shorthand and telegraphy were both skills which had to be studied and practised for several years before they could be fully mastered.

Moreover, much of this new technology was performing work which had been described as 'mechanical' even before machines had been designed to carry out these repetitive and essentially monotonous tasks. A memorandum sent by the Controller of the Stationery Office around the Civil Service Departments in 1917, for example, informing them of the technology currently being used in the Service, argued that the introduction of machines would result in a, '... reduction of monotonous labour which tends to deaden latent creative and critical faculties'.[32]

The addressograph was an excellent example of this. As the name suggests, the machine was designed, via a stencil and cartridge system, automatically to address envelopes. The machine was especially useful in banks as it could be adapted to print out cheques. The machine was a great labour-saving device when every six or even three months the registrar office sent out dividend payments on behalf of companies, often to thousands of shareholders. Lists of shareholders, dividend warrants, and addressed envelopes could be printed out at a fraction of the cost and time it would take to perform the task manually.[33] Before the introduction of the machine this monotonous but essential job had to be carried out by hand. It can thus be seen that the addressograph was effectively mechanizing a mechanical job which had earlier taken up the time and labour of clerical workers.

An example of the benefits of mechanization to the clerical worker can be seen in the introduction of adding machines to write up the Dividend Pass Books in the Town Office of Glyn's Bank in 1903. The experiment was said to have been a success and to have, '... relieved the Pass Book writers of a great deal of their Evening Work'.[34] The following year the use of the machines was applied to the Clearing Books and Ledgers. The system was popular with customers as the figures were plainly written and could be easily read. As a result of this experiment, the workload on the clerks at Glyn's using the machines was decreased at a time when the expansion of work in other departments meant that the number of clerks, despite increases in recruitment, was failing to keep up with the added workload. The introduction of this new technology was thus beneficial. No clerks were sacked as a consequence of its introduction.

Re-skilling

What has been missed in the whole discussion of the impact of technology on the late Victorian and Edwardian office is that much of the new machinery and procedures simply changed the way in which office labour was carried out. Old procedures and skills were replaced by more modern methods which required new skills. Listing all the new technologies and giving them marks out of ten for their putative degree of complexity, a system, for example, used by Cohn in his examination of the subject, fails to appreciate this.[35] In many cases what was happening in the office between 1880 and 1914 was not deskilling but rather a process of re-skilling whereby clerks were learning new skills as a result of new technologies which were replacing older ones.

A good example of this can be seen in the use of adding machines. This technology is used by Cohn as evidence of deskilling.[36] Formerly clerks were able to add-up long columns of figures mentally. This was a traditional clerical skill known as casting, and was seen by Cohn as being made redundant by this machinery. Clerks now simply had to enter the various figures, which would be printed on a slip of paper, pull a lever, and the sum total would appear.

An illustration of adding machines in use in this period, which casts doubts on this evaluation, was provided by W. Howarth in his chapter on the London Clearing House in his work on the banking and clearing systems of Britain.[37] Howarth estimated that about 245 million pounds worth of cheques were cleared by the House each week in 1900. Arithmetic, particularly addition, was a fundamental skill of the clearing house clerks whose job it was to calculate, by adding up cheques, how much money the banks owed each other as a result of cashing each other's cheques. It is no surprise, therefore, that adding machines were introduced relatively early into this financial institution. At the time of writing Howarth reported that the Clearing House had 170 of these machines.[38]

Discussing the use of adding machines at the London Clearing House, Howarth wrote,

> ... Whereas in the old days one would see the clerks entering the drafts they had received in books at lightening-like speed, and then casting up the totals afterwards – now all is changed. On the five floors one sees men sitting each with a little machine in front of him. This is that marvel of mechanical ingenuity – a calculating machine ... It is indeed a busy scene when the clearings are on. On each floor there is the never ceasing click, click, of the machines, the nimble fingers of the clearers, with one hand turning over the cheques, with the other playing with the keyboard, listing and totalling at a great rate – some much more expert than others, since in this, as in typing, practice is everything.[39]

Mental arithmetic was not strictly required in order to use these machines. However, one sees in the above account the use of new skills such as agility and speed in entering figures, and the ability to turn cheques, register their amounts and enter at the same time. As Howarth said, this was something which needed practice. Proficiency in using these machines was learnt over a period of time. Rapidity and accuracy, however, were still what was overwhelmingly demanded of clearing house clerks. The introduction of adding machines simply meant that new skills had to be learnt to achieve this.

In addition, it is ridiculous to argue that this technology meant that clerks simply jettisoned their arithmetical skills. Adding machines were not used to perform all calculations. Trial mental calculations were performed to check that correct amounts had been entered. The persistence of mental arithmetic can be seen in the following lines by Howarth,

> ... The rapidity with which the mental calculations are made is simply marvellous; the clearers run up column after column of figures with their eye, dotting down totals as they go on, and, with the majority, it is the strange exception to find an error. Of course, when the calculating machine is used an enormous amount of brain work is

saved, and as a matter of fact, it is practically impossible for the instrument to make a mistake in a total except, by chance, the 'clearer' types the wrong amount of a draft.[40]

The overall impression would appear to be that the clerks of the London Clearing House did not forget their arithmetical skills, and that these simply became downgraded as they re-skilled using the new technology available.

The example of adding machines reveals a certain trend. Its inauguration meant that clerks had to learn new skills to operate the machine effectively. Practice over a period of time was vital to gain proficiency. In addition, older skills such as mental arithmetic were not abandoned but simply downgraded. Re-skilling rather than deskilling appears to have followed the introduction of the adding machine, and by connection other complex office machinery. Such technology can therefore not be seen as having a harmful effect on clerical workers. Nor is there evidence that older clerks were unwilling to learn how to use these technologies.

Technology as Tool and Facilitator

In his letter in support of technology, R. G. Acock located the advantages of technology in the overall changes that had taken place in the clerical profession,

> Office work at the present day is more of a fine art than it used to be. A clerk must be something more than a writer. His work involves more special training, according to the special branch he intends to take up. The clerk is essentially a brain-worker. It requires something more than a mechanical operation to use a calculating machine, or any of the more up-to-date 'office machines'. Present-day office methods tend more and more to retaining the clerk who uses his brains, whether it be in typing a letter or keeping books. The clerk finds that knowledge in regard to everything relating to the business world and office appliances is the best asset he can possess. Under present conditions, and still more so in the near future, will the lie be to the legend: 'Any fool can be a clerk'.[41]

Acock was essentially making two points here. The first, seen in the opening chapter, was that specialization was the defining feature of the modern clerk. The second was that this specialization involved the clerk making more use of his mental abilities. Technology was seen as simply facilitating this process. It was a tool, a means to an end, rather than an end in itself. This latter point was stressed by Lawrence R. Dicksee when he argued that, '…the mere mechanical utilization of manual dexterity produced nothing but disastrous results'. It was the mixing of manual skill with a thorough knowledge of the office work which produced a fully accomplished clerk.[42]

The point which both these men made in relation to the impact of technology on office work seems to have been missed by commentators. New technologies should not be seen as some autonomous historical phenomenon which impacted on clerical workers towards the ends of the nineteenth century and completely transformed their working lives. They were simply tools which clerks applied to the actual content of their work. At the Home Office, for instance, four calculating machines were used in the statistics branch where clerks carried out work, which was described by the Permanent Under-Secretary of the Home Office, Sir Edmund Troup, in 1912 as requiring carefulness and a good deal of intelligence.[43] These machines were used to facilitate highly complex and innovative clerical work. They were upgrading rather than downgrading office labour.

The whole question of whether deskilling was taking place should therefore take far more into consideration the actual work that clerks were doing, and what prior knowledge was needed to perform it. As Dicksee argued, clerical work had as much to do with what a clerk knew about the subject or task he or she was dealing with, as with the skills which were applied to it in order for this work to be realized. This point was precisely made by Miss E. A. Charlesworth, Chief Superintendent of typists at the Local Government Board and representative of the Civil Servants Typist's Association. Asked at the MacDonnell Commission, 1912–13, established to investigate the staffing and work of the Civil Service, about the time it would take an average girl to learn to type at a rate of 70 to 90 words a minute, Charlesworth answered,

> It would take her a year, I think. But I think experienced people in this work do not attach much value to the number of words a minute that you can copy. It is an easy thing to master the manipulation of the machine; a child can do it just the same as anyone, almost, can learn to sew; but to produce a garment is quite another matter. I think, in typewriting it is the same thing. A child can very soon learn to move her fingers quickly over the keys; but what her production would be like is a very different thing.[44]

It is in this respect that serious questions can be raised against the whole argument that clerks were being deskilled by technology before the First World War. As has been argued in the first chapter, as society and the economy became more elaborate, clerical work became more complex. One major aspect of this, as Geddes, Acock, and other contemporaries argued, was that the clerk became more specialized. How, therefore, could clerks have become deskilled in this period?

The Clerical Perception of Office Technology

What was the male clerical perception of the mechanization of the office? While the introduction of the typewriter or adding machine may have been no inauspicious development for the clerk, there may still have been hostile reactions and feeling of dread towards these changes. Was, for example, Murray Fernie's reaction typical of a large number of male clerical workers?

Clearly there was some opposition to mechanization. Some sectors of the clerking profession such as male copy clerks, many of whom were temporary workers and on the margins of the profession, were adversely affected and therefore could have been expected to oppose its introduction. Others, such as Fernie, may have been opposed for ideological reasons. Within the clerical trade union movement, for example, there were certainly elements who saw in technology attempts by management to extend their control over the workplace and their employees. Many more, particularly from an older generation, may have felt apprehension at the introduction of what would at the time have appeared to be revolutionary technology and the change to the work routine which accompanied it. The question, however, is how representative was this group of clerks in general?

The evidence would suggest that while such opposition did exist, it was limited. In clerical journals, for example, there was very little real hostility to mechanization. Only in the *Clerk* does one find some opposition, and even here this was tempered by letters such as Acock's which supported technology, and intermittently, articles on the advantages of technical education. Similarly in the diaries and interviews there is no trace of any such hostility. Indeed, George Rose, for example, was enamoured with the whole concept of the telephone and the opportunities which this offered him to organize his social life from the offices of the Commercial Gas Company in Stepney, East London.[45]

Support, in fact, can often be detected. Technology was welcomed by some as a sign of progress and modernity. Acock's sentiments can be found elsewhere. The *Office* magazine and other similar journals almost worshipped the very idea of technology. The opening edition of the magazine on 22 September 1888 wrote,

> Typewriting and shorthand writing are sister arts and time-savers; the copying press and other mechanical contrivances for multiplying copies of documents are of no less importance. None of these arts and contrivances have, until now, been brought to public notice, and advocated and encouraged through the channel of a bitter press.[46]

Cohn noted the existence of an extensive number of journals around the beginning of the twentieth century which catered for shorthand, a skill which was closely connected with new technologies such as the typewriter and copying machines.[47] Clerical journals, in general, tended to convey a positive attitude to the mechanization of the office. The *County Magazine* at the London and County Bank, for example, reported in 1909 that, '... The contest arranged by the Burrough's Adding Machine Co. for speed on the 'artificial brain machines', was a great success, both for its uniqueness and the conviviality of the evening'.[48] Although the bank's representative only came fourth, it was with evident pride that the journal announced that the American record of 4 minutes 16 seconds was beaten by at least 50 per cent of the competitors.[49] Such speed competitions in using adding-machines, as well as shorthand and typewriters, seem to have been a relatively common phenomenon in the office world.[50] Prize-money was offered for fastest times, and many were organized by commercial companies eager to market their new products. The continued existence of these events and the positive reporting they received in the clerical journals suggests that they were popular, and by extension so was the technology which they tried to promote. Overall one can argue that it was this opinion, rather than the converse, that was more representative of clerks' attitudes to the mechanization of the office.

Women

Women as Secondary Labour and Synthetic Turnover

Murray Fernie's disquiet towards technology also extended to women. Non-unionized clerks reflecting on the impact of the increased mechanization of the office would, in his opinion, became, '... troubled with an uneasy feeling regarding female competition, which in some vague and undetermined manner he thinks should be stopped'.[51] Hostility towards the increased feminization of clerical work was certainly evident in the *Clerk*, despite its advocacy of equal pay and rights for female clerks, and the existence of a woman's page in the magazine. In the first edition of the magazine, an article entitled 'Tuppenny Girl Clerks' argued, 'Over and over again women are substituted for men because of cheapness, but sooner or later women will realize that in accepting this inferior position they are dragging down their fellows'.[52] Throughout the period, despite the protests of female contributors such as Mary E. Taplin, articles and letters continued to appear complaining and warning about the increased use of women in the office.

Were female clerks so damaging to male clerks during this period? Did, for example, their willingness to accept lower incomes result in the decline in salaries and general working conditions for male clerks? As has been argued, many writers on the subject have been prepared to accept this scenario. Research by Cohn, and more recently by Ellen Jordan, has, however, seriously thrown this whole picture into disarray. Cohn looking at the Post Office and the Great Western Railway, and Jordan at the Prudential, have argued that primary and secondary labour markets using female labour were firmly established in these organizations between 1870 and 1914. All these organizations, common to most offices, had incremental pay structures. While these pay structures were economically beneficial in the primary labour markets, increased pay over time reflecting the growing expertise of the staff which in turn helped to retain such workers, they made no sense in relation to the secondary markets. These sectors had relatively low learning curves. Workers here would be far more likely to be still holding entry-level jobs long after having joined the organization.[53] In this context, paying sustained yearly increases to staff made no economic sense and was, in contrast to the primary clerical workers, a costly source of expenditure.

The solution to this problem was to find a source of labour who would voluntarily leave after a period of time, usually of around six to seven years. This was long enough for them to master their area of responsibility but not prove too costly to employ. Boys and youths had commonly fulfilled this role. Some were dismissed, some left of their own accord, and others were retained when they matured into adulthood. The sheer increase in the size of the clerical market, the increasing public opposition to boy labour at the turn of the century and the fact that they could only be retained for relatively short periods of time made them, however, increasingly unpopular with employers.[54] It was in this context that young, single women became increasingly used as a source of secondary labour. What made this possible was the imposition of the marriage bar. When they married, female clerks were forced to give up their positions. A system which Cohn terms 'synthetic turnover' was thereby instituted which ensured that the vast majority of women would work for an organization for around seven years, a period which was far more appropriate to the needs of the employers.[55] Those female clerks who did not get married were able to take up senior managerial positions supervising clerical workers of their own sex. Furthermore, female clerks, predominantly from the middle classes, could be selected from a social milieu which was felt to be more appropriate to the office environment.[56] The whole system thus appeared, as least for the companies and offices concerned, to be a virtuous circle.

Cohn and Jordan's conclusions have largely been borne out in the archives examined in this study. At the L.C.C., for example, women were first introduced in 1898. On 14 July 1898, the Clerk of the Council, C.F. Steward, wrote a report to the Establishment Committee recommending the employment of females clerks,

> ... On entering the Service the [male] Junior Clerks receive a commencing salary of £80 a year and naturally look forward to rise in course of time to the higher classes and to perform the more important work devolving upon officials in those classes. The necessary copying or typewriting work has, however, to be done and, as above pointed out, forms a portion of duties of clerks who have been for some years in the service and who are in receipt of salaries of £100 a year or more. A copying department composed of Lady Clerks would gradually relieve some, at any rate, of the departments of the ordinary copying and typewriting, and would result in a considerable saving in as much as the pay of Lady copyists would, if the scale in government offices is adopted be from 16/– to 25/– a week, with a somewhat higher salary for a superintendent.[57]

Within less than a year of lady clerks being taken on, a report appeared before the Establishment Committee asking it to recommend to the Council that women should resign upon marriage. It was pointed out that this was standard procedure in Government offices. It also requested that a gratuity be given to lady clerks on resignation who had served no less than six years.[58] As Cohn has observed, such gratuities were given in order to ensure that female staff were kept on for the optimal time.[59] Both recommendations were carried.

While the L.C.C. was busily hiring female clerks it was attempting to scale down its use of Boy Clerks, a grade of clerical workers aged 14 to 20. A report from C.F. Stewart on 14 July 1898, recommending the use of lady clerks, clearly shows that the two were firmly related,

> The Council on 28th January, 1896, instructed us to consider and report what, if any, office in the clerical establishment of the Council were suitable for women, and what arrangements should be made to enable women to become candidates. On 23rd February, 1897, when we reported to the Council on the question of gradually abolishing the class of boy clerks, reference was made to the above instruction, and the opinion was expressed that a considerable amount of copying and typewriting work could with advantage be allotted to a copying department composed of lady clerks.[60]

Boy clerks were gradually reduced at the L.C.C. and absorbed into the new Minor Establishment grade of 1906. The recruitment of female staff into the L.C.C. was seen as a means of removing juvenile clerical labour. It was supported by the argument that by the use of lady clerks, male clerks could be more appropriately applied to work which would better justify their salaries. This did not mean, of course, that all women fully and passively accepted this scenario. Miss E. A. Charlesworth at the Civil Service, for example, was adamant that the work of female typists was far superior to the work of boy clerks, and argued that women were just as capable of doing the same clerical work as men.[61]

Income

In relation to the supposed harmful effect of female clerks on male salaries, there is strong evidence, as has been argued in Chapter 4, that male clerical incomes rose rather than fell over this period in London. Rises in clerical incomes during a period of rapid feminization clearly discount the whole argument that such a phenomenon was damaging to the financial well-being of the London male clerk. Conversely, they support the thesis, put forward by Ellen Jordan, and suggested above, that the increased employment of female clerks was in the interest of male clerical workers as the low incomes of women subsidized continuous incremental increases for men.[62]

Another area which should be incorporated into the discussion is household income. Meta Zimmeck, in her essay on female clerks, argued that the justification for paying female clerks less than male clerks was partially the argument that men had, or would have, dependents, and therefore received a 'family' wage. Women, on the other hand, did not, and therefore received a 'single' wage.[63]

What Zimmeck fails to note, however, as have all commentators on the subject, is that unless one lived on one's own in this period, which was uncommon, *all* incomes were household incomes. Until individuals got married and set up their own home, all income that was earned by individual household members would be put in a common household 'pot', usually controlled by the wife and mother, who then used it for the common benefit of the household. Individual contributors were allowed to keep some 'pocket money' which would go towards entertainments, holidays, travelling or lunch money.

Paul Thompson and Thea Vigne's interviews show that this system was ubiquitous amongst clerical and working-class families. Even boys doing paper rounds were expected to contribute. As a child for example, Geoffrey Rogers, whose father was a clerk, and who became a clerk himself, had several jobs: delivering newspapers, as a baker's delivery boy, and as an odd job boy at a large house. In all of these he gave his mother his wages and was given back a proportion as pocket money. When he left school and started clerical work he continued to give his salary to his mother.[64] Exactly the same system can be seen in the case of Alfred Henry Pyle who continued to give his salary to his mother until he got married and set up his own home.[65]

The same system applied to female working members of the household. The whole idea of 'pin-money clerks' – single female clerks who had no family responsibilities and spent all of their money on clothes and entertainment – can be dismissed.[66] The vast majority of female clerks lived at home with their families. Earning such small salaries made it impossible for women to live on their own. Meta Zimmeck, for example, notes that some firms made their employment of female clerks who came from outside of London conditional on them having signed statements that they were living with friends or families.[67] It should be remembered that 'pin-money clerks' was a term of abuse used by male clerks protesting against the employment of women clerical workers. They were the same group who argued that clerical salaries were decreasing as a result of such practices. The whole nomenclature should be seen for its propaganda purposes rather than for its depiction of reality. In addition, the number of women who set up home on their own, or with other women, was limited. Detailed census research on Hackney, Dalston, East Dulwich, Acton, Ealing and Chiswick failed to show any female clerical workers living alone, or with other women.[68] What it did show, however, was a multitude of such single females living at home with their families, many of whom were clerical workers themselves. These were families such as Geoffrey Rogers's, living in South London, whose father until 1918 was a clerk, who was a clerk himself, and who had three sisters (out of four) who became clerical workers, and at least one brother (out of three) who was a clerk in the military before he emigrated to Canada.[69]

The import of this is that if one looks at incomes as based on the household rather than the individual, as collective rather than atomistic, the employment of young single females as clerical workers was beneficial to families whose heads of household were clerks, or who had clerical household members. Female clerks augmented family incomes, and were thus advantageous to many male clerical workers. Why else would clerical fathers have been so keen to have their children of *both* sexes receive the best education possible? Elsie Barralet, for example, went to the Technical School in Leyton, Florence Johnson received a secondary education until she was sixteen and then went to a typing school for two years before getting a clerical position with the Metropolitan Water Board. Both of Arthur Whitlock's daughters went into clerical positions in 1920 and 1923. This, more than seventy-five years later on, was firmly linked in his mind with the education they received, '... The older daughter because of the school she went to, she got a job at the L.C.C. ... The other daughter, with her commercial education, got on just as well up in the City'.[70] After the First World War, Sylvia Ward's father, who was a bank clerk and whose health was already delicate because he had suffered from scarlet fever as a child, had physically worn himself out during the hostilities of commuting into the City from Sidcup every day, working, bringing up a family, growing food on an allotment every weekend, serving as a special constable in London, and acting as a physical instructor for the National Volunteers. Sylvia recalls how the doctor told her mother that he should get his two girls working as quickly as possible or else he would have a heart attack.[71] Sylvia duly got a job with her mother's former employer at the Prudential. The opportunity that existed for his two daughters to work in what was seen as a respectable profession for middle-class single women was clearly advantageous for Sylvia Ward's clerical father.

It can, therefore, be seen that there are strong grounds for questioning the whole idea that the feminization of large sectors of clerical work was detrimental to male clerks. Despite the increase in female numbers, male clerical incomes went up, not down. Women were used as secondary clerical labour, and although in many areas men were too, such as Assistant Clerks in the Civil Service, or the Minor Establishment at the L.C.C., it was in the typing and copying sectors that women were concentrated where they offered no serious competition to their male counterparts. In addition, the marriage bar ensured a high turnover of women which precluded them from being given responsible positions which had high learning curves and good prospects. In many cases, it was this concentration of women in entry-level jobs which subsidized the pay increases and opportunities for better positions for men between 1870 and 1914. Finally, as clerical incomes were household incomes, and as many female clerks still lived at home with family members who were often clerical workers, their introduction into the clerical labour force in many cases had direct financial benefits for male clerks.

Angel in the Office: The Hostility of Male Clerks to the Breaking of Gender Boundaries

Female clerks not only had the potential to damage clerks financially, their increased employment also posed the danger of upsetting the gender boundaries of the nineteenth century middle-class Victorian world which confined women to the private sphere and men to the public.[72] Gregory Anderson, for example, has shown the fears expressed by male correspondents to the *Manchester Guardian* in 1886 over the question of women in the office.[73] Similarly, Jane E. Lewis has argued that, 'While middle class men ... had no hesitation in relying on the arduous work of their female domestic servants they had no intention of permitting either their wives or daughters to engage in paid employment'.[74]

One factor which softened clerical opposition to the employment of women was the attitudes of male employers and senior management. This group effectively shared the same deep-seated attitudes towards women as their clerks. Their use of female clerks was subsequently constrained by these beliefs. They did not, for example, use female clerks almost exclusively for secondary labour out of consideration for their male employees, but because they believed that women's inherent gendered qualities made them able to perform only certain types of office work. As Lewis has argued, women were not only employed because they were cheap, but because they were also thought to possess certain gender characteristics – a quickness of eye and ear, a nimbleness of hand, a character which made them more inclined to sedentary employment, patience which disposed them more to repetitive and monotonous work – which were thought to make them highly suitable for the growing number of secondary clerical positions which were then becoming available.[75] On the other hand these qualities were thought to preclude them from the more demanding, 'intellectual' positions which were duly given to men. Mr Stanley M. Leathers, who as First Civil Service Commissioner was responsible for admission into the Civil Service, stated in 1912 that entrance examinations had a 'deleterious effect on the health of women'. This was used to legitimize the higher rate of rejections for women in the Civil Service and was supported by Dr Wilson, the Chief Medical Officer of the Post Office.[76] The mechanical/intellectual distinction which had been envisaged by Northcote and Trevelyan for office work in the mid-nineteenth century was effectively realized in terms of gender less than fifty years later.[77]

Another factor that mitigated the impact of the feminization of the office for male clerks was that for the most part female clerks accepted the gender stereotyping that was being actively imposed in the office. They accepted the fact that although they were office workers, they were also future wives and mothers, and that primacy had to be given to the latter rather than the former. There was subsequently, as Jane Lewis has admitted, a willingness to accept many of the limitations which employers and managers, no doubt with the support of the majority of their male clerical employees, ringed around them.[78]

A final factor which should be taken into consideration when discussing the reaction of male clerks to the increasing feminization of the office is that many of these individuals were actively involved in the process itself. 20 per cent of the fathers of female applicants for Class II typists at the London County Council, 1905–14, were in clerical and civil service occupations.[79] Similarly in the competition held in April 1911 for women and girl clerks at the General Post Office, 37 per cent of the fathers of applicants for women clerkships and 33 per cent of the applicants for girl clerkships were in clerical and civil service positions.[80] Moreover, in a period when access to clerical work was very much restricted by who one knew, many male clerical workers were able to secure work for daughters, sisters and other female family members. It is important to note that throughout this period it was predominantly parents who decided what work their children would do. As Geoffrey Rogers said about the decision that he would become a clerk, '… I didn't have any option, I was just pushed into it'.[81] Similarly, Sylvia Ward was 'found' work as a clerk at the Prudential following the doctor's warning about her father's health.[82] Clerical parents thus actively chose clerical professions for their daughters.

George Rose, for example, was not opposed in the least to his sister Margie finding employment as a clerk in London in 1910, even though this did result in her coming to live with him. He even admonished her for not trying hard enough to succeed in her office work. As he wrote in his diary,

> That waltz you play so often, Margie, is extremely bad for you. It is voluptuous and sensual, and without a spark of intellectuality. You may take this as certain; that so long as you find such stuff exercises a sway over your foolish little heart, reducing it to the state of a flabby, pulpy inorganic thing, then so surely will you never improve yourself (as you talk of wanting to do). You will never learn shorthand, and you will be ready to throw your palpitating little coalition of weak sentimentality into the arms of the first handsome, soldierlike fool who cares to attract you.[83]

A week earlier he had written concerning her, '… as she has also failed to make enough progress in shorthand to justify Mr Muntzer in appointing her to Ethel's [a female clerical friend of Rose] place next June one of the best chances of her life seems about to be lost'.[84] This was hardly the writing of a man who was opposed to women entering the office, and one could be sure in the case of George Rose that if he had an axe to grind, he would certainly do so assiduously in his diary.

So long as women were segregated into the secondary labour clerical market, so long as they did not compete with men, were not given the same opportunities, and were forced to resign on marriage, opposition towards them by male clerks was muted. In a period when male clerical incomes, opportunities and numbers were increasing what else would one expect? Opposition was, as has been seen, expressed in the *Clerk*, but then the N.U.C. only represented a tiny fraction of clerks in London and the rest of the nation. Its lack of support, and its failure to arouse support by its implicit critique of female clerks may be seen as further evidence of the lack of major disquiet amongst male clerks towards increased feminization. As even Gregory Anderson admits, by the turn of the century, with the realization that there was no actual threat, opposition to female clerks in clerical circles was quietening down.[85] It was only in the Post Office, where as has been seen, women were used in more responsible positions, that opposition amongst male clerk was much more vocal.[86]

Conclusion

At the MacDonnell Commission in April 1912 Mr Edmund Phipps, Principal Assistant Secretary of the Elementary Education Branch of the Board of Education was asked if he thought there would be any objections to the recruitment of youths into the Assistant Clerk Class of the Civil Service at an age when their education was imperfect. His answer is revealing and contains may of the arguments presented in this chapter on the effects of technology and women on male clerical workers,

> ... I think so. I think that the old conception was that the abstractor [assistant] class would do nothing but such very simple duties as made it matter very little what sort of person they were. I think nowadays we have got away from that; we have steadily shifted the simpler jobs out of the way. Thus, we have employed women typists to do the great mass of copying that was supposed to be the regular work of abstractors; we use telephones more, we use printed forms instead of copying, we use carbon copies in type-writers. Therefore we do away with such simple work. So the abstractor clerk is doing undoubtedly very much superior work, certainly in the Board of Education and other offices, than his class was ever designed to do, and I think it is a very serious thing for the Service to have a great mass of men brought in at a salary which will rise to £150, which they will reach between 40 and 50, who have no prospect beyond that.[87]

As a result of the increased application of technology and female labour to the civil service the assistant clerk, the lowest permanent grade, had had its work upgraded. On the basis of this, the grade pressed for an increase in their salary scale which was in the event granted by the Commission. Here is a clear refutation of the argument that women and technology deskilled and downgraded clerks before the First World War.

The feminization, rationalization and mechanization of the office between 1870 and 1914 in many cases revolutionized the working environment for the male clerical worker. It created the modern office. It did not, however, result in the downfall of the male clerk or his demise into a white collar proletariat bereft of status, skill or financial income. In fact the very reverse appears to have happened. Against the background of these changes, clerical incomes, skill levels and opportunities increased. Clearly there was some link. Technology upgraded work by obviating the need to perform unskilled, repetitive work. It demanded in some cases the learning of completely new skills, and in others the need to re-skill in order to perform the same office tasks. Similarly women clerks upgraded male clerical work by having inferior work downgraded to them. They also contributed to increasing male incomes by acting as a cheap source of labour in secondary clerical labour markets, and by augmenting family incomes.

What is as important is that the inauguration of the two did not meet with the degree of hostility from male clerks that has been suggested. If one wants to look for opposition in the complaint literature of this period one will certainly find it. The same is the case for the Victorian and Edwardian press. These papers, particularly the emerging sensationalist press, in their aim to increase sales, were keen to foster an atmosphere of controversy and crisis rather than one of consensus and calm.[88] This is not to argue that there was no opposition, it is only to say that its degree should not be exaggerated. Clerical journals did not universally condemn the changes. Diary entries and interviews fail to give a sense of foreboding or opposition. Company records do not, on the whole, suggest resentment. It would appear that male clerks were quite sanguine about changes which were clearly, in most cases, in their interests.

6 EDUCATION, MERIT AND PATRONAGE: THE LONDON CLERICAL MARKET

Key to any analysis of clerical workers in London in the late Victorian and Edwardian period is a discussion of education. Clerks were essentially 'brain workers', a term which, as has been seen in previous chapters, was as much ascriptive as it was prescriptive. In terms of a clerk's usefulness, market value and relative status, intellectual capital was almost as important as vocational skill. In many cases the distinction was immaterial. In this sense, a clerk's education was central to his professional career. As Sidney Webb, former chairman of the Technical Education Committee of the London County Council (L.C.C.) and a major commentator at the time on education, noted in his work on London education in 1904, what a clerk was professionally capable of rested in large part on the education he had received.[1] The knowledge of languages, the business organizations of other countries, the intricacies of currencies and international exchanges, foreign tariffs and port dues, new taxes or commercial laws, the ability to calculate actuarial probabilities and insurance risks, even the capacity to apply one's intellect to solve a minor problem, all of these skills and items of knowledge could not be simply 'picked up', but to a large extent were dependent on the mental training that one had learnt at school and college.[2]

Education is also an important topic in relation to clerks because of the putative effects that expanding state-provided education were said to have had on the profession. Whereas it was argued that earlier in the nineteenth century clerks had a relatively high and secure status due to the scarcity of their essential skills of literacy and numeracy, the provision of these by the state following Forster's Education Act in 1870 and later legislation was said to have made them widespread and thus undermined their position. The result, it was argued was an over supply of clerks in the market and a subsequent fall in the market position of the clerical worker.[3] Murray Fernie, who as has been seen in the previous chapter protested against the spread of technology in offices, also remonstrated against state sponsored education. In his opinion, '... the typewriter has accelerated that lowering of clerical remuneration which *has been steadily going on since the passing of the early Education Acts.* [my italics]'.[4] The National Union of Clerks and

The Association of Women Clerks and Secretaries both demanded legislation to raise the school-leaving age so as to postpone entry into office work. They also wanted counselling in schools to warn students against considering work in an 'overcrowded' clerical market.[5]

Nearly seventy years later Gregory Anderson echoed these sentiments. Anderson argued in his conclusion that in the latter half of the nineteenth century the clerk had embarked upon his steady decline into proletarian oblivion, and made a strong link between this voyage and the widespread availability of elementary education;

> ... While there existed, as there did before the 1870s, a marked differential between educated, literate clerks and the great mass of the relatively uneducated working class, clerks were secure. Once popular education expanded, however, that essentially fragile differential between clerks and the rest of the working class was further narrowed when the relative economic position of many workers, given the rise in real wages, improved in the last decades of the century.[6]

Education was thus key to the relative status of the clerical worker between 1870 and 1914. Much of the current argument on the demise of the clerk for this period rests on the simple premise that more state provided education led to a proportionate decline in the position of the hapless office worker.

Having given the background to the importance of education for clerks in the later half of the nineteenth century this chapter will concentrate on asking whether the provision of universal elementary education by the state after 1870 was so detrimental to the overall welfare of the clerk. It will argue that while near universal elementary education did indeed have wide ranging effects (not necessarily negative) on the clerical profession, not enough attention has been paid to the spread of secondary education, particularly in London, in the same period. While elementary education may have made basic clerical skills more widely available to a greater populace, the improvement and expansion of secondary education meant that many clerks were able to counter this and perpetuate an intellectual, social and cultural distinction between themselves and the working classes.

The expansion of secondary education between 1870 and 1914 and its effects on the clerical labour market will consequently be analysed in detail. To begin with, the growth of secondary education in London between 1869 and 1914 will be examined. Following this, the centrality of secondary education to clerks will be discussed. An examination of the recruitment structure of the London clerical labour market will follow in order to understand what role secondary education played in assisting its students in finding clerical work. In relation to this, the increasing importance of public examinations in the second half of the nineteenth century will be commented upon. After this, the educational backgrounds of successful second division clerks in the Civil Service and in Glyn's

Bank and the occupations of their fathers will be analysed to demonstrate the growing importance of secondary education to clerical work.

Secondary Education

The Growth of Secondary Education in London

In 1903 the London Education Authority was created. The London School Board along with many of the city's endowed grammar schools were now incorporated with the Technical Education Board (of the L.C.C.) into one over-arching educational body under the control of the London County Council.[7] For the first time in its history the capital had an institutional body which was responsible for the provision of education from elementary schools through to grammar schools, technical colleges, the polytechnics, specialist schools and the University of London. What was more, the body had full statutory powers to raise taxes in order to fund its educational policies.

Such was the backdrop to Sidney Webb's comprehensive survey of the educational institutions that the new authority had under its control, *London Education*.[8] In addition to meticulously discussing the future educational needs and challenges of London and its inhabitants, Webb also provided an in-depth study of what had been achieved in educational provision in the capital over the last forty or so years. The result was impressive. From a system which had previously relied on the voluntary sector with sparse governmental support had evolved a partnership between public and private bodies which, while not perhaps universal, had made great inroads into providing education for a broad range of London's populace.

Discussing the achievements of the former London School Board, Webb reeled off an extensive range of statistics made possible by the 1870 Education Act; half a million additional children in elementary education on top of the 300,000 who had previously been catered for by the voluntary sector, 500 new public buildings occupying 600 acres of valuable land, a school in every one of London's electoral districts, four to the square mile of the whole of the city's surface, a total of 14 million sterling expended on the whole enterprise.[9] It was not only a question of quantity, however. Under state provision and inspection, standards had been raised and education had come to be seen not as an act of charity but as a crucial requirement for the well-being of the individual and more specifically for the state and society. It was indeed this principle which was said to have been inscribed in the 1902–3 Education Acts.[10]

As well as discussing elementary education, Webb also examined the state of secondary education in London. The capital had no less than 25,000 boys and girls in its secondary schools, a figure, according to Webb, larger than either Paris or Berlin.[11] In addition to this figure was a further layer of private 'commercial academies' and colleges for 'young ladies of the genteel suburbs'; a group that Webb saw as complementing rather than competing with public provision.[12] In addition to growth in student numbers, from an estimated number of 12,500 in 1892,[13] many of these schools had been equipped with modern buildings, science laboratories and suitable equipment. Efficiency still, however, varied between the schools and staffing in many remained a weak point.[14]

Nevertheless, the change in secondary education over the previous thirty-five years in London and the nation as a whole, while not up to the same degree as elementary education, had been substantial. The change had begun in 1869 with the passing of the Endowed Schools Act. The Act, which can be seen as pre-cipitating the beginning of the modern grammar school in England and Wales, established the Endowed School Commission whose job it was to reform exist-ing educational endowments in the country, particularly those that related to the grammar schools.[15] While the act did not specifically set out to create a tier of secondary education, or concentrate on this area *per se*, it had been heavily influenced by the report of the Schools Inquiry Commission, 1868 which had spoken of the importance of the grammar school endowments and the need to reform them, the Taunton Report of 1868 which had established a template for a modern secondary school system, and by the call of Mathew Arnold in the 1860s for the need of such a system of national education to cater for the needs of the growing middle classes.[16]

The reform of the grammar schools and the expansion of secondary educa-tion had direct relevance to clerical workers in London. Clerks as members of a loose but broad-based middle class, were a major group who benefited from the work of the Commissioners and the general reform of the grammar schools which were so clearly directed towards this social stratum. It was not only the extra resources that went into grammar schools which changed them but the whole ethos which the Commissioners brought which wrought such a dramatic change in the schools. Individual merit, the guiding public principal of Britain's middle classes, became the principal criteria of who should receive the benefits of the endowments, and not the older ideas of charity, dependence and personal patronage which had sustained the former order. As W. E. Forster, vice-president of the committee on education, explained in the second reading of the Endowed Schools Bill on 15 March 1869,

> ... Free education should not be given unless it was the reward of merit. The poor should benefit from endowments, not by favour but as the reward of their own achievements. The interests of the middle classes, who needed good education for their children, should be carefully preserved. The ideal of the future should be that no one class should guide the destiny of England, but that England for the future is in truth to be self-governed; all her citizens taking their share, not by class distinctions, but by individual worth.[17]

The upshot of this was that resources were taken away from poorer social groups who were often boarded and clothed as well as educated by endowments such as at Emmanuel Hospital, Westminster, and diverted to relatively less poor but more 'deserving' members of a rising lower-middle class.[18] This was done by the establishment of a series of scholarships and exhibitions. These granted free admission (or substantial discounts) to successful candidates to grammar schools. In some cases financial assistance was also given to students. The system was continued by the L.C.C.'s London Education Authority in 1903. The L.C.C.'s *London Statistics 1912–13*, for example, shows that there were 8,544 Council scholarship holders in secondary schools in London in 1913, over one third of the total number of pupils.[19] The main beneficiaries of this were children of clerks, shopkeepers and some skilled workers, groups from which the new recruits of the rapidly rising white-collar workforce were recruited, and which would later come to be seen as the 'lower-middle class'. Llewellyn-Smith and Acland, for example, estimated that 74 per cent of students at three secondary schools they studied in East London were from 'middle class' backgrounds; a group which he described as being predominantly made up of licensed victuallers, shopkeepers, managers, agents, officials and clerks.[20] Similarly, out of the 420 boys at Owen's School in 1898, 129 had fathers who were clerks, agents, warehousemen and civil servants and the fathers of 115 were tradesmen and shopkeepers.[21]

The Centrality of Secondary Grammar Schools to the Clerical Workforce

It can thus be seen that those groups who benefited principally from the reform of the grammar schools in London, and who supplied most of its students, were clerks and shopkeepers, together with some skilled workers. There is a large amount of circumstantial evidence which suggests that many of the pupils of these grammar schools went into clerical occupations. Discussing secondary education in London, for example, Sidney Webb noted, '... From the secondary schools comes a large proportion of those who enter city offices as clerks; practically all the bank and insurance staff and the civil service, and nearly all the sons of business men who are destined to succeed to their fathers' positions.'[22]

An interesting source which provides an insight into the future careers of the pupils of grammar (and other secondary) schools in London is the *Report of the Special Sub-Committee of the Technical Education Board of the L.C.C. on Commercial Education, 1897.*[23] In addition to businessmen, the evidence of educationalists, including headmasters and teachers of secondary schools, was recorded in relation to attitudes concerning commercial education. Information was also given regarding the curriculum of some of these schools. One of the witnesses, for example, was Dr. Wormell, headmaster of the Central Foundation School in Cowper Street on the borders of the City. Talking in relation to his own school he noted that, '... over two hundred boys per annum go out to commerce in direct answer to applications'.[24] Mr. R. E. H. Goffin, Headmaster of United Westminster Schools, stated in a letter to the Committee that it had former students in almost every bank in London. He also wrote of his experience of the type of education required by, 'banks, railways, insurance companies, actuaries, accountants, &c., and...for librarians and municipal officers ...', clearly suggesting that these were careers that his pupils went into on leaving school.[25] What is interesting to note in this report is the degree to which schools tailored their education to those students planning a career in business or public administration. Llewellyn-Smith and Acland's observation that some schools provided lessons in bookkeeping and shorthand, in addition to the staple subjects of English, foreign languages, mathematics, drawing and natural science, was confirmed in the information provided by schools to the Technical Education Board of the L.C.C.[26] The Central Foundation School had, for example, a civil service, technical and commercial department.[27] The same structure existed at the boys school of Regent Street Polytechnic and undoubtedly did so in other schools in London.[28] Asked about his opinion on the teaching of distinctly commercial subjects at schools, Dr Wormell answered,

> ... we might recognize a certain number of schools having more distinctly commercial curricula than others, and boys whose minds are made up as regards the future should select such schools. This does exist to some extent. If you take a map of London and get the boys to mark their place of residence you will find that the different schools draw students from all parts of the metropolis. The object of the parents in selecting schools at some distance cannot be on account of the small fees, because of the railway fare; they obviously have chosen certain schools because they appear to suit their requirements. I think we might take advantage of this fact and acknowledge the commercial curricula in a few schools ...[29]

At University College School classes existed for bookkeeping, French correspondence, political economy and commercial history and commercial geography. Shorthand was available for a 'small fee' after school hours. The headmaster of the school stated that,

> ... A sharpish boy of 14 or 15 intending to enter an office between 16 and 17 would probably have made distinct progress in Latin, French, German, mathematics and arithmetic, besides his English subjects. I then let him drop Latin, give rather more time to modern languages, including if he will take it, a little Spanish and put him to commercial geography and political economy instead of ordinary history and geography, in which he may be supposed fairly proficient. He will almost certainly want to take bookkeeping, which is probably good for him, as giving habits of neatness. But a good many of these boys are not very sharp, and for them I do not crowd in so many subjects.[30]

Similarly at Sir Walter St John's School, Battersea, all boys intended for commerce took German in addition to French. As soon as the boys reached the upper fifth form they were given the option of spending half their time at 'strictly commercial work' which included shorthand, bookkeeping, typewriting and office routine, subjects required for the Civil Service Examinations or subjects necessary for the Cambridge Local and other similar examinations. For commercial subjects visiting masters were employed to ensure that these subjects were well taught, though it was noted that this had not been a success.[31]

Another factor which suggests that secondary grammar schools and other types of secondary institutes including private, county and technical schools were providing a large number of clerical workers in London is the fact that the age for clerks beginning work appears to have been rising over the period, from on average around fourteen to sixteen. Asked, for example, whilst appearing as a witness for the T.E.B.'s inquiry into commercial education, if he had noticed any tendency to raise the age for taking clerks into business, Professor W. A. S. Hewins, Director of the London School of Economics, answered that with the absence of statistics on the subject he could not express an opinion. Not to be put off by this, Rev. C. G. Gull, a member of the interviewing panel, representative of the Incorporated Association of Headmasters on the T.E.B., and headmaster of the Grocers' Company School, Hackney Downs, riposted that, '... he believed that there was a tendency to induce students to remain at school until they reached 16 and a half years of age'.[32] Mr Easterbrook, fellow panellist and headmaster of Owen's School, Islington, agreed with this, stating that he, '... believed that the good firms were not taking clerks into business as early an age as formerly, but the inferior firms endeavoured to get them as young as possible'. Reverend Gull added, '... in his own school he noticed that the age of leaving had been increased by twelve or fifteen months'.[33] Such an opinion was shared by the MacDonnell Commission which recommended that the Civil Service should recruit at an older age in order to reflect changing trends in education.[34]

It can therefore be argued that from the 1870s onwards the expansion of secondary education in London, principally via the rejuvenation of the grammar schools, benefited more than any other group clerks, tradesmen and some skilled workers. It did this by providing a secondary education which was exclusive in that it disqualified most of London's children from attending, but inclusive enough, at around £4 to £8 a year for many of these schools,[35] to admit large numbers from the first two groups. Scholarships from these schools and later on from the L.C.C. were also of great assistance, particularly to the children of skilled workers.[36] Improvements in secondary education preserved a middle-class status for scores of families who hovered on the social threshold by bequeathing an education which gave them a distinct standing. As Felix Owen, whose father had paid for him to go to West Ham Grammar School for eighteen months, and who was able to procure a job in the City as a Junior Broker in 1918, stated,

> I left school a bit earlier than I should have done, you were kept on at school until you were fourteen, I left St. Peter's and Paul's at thirteen and went to West Ham Grammar School for about eighteen months ... I think mainly the object was if I got put down on my C.V.'s in future educated at St. Peter and Paul Elementary, West Ham Grammar School, it gives you a bit of kudos you see ...[37]

In addition, by providing in many of these schools a more modern education, with some even giving rudimentary commercial training, secondary education ensured that the provision of universal education after 1870 did not adversely affect too much existing clerks. This, combined with the rapid expansion of clerical numbers, meant that these clerks were able to retain the lion's share of the best positions for themselves, their sons and daughters. The report of the T.E.B. into commercial education clearly saw this distinction when it attempted to categorize the grades of those employed in the world of commerce or business into three groups. The first were, '... the great army of office boys, junior clerks, shorthand clerks, copyists, typists, junior bookkeepers, ledger clerks and accountants'. The second were, '... employees in more responsible positions, such as senior clerks, correspondence clerks, managers of departments, agents, dealers and travellers'. The third were, '... the great employers of industry and the heads of large firms and business houses'. While the report admitted fluidity between these groups, it nevertheless insisted on a distinction in education between them. Primary would suffice for the first, secondary for the second and university for the third. Education was thus key to advancement, those receiving one grade free from worrying over the social incursions of the group below them.[38]

The Increasing Importance of Public Examinations

In tandem with the growth in secondary education, a further significant development over this period was the growing importance of examinations. Public examinations in England and Wales can be seen as beginning around the middle of the nineteenth century. Recruitment by examination originated in The East India Company and the Home Civil Service in the 1850s. It was followed later by other branches of the Civil Service, the Military, the railway companies, banking, insurance and local government. Accompanying and complementing this development was the establishment of a number of national examining boards. In 1853 The College of Preceptors initiated public examinations across the country as a whole. The Royal Society of Arts followed suit in 1854. In the latter half of the 1850s the universities of Oxford and Cambridge, and the Department of Arts and Science began their own examinations.[39] These examinations became increasingly important for applicants for clerical work. Holders of such qualifications, for example, became gradually exempt from certain entrance examinations.[40] In addition, some firms began to demand these qualifications for positions within their companies. Glyn's Bank for example, around 1875 stipulated that, 'Decided preference will be accorded to Candidates who are acquainted with London and have already had some experience of office business; and also to those who have passed the Local Middle Class Exams of Oxford or Cambridge, or of the Society of Arts, or the Science Examination of the Privy Council'.[41]

On the one hand, the rise in the importance of examinations in Britain in the latter half of the nineteenth century can be seen as the consequence of an increasingly complex, bureaucratic and impersonal society. On the other they can be viewed, in much the same way as the reform of the grammar schools, as heralding the rise of a more individualist, meritocratic society. Impersonal systems of qualification would obviate, so it was hoped, the need for a system based on dependency and patronage. This was certainly the dynamic behind the Northcote–Trevelyan report commissioned by Gladstone, the then Chancellor of the Exchequer, in 1853 into the recruitment of civil servants. The report, presented to Parliament in February 1854, led eventually to the establishment of the Civil Service Commission in May 1855 and the principle of entrance by examination.[42]

The supposed meritocratic link between the rise of an examination system which acted as gatekeeper to a nexus of power relations, and the reform of the grammar schools and development of a modern secondary education system can be seen in the fact that public examinations were taken almost exclusively, with the exception of the government's Science and Arts examinations, by students of the latter. Such examinations and the privileges which they brought with them were effectively limited to the minority who went on to receive a secondary education. An insight into the students taking these examinations is given by a list of the type of schools candidates who sat the December 1893 Cambridge Local Examinations, compiled by J. N. Keynes, the then secretary of the Cambridge Local Examinations Syndicate; 2,350 candidates were from endowed schools, 1,214 from 'Other Public' (most probably private foundation schools which were mostly non-profit making private establishments with a board of governors), 1,536 from private schools and only forty-five from higher grade elementary schools.[43]

What is in fact clear from these figures is that, in effect, one form of privilege was simply being replaced by another. Only a minority were receiving secondary education, which entitled them to dominate a public examination system that was increasingly important for entrance into higher-status jobs. The important point here is that substantial numbers of clerical workers had become part of this exclusive group.

Recruitment Structure of the Clerical Labour Market

Asked during his interview for the *Millennium Memory Bank* if he felt that his education was better than a lot of people had received when he was a child, Felix Owen answered,

> Well I mean, my final eighteen months at the West Ham Grammar School, I can see what my father's idea was. I mean, that's been of great value to me all through my life. Much more so if I'd had to put down on my application for a job – Where educated? St. Peter and Paul Elementary, that sounds fine, but if you can say St. Peter and Paul elementary school and West Ham School, that sounds even better, I mean you will get the job. If there was any doubt, one way or the other, you would get the job in preference to somebody else who had not been given that little bit of extra.[44]

How exactly did this work? What were the dynamics of advantage which a secondary education gave? In order to answer these questions it is important first to examine the actual recruitment structure of the labour clerical market in late Victorian and Edwardian London. It is only with a fuller understanding of this that one can appreciate Felix Owen's comments.

Meritocracy may have been the guiding public light of many of the middle classes throughout this period, but patronage still remained the basis for a large number of those who looked for a berth as a clerk in London. *Business Life*, for example, wrote in 1902 that, 'One of the chief reasons why many who have acquired proficiency in commercial subjects fail to obtain a situation, although they assiduously watch the daily papers is owing to the fact that the best positions which fall vacant are never advertised at all'.[45] The clerical market in London for this period can be broadly described as a closed shop which was only very gradually developing, under the pressure of expansion, into a transparent and open labour market. Only the lowest clerical positions such as copyists or office boys, usually in small and emerging firms, were actually advertised. The more attractive positions, particularly in the banks, insurance companies and major commercial firms still tended to be passed on by word of mouth and personal contacts. With the exception of the Civil Service, including the Post Office, who one was acquainted with mattered just as much as what one actually knew.

An extremely good example of this system of patronage is the case of George Rose from the Essex market village of Chipping Ongar. Rose's diaries open in 1900 when he was 17 and still living at home and working in Ongar.[46] He was effectively doing two jobs at this time. The first was working for Mr Henry Child, who owned the local drapers in Ongar, and appears to have been one of the local business magnates. The second was working in his father's tailors shop, usually in the late afternoon and evening. In addition to owning the local drapers Henry Child was a director of the Ongar Gas Company and also held shares in the Ongar Waterworks Co. Ltd, of which his son William was secretary. Although not stated, it would appear from Rose's description of his activities in the 1900 diary, that he did clerical work for both the Gas and Waterworks, in addition to the drapers. This included bookkeeping, checking meters, and preparing, writing out and delivering bills.

In late 1900, Henry Child's son William prematurely died, and in December the Child's drapery business closed down. With this went Rose's various jobs. Rose was not, however, to be out of work for too long. His diary entry for 29 December reads,

> The year is closing, this book is closing, and my past three years of life is closing too. Today is the last, thank God. After all, the old place is full of recollections of Harry Child's poor fellow, naturally I can't help feeling backwards. What a variety of emotions I have experienced there, I have had practically three masters, I look back at the work with nothing but loathing but there is little pleasure in the thought of the departed family Cecil, and little Nora and Trevor. Well it's Mr Wightman now and it's sacrilege almost, however I left tonight at 9.20 and posted a few letters for him, then father dictated a letter to Mr. Jones. Oh dear.[47]

Rose woke up at 7:00 a.m. in the morning of 1 January 1900, breakfasted, and received a letter asking him to come to the offices of the Commercial Gas Company in Stepney, East London. He was given a long column of pounds, shillings and pence to add up, and on doing this commenced a job which was to span his working life.[48] The Mr Jones that Rose's father had earlier written to was Stanley Jones, a director of the Commercial Gas Company, who was described by Rose in the diary as 'my employer'. Stanley Jones was a relation (presumably the son, as they lived at the same address) of the local Ongar businessman, Henry Edward Jones. The latter was a director of the Ongar Gas Company and had helped establish the Ongar Water Works Company in 1897, both companies which Rose had worked for earlier via his connection with Henry Child.

Clearly, Rose's employment at the Commercial Gas Company, a well paid, secure position with good promotion prospects, was due to his family connections within the close-knit village of Ongar. The use of the term 'Ongarians' in relation to work[49] and the frequent references of fellow clerks who came from the Essex village in the diary suggest that the nexus between London and Chipping Ongar was made use of by other families in the Essex village.

Other examples of these personal connections are common in the sources. Felix Owen, for example, got his first job with a firm of insurance brokers in Leadenhall Street via his father who was a timber merchant and insured his timber cargoes through this firm. As Owen said, '... getting a job in those days was very much a matter of influence'.[50] Andrew Carlyle Tait, who like Felix Owen lived in Ilford, Essex before commencing work, obtained his first clerical position at the wholesale and export stationers and manufacturers, Spicer, James and Sons in the City in September, 1904. Tait's father owned a bookshop in the City and used his connections with the stationery firm to secure a job for his son. Tait noted in his diary in July, 1894, that, '... I expected yesterday that when our summer holidays were over I should have to go up to Mr. Spicer's in Thames Street whom Pa has spoken to about me, about the beginning of September'.[51] In the event, Tait was forced to go the day after he left school for an interview at the company.

Contacts came through sources other than one's father or other family members. Church or Chapel were important centres of patronage and personal connections. Jim Hancock's father, for example, was given an introduction to the London County and Westminster Bank through his father's connection with the Congregational Church,

> ... There was a Mr. Campbell, a bachelor, who used to come to the family every Sunday for lunch at Stoke Newington after church. And he had come down to make his fortune in the 1880's with a Mr. Nebittson who had become a very successful banker and who had been made Lord Glenn Dynne. And he, well it was arranged that he would be a referee for my father in the application for the London County and Westminster Bank. And this was sufficient for my father to be given the chance of a job.[52]

Living nearby in Homerton, Hackney, William Evans was able to obtain his position in the office of the solicitors Ashurst Morris Smith & Co., via his connections with a Mr Botwright, an employee of the aforesaid company and fellow member of Clapton Park Congregational Church in Lower Clapton.[53]

Family members too were very useful. Not only fathers, but also uncles, brothers and other relations would often help to procure positions for relatives in the offices where they worked. This is evident in the clerks' registers of companies such as the Prudential, the Great Western Railway, and Glyn's bank where the same names and phrases next to employees such as, 'Son of Robilliard, Clerk at Glyn's in Town Office' are common.[54] As a book written in 1933 to celebrate the rebuilding of the bank commented,

> ... Just as throughout its History the House has always welcomed as Partners the descendants of the old banking families which were connected with its formation, so in choosing its clerks, despite the keen competition to enter the service of the House, preference is always given to the sons and daughters of members of the staff and of the customers; and as a result of this it is not uncommon to find that three generations of a family have been in the employ of the Bank.[55]

In a period when trust and knowledge of background was crucial, especially for those dealing in large sums of money, such a system was hardly surprising.

Another important source was school itself, particularly via the Headmaster. Schools not only facilitated their students by the education they provided, or by, as in Felix Owen's words, the 'kudos' they gave, but also directly helped to procure for their students positions in companies, particularly clerical ones. This was done in several ways. One was by simple advice. Headmasters would advise parents on which would be the best career plans for their children or even which companies they should direct them towards. As *Business Life* commented on the subject, '... There is not a school in the country whose Principal is not from time to time consulted by the parents of the Scholars in his charge as to the field of occupation for which a boy is most suited'.[56] In relation to its own educational establishment, the Pitman's Metropolitan School, the journal wrote,

> ... Mr de Bear [the Principal of Pitman's Metropolitan School] estimated that the number of parents and others who seek advice of the Management in the course of a year must amount to many thousands. It is one of the most important parts of the work performed by the heads of the departments of the School, to watch carefully the development of the students, in order that they may be placed in the business world to the best possible advantage, as soon as they have attained proficiency in their studies.[57]

In an employment market tightly restricted by personal contacts and patronage, this advisory role of the Headmaster was clearly an important function for parents in addition to his more pedagogical duties.

Headmasters were also important in that they provided personal references for their students when applying for positions. This was a function, for example, that Dr Wormell of the Central Foundation School, told the panel of the Technical Education Board of the L.C.C., he carried out for the hundreds of boys who went from his school every year into commerce.[58] In a period when, for instance, three character testimonials were needed for a position on the Great Western Railway, this was clearly of some importance.[59] In addition, from evidence from companies to the Technical Education Board concerning recruitment, there appeared to be a tendency for various companies to recruit from specific schools. Mr Thomas P. Chappell, of Messers Chappell and Co., Ltd, music publishers and pianoforte manufacturers, for example, told the Board that the best clerks in his company came from the Philological School in Marylebone.[60] Mr Lorimer, of Messers Lorimer and Co., manufacturing chemists, wholesale druggists and exporters, Islington, stated that several of his employees, who started as youths at the age of 16 or 17, came from University College School. He also stated that there was a preference to employ girls in the company from Owen's School.[61]

Companies would also apply directly to schools for applicants. The furniture company Messers Maple and Co., of Tottenham Road, for example, recruited their clerical staff from charity schools such as Spurgeon's Asylum and the Orphan Working School. This recruitment policy was said by its head, Sir J. Blundell Maple, to be in operation in other firms such as Messers Debenham and Freebody's and Messers. Schoolbred and Co.'s.[62] The system was not, however, confined to the Charity Schools. The 200 students who Dr Wormell stated went every year into commerce from the Central Foundation School were recruited directly on this basis.[63] It can also be opined that other secondary grammar schools such as Owen's and Roan's received similar applications. It is interesting to note, for example that, when the London Chamber of Commerce decided to establish a system of commercial examinations in order to try and improve the quality of recruits going into business and commerce in 1887, it convened a congress to discuss the matter which consisted of businessmen and representative schoolmasters. The latter, judging by the schools where the subsequent examinations took place, came almost exclusively from the grammar schools.[64]

Contacts and Examinations, patronage and meritocracy; paradoxically these two diametrically opposed factors determined for many who and who did not perform office work, a key factor for those desirous of obtaining and retaining middle-class status. What is interesting to note is that the contradictions between the two were neither acknowledged nor appreciated at the time. In 1904, for example, an article appeared in the Pitmans journal, *Business Life*, entitled 'Capacity versus Influence'. As the title suggests, the article asked the question what was more important in obtaining work, ability or contacts?

> Whilst interviewing the manager of a large firm of merchant bankers, who had been making enquiries recently with a view to engaging two juniors for positions in the bank, we took the opportunity of ascertaining his views upon the subject of influence in the City. 'Which is the most important factor', we asked, 'in helping a youth on to success in business life, the patronage of influential friends, or individual capacity?' The manager expressed his opinion that if he were asked to give a direct answer to the question, he should say that capacity was of more importance than influence, but he thought that given a youth who had been properly trained for business, it was distinctly advisable that he should be procured the best possible introduction which influence or recommendation could afford him.[65]

The answer was that both were important. You had to have ability *and* contacts in order to procure a position in London, especially in the City. The two were often supplied by secondary education, particularly the reformed secondary grammar schools. In addition to acting as an important mark of social status, many of these schools provided contacts whether through the headmaster or the institution itself. In addition, these schools afforded information via personal acquaintances, teachers or the principal himself on how the system worked that granted admission to the more sought-after positions. At the same time they provided the education that was required to pass examinations to prove that one had capacity required for certain kinds of clerical work. In effect they were suppliers of social, intellectual and cultural capital. It is in this respect that these schools smoothly dovetailed into the whole recruitment structure of clerical work between 1890 and 1914, and why, as has been shown, there appear to have been such close connection between them and the wider business community.

Social Background of Clerks at the Home Office and Glyn's Bank, a Comparison

The importance of a secondary education to office work can briefly be seen by an analysis of the backgrounds of two groups of clerical workers. The first were second division clerks at the Home Office, the second, officials at Glyn's Bank. It must be emphasized here that the aim is not to establish typicality. These clerical positions were not representative of all clerks. They were well paid, were extremely secure jobs, had good promotional opportunities, paid holidays and pensions.[66] They were consequently positions which were widely sought after. It is precisely here that one would expect to find a high number of clerks with a secondary education.

In the civil service entrance was meant to be purely based on merit. Second division clerks were responsible for the more senior and supposedly complex clerical tasks of the Civil Service. They were sandwiched between the first division clerks above them and the assistant and boy clerks below them. The class, created by the Playfair Commission in 1876 were males, recruited between the ages of 17 and 20 by a competitive examination in subjects said to be of 'an ordinary commercial education'.[67] The entry examination was, however, competitive in the extreme. As *Business Life* commented on the examinations in general,

> ... the [Civil Service] examinations are in reality competitive tests, in which the candidate is not merely required to attain a fixed standard of proficiency, but must beat his or her fellow competitors. In this connection, due weight must be given to the fact that the proportion of candidates sitting in relation to the number of vacancies announced is always very large. In a recent examination for girls, no less than four hundred candidates competed for forty vacancies.[68]

Similarly in 1885 the *Thirtieth Report of the Civil Service Commission* noted that,

> There does not yet appear to be any diminution in the attractiveness of these appointments for the general public. Thus, whereas the number of competitors in 1876 was 370, it rose in 1879 to 1,269, and in 1885 to 2,075, the proportion being 10.3 candidates to each vacancy.[69]

Faced with such staunch competition, preparation for anybody entertaining a serious hope of passing the exam was essential. As *Business Life* continued,

> The student, having determined to try for a Government appointment, should at once place himself in the hands of an experienced coach. To enter into preparation for a Civil Service examination with out such expert guidance would in most cases be a very hazardous undertaking ... A competent instructor will be able to tell the student much that he will find indispensable to know, and he will put him through a series of model examinations, using tests almost identical in nature with those which the examiners themselves chose.[70]

Preparation was sometimes provided at school, as in the case, as seen above, of Sir Walter St John's School, Battersea, or the boys day school at Regent Street Polytechnic. As many of the candidates were already working in other clerical occupations, a more typical method would be to attend evening lessons, either at the many classes held in the Board schools throughout London, the Polytechnics or private commercial colleges such as Pitman's. Even in this case, however, the overall threshold of the examination meant that a secondary education was imperative.

The centrality of secondary education to passing the competitive examination for the Second Division can be seen in the *Report of the Royal Commission on the Civil Service, 1912–13*. The report provided extensive information on the schooling of successful candidates and the occupations of their fathers. Of the 100 successful candidates of the September 1911 examination for the Second Division, twenty-four had been educated in London schools. The other seventy-six had been educated at schools all over the country, including Dublin, Liverpool, Leeds and Edinburgh, reflecting the national attraction of Civil Service positions. Out of the successful candidates schooled in London, all had received secondary education. Most of these had attended secondary grammars.[71] The education of successful candidates outside of London broadly reflected this. Compared with figures from 1885, however, out of 221 successful candidates, nearly half had only received an elementary education. The rest were divided between private schools (fifty-eight) and endowed grammars and private foundation schools.[72] As the Report of 1885 commented, '... The statistics given in the Appendix, relating to the 221 Clerks appointed in the year 1885, show that as many as ninety-five received their education in National, British, Wesleyan or Board School; while of the remainder, only about a dozen were educated at schools of so high a class as that to which Dulwich College and the City of London belong'.[73] What is clearly evident from the information contained in these two reports is the increase in both the quality and extent of education that these successful candidates were receiving over the space of twenty-six years. While few of the successful candidates of 1911 were attending such first grade schools, far more were attending second-grade secondary schools such as Owen's School or Parmiter's.

In relation to the occupations of the fathers of successful candidates in 1911 the largest groups were Merchants and Shopkeepers (twenty-two), and Artisans (seventeen). In relation to clerks, there were six successful applicants whose fathers were civil servants and another six who were mercantile clerks. In addition there were three railway employees and four accountants who may have been doing clerical work, and one secretary. This would make a possible twenty clerical workers.[74] The dominance of shopkeepers, artisans and clerks as recruits into the growing civil service is commensurate with the groups from which the growing clerical workforce of London and the nation as a whole was being drawn. It also tallies with the groups who were the main recipients of expanding secondary education in London.

In contrast to the Civil Service, admission into Glyn's bank, like most of the financial establishments in London in this period, rested more on patronage. According to a booklet outlining the regulations for entrance into the banks, *c.* 1875, aspiring candidates had to have their name entered on an application list. This could only be done, however, with the recommendation of a customer or someone connected with the house. When a vacancy became available three candidates would be selected and interviewed. Living in London, previous experience of office work and having passed public examinations were all important factors at this stage.[75] Capacity and patronage were thus both requirements for being admitted into the bank. Unlike the Civil Service, however, the former was useless without the latter.

Information on the schools that clerks went to and their fathers' occupations can be found in the Clerk's Register of the bank. In relation to schools the types of establishments that clerks went to who entered the bank between 1900 and 1910 can be seen as follows;

Table 6.1: Types of Schools Attended by Clerks who Joined Glyn's Bank 1900–10.[76]

Type of School	Endowed Grammar	Private/ Private Foundation	Higher Grade Elementary	Elementary Board/ Church School	Technical/ County High School	Not Known
Numbers Attending	54 (54.5%)	25 (25.25%)	1 (1%)	11 (11.11%)	2 (2%)	6 (6.1%)

Here again one sees a broadly similar picture. The vast majority of boys who were being taken on at Glyn's bank had received a secondary education, the majority of these having attended secondary grammar schools. The eleven clerks who had only received an elementary education could be put down to the patronage system. Whereas the system clearly favoured more affluent members of society with business connections to the banks such as customers, companies with whom the bank did business or partners, it could also benefit poorer individuals who had connections with these groups. Sons of servants were one obvious example. This is commonly seen in the Clerk's Register with such phrases as, 'Former Head Gardener of Lord Hillingdon [one of the partners] who introduced him' or 'Lord Portman's huntsman – who introduced him'.[77] In addition, the bank with major connections with railway companies both at home and abroad, regularly recruited clerks from this sector. This could also account for those who had not had secondary education. A report from the Great Western Railway, for example, entitled 'Junior Staff Report', *c.* 1911, stated that, 'An analysis of Junior

Clerks recently appointed shews that 81% were educated at Council School, 14% at Grammar Schools and 5% privately'.[78]

The occupations of clerks' fathers at the bank can be seen in table two below. Clerical I relates to clerks proper. Clerical II relates to those doing white-collar work, mostly commercial salesmen, warehousemen and shop/drapers assistant. Tradesmen includes farmers, of whom there were several, and artisans/skilled workers includes the work of 'dependents' mentioned above such as gardeners and huntsman. On several occasions a grandfather's or uncle's occupation was given instead of a father's. These have been included.

Table 6.2: Occupations of Fathers of Clerks at Glyn's Bank, July, 1884 to March, 1914.[79]

Occupational Type	Number	Percentage
Clerk I	82	29
Clerk II	37	13.1
Professional/Managerial	98	34.6
Tradesmen	33	11.7
Artisan	24	8.5
Labourer/Unskilled	2	0.7
Other	7	2.5
Total	283	100

While similar to the second division of the civil service there were some interesting differences. The number of sons of tradesmen and artisans was much lower, although in the case of the former, this may be due to some degree to different uses of categorization. It is interesting to note the large number of sons of clerks working at the bank. This probably had a great deal to do with the patronage system. Many of the clerks at Glyn's were sons or relations of clerks already working there. In addition, the differences from the second division of the civil service may be due to the idiosyncrasies of the London labour market, in particular its large number of white-collar and professional workers compared to other cities.

Despite these differences, however, there are several things which are clear from the information furnished by the two institutions. The first is that there was no apparent break down in the social make up of groups entering these clerical positions, nor was there equally any 'invasion' of 'inferior' social classes into these much sought-after jobs. They remained the preserve of lower-middle-class groups with a relatively large contingent of skilled workers, many of whom were probably scholarship holders.[80] In addition, it would appear that a secondary education was a sine qua non of gaining a foothold into Glyn's and the Civil Service. In the case of the latter, all the successful candidates from London for boy clerkships were from these schools.[81] David Milne, Representative of the Association of Assistant Clerks at the MacDonnell Commission, stated in relation to this that, '... since 1900 ... the examination has become much more severe, and it hardly seems likely that a boy who has received no education beyond that given in an ordinary elementary school would have much chance of success in the boy clerks examination'.[82] For Glyn's and other London banks, a relatively advanced education was also important for an industry where administrative errors could cost a great deal of money. In many respects, however, these two requirements, a relatively high social status and a secondary education, were related. The latter was usually a result, and in many cases a requirement, of the former. They were part of the patronage/meritocracy nexus that was so important to the clerical market of late Victorian and Edwardian London.

This system was no less a part of the Civil Service entrance examination system, despite the hopes of its founders. As the article from *Business Life* made so clear, knowing how the examination worked, being able to spare the time and money to do this, knowing the best tutors, and obtaining information on the best preparation colleges were all crucial for passing the exam and entering the Civil Service. This point was precisely made in the questions and answers of the Bishop of Southwark and Mr David Milne over a system of entrance examinations for the Civil Service which the latter had proposed,

> (Bishop of Southwark) ...When you spoke this morning about the examination that you propose, would any system of preparation be required for that examination by these boys of 16? – Yes, I should take it that there would be.
>
> That is to say, they would have to have some special training, even if they were at a continuation school, if they wanted to be successful in this competition; they must, somehow or other, get some special training? – It is so to-day in the Civil Service; there is a special period of cramming to be undergone.
>
> They would have to go to Clark's College or some similar institution? – Yes to a college of that nature.
>
> And the better the special training the boy can get the more chance he has of success? – That is about it.
>
> Then, if he cannot afford to pay for it, however clever he may be, that means that he will not get in? – Yes, that is what it comes to, I'm afraid.
>
> So that the open competition system is really putting a premium, unless you have a very extensive system of scholarships, upon those who have got most money? – That is so; that holds good today.[83]

Competitive examinations, it would appear, were never purely a matter of testing ones abilities.

Conclusion

While it cannot be denied that the introduction following 1870 of universal elementary education had implications for the clerical market in London, the extent of this should not be exaggerated. There was no 'swamping' of clerical positions by a new army of recruits fresh from the Board Schools which were springing up all over London. Many of the expanding clerical positions were certainly being filled by these individuals. This is what one would expect in a society which was becoming more complex, in which work was becoming increasingly bureaucratic and implementing increasingly finer divisions of labour and to which Forster's Education Act was in part a response.

Yet there are several things one should bear in mind. London was already educating large numbers of young people before 1870 in its Anglican and nonconformist schools, in addition to a number of other institutions such as endowed schools, ragged schools and orphan schools. Many of the new recruits into the clerical market continued to come from these schools and undoubtedly more would have if the State had not entered the educational arena. Moreover, it was not until 1880 that schooling was made compulsory, and then only until the age of ten. After 1899 this was increased to twelve. In addition, as was noted by Sidney Webb and the report of the Technical Education Board of the L.C.C. on Commercial Education, many of these elementary students went into positions which were the lowest rungs on the clerical ladder. Finally, as this chapter has stressed, attention must be paid to the expansion of secondary education in London in this period if one is to fully understand how expansion in schooling in the capital affected the clerical market. It is perhaps a failure to do this which has made earlier comments on this area distort and magnify out of all proportion the impact of Forster's Education Act on clerical work.

In relation to the extension of secondary education in London after 1870 this chapter has tried to show that the main beneficiaries of this were poorer members of the middle classes, in particular clerks and tradesmen, who appear to have made up the largest social group who sent their children to these schools. This was important in that such an education gave their recipients significant social status. Large numbers of these pupils went into careers in more prominent and better paid areas of clerical work, particularly in the City, such as the banking, financial and insurance sectors as well as public administration. There were close relations between these sectors and certain secondary schools which assisted in procuring for their pupils such clerical positions. These schools were well integrated into the patronage network that was so important in obtaining clerical work in London. In addition, the spread of public examinations benefited students of these schools. Most of the candidates who took these examinations had received a secondary education, and these qualifications in turn were increasingly being demanded by companies and local councils for applicants hoping to gain work with them. Such an education also benefited candidates for competitive Civil Service examinations. Secondary education was thus important in that it provided social and intellectual capital which could be used to advantage in the London clerical market.

The picture which thus appears is that as elementary education became more available certain groups of clerical workers and other sections of an evolving lower-middle class simply moved up the educational ladder into secondary education. In effect, what was taking place was educational inflation. Exclusivity was subsequently maintained, assisted indeed by the growing importance of merit proved by examination. The difference in the quality of education received by the successful candidates for Second Division Clerkships in the Civil Service between 1885 and 1913 is compelling evidence for this, as is indeed, the fact that the schools which clerks had attended began to be recorded in the Clerks Register at Glyn's from 1900 onwards.[84] It is this which partially explains why there was no collapse in clerical salaries in these sectors, and in fact why they continued to increase. In addition, improvements in secondary education helped maintain the status of many clerical positions by restricting entrance to selected social groups. In relation to this, it also served as a mark of social distinction. As David Milne told the MacDonnell Commission in relation to his members, '... You must remember that assistant clerks are drawn from boy clerks, the majority of whom are secondary school boys and have been brought up in a fairly comfortable and decent home'.[85] Social and financial status were in effect secured for many by the expansion of this area of schooling.

The spread of secondary education was thus of direct relevance to clerical workers from a social and professional basis. Yet to concentrate solely on this sector of schooling when examining the effects of expanding educational opportunities on clerical workers would fail to take note of other equally important pedagogical developments. Between 1870 and 1914 there were two important developments in education affecting clerks in London who had already embarked upon their professional careers. The first was the growth and spread of commercial education. The second was a great expansion of continuation classes, particularly at night school. It is these two areas that will be discussed in the next chapter.

7 COMMERCIAL EDUCATION AND THE CLERK

On 17 May 1897 the Technical Education Board of the London County Council selected a special subcommittee to examine commercial education in London. At the beginning of the extensive report which followed it was stated,

> In conducting our investigation upon the subject of commercial education we have been greatly impressed with the feeling that the matter is one of supreme national importance. The great increase of foreign competition which has been felt by those engaged in almost every branch of commerce and manufacture has aroused a widespread feeling of alarm in the community. It is becoming more and more clear that among the principle causes which are threatening us with a grave diminution of international trade must be placed the better education enjoyed by many of our competitors.[1]

The T.E.B.'s report was part of a major discussion which took place in London between the 1880s and 1914. It was one which involved the press, politicians, academics, businessmen and even royalty.[2] This discussion over commercial education was an appendage of a wider debate concerning technical instruction, which in turn was part of a much broader discourse over national efficiency, an issue which dominated British society at the time.[3] Since the 1870s, and especially following the 1890s, British business and commerce were coming under increasing strain. The reasons for this are complex and manifold. They can, however, be briefly summarized as a perceived failure to respond to overseas competition, especially from the US and Germany, a lack of willingness to adapt to the conditions of the Second Industrial Revolution, an economic age defined by the application of sophisticated science and knowledge to production, and an inability to develop modern, manufacturing enterprises with their emphasis on scale, modern manufacturing techniques, organization and scientific management.[4] The overall consensus was that Britain's failure to rise to these challenges lay in its outdated system of education, in particular its failure to provide adequate technical education.[5]

In London much of this debate centred around commercial education. As the national centre of trade, commerce, finance and communications this was not surprising. In addition, London's emerging global position and nexus of an

Empire which came to dominate its conceptual makeup and everyday life, meant that for many the perceived hegemonic status of the capital was intricately connected with this issue.[6] In the words of the T.E.B.'s report, the question was vital to London as it was the greatest commercial centre in the world, was the heart of the British empire, and possessed more clerks than any other city on earth.[7] For the Board there existed a clear relationship between metropolis, empire, commercial dominance, clerical workers and the importance of commercial education.

This chapter will examine developments in commercial education in London. It will first define the contemporary usage of the term. The growth of commercial education will then be analysed from the perspective of changes in the clerical profession. The introduction of new technologies and techniques, the attempt to professionalize, and the breakdown in more traditional training techniques, and in conjunction with this the growing bureaucratization of office work, will be examined. It will then briefly chart the progress of commercial education in London. Four important institutions in its development will be examined, viz., the Polytechnics, the evening schools, the London School of Economics and the private commercial college, Pitman's Metropolitan School. Finally the attitude of employers and clerks to the topic will be discussed.

Much of the development in what was termed 'technical education' in London was increasingly covered by commercial education. To omit commercial education is therefore to give an incomplete picture of technical education in London. Commercial education also crystallizes many of the themes that have been discussed in previous chapters. It concentrates attention on the growing specialization of clerical work and the attempt to achieve higher professional status, its bureaucratization and the increasing importance of new technologies and techniques. A discussion of the subject, however, does more than this. It enables us to look into the psyche of the clerk and examine important aspects of his professional and overall identity. For the clerk the idea of commercial education represented key values – individualism, merit, character, promotion and, most importantly, self-improvement. It thus acts as a gateway into the conceptual makeup of the Late Victorian and Edwardian clerks which in turn helps us to understand why it was so important to many in this group and sheds light on why clerks came to dominate the further education movement in London.

Modern historiography has commented abundantly on the issue of technical and higher education.[8] In relation to London, the state of higher education, and in particular the growth of the polytechnics and the work of the T.E.B. has been the subject of a recently published collection of essays.[9] In all of this, however, the issue of commercial education seems to be strangely missing. In relation to the latter work, comment concentrated more on technical education for artisans and manual work rather than on commercial education and clerks. With the exception of a chapter in Gregory Anderson's *Victorian Clerks* and another in R. Guerriero Wilson's *Disillusionment or New Opportunities?*, nothing of note has been published concerning it.[10] Furthermore, Anderson's comments themselves are a cause for concern. Though providing valuable information on the development of commercial education in the north-east of England in the Victorian period, these developments are depicted as nothing more than a last-ditch, desperate attempt by clerks to protect themselves against an inevitable, encroaching proletarianization. Anderson's overall thesis of social decline amongst clerks prevents him from appreciating the impact of more formalized commercial education and training on clerical workers. The historiography in sum is therefore almost silent on a subject which appears to have been widely discussed, particularly in London, and where it does speak out, it is in many respects quite misleading.

The Meaning of Commercial Education

In the latter half of the nineteenth century commercial education was seen as a branch of technical education rather than a subject in its own right. At its most basic level technical education denoted a pedagogical system which was opposed to a purely academic education based on humanistic principles. It encapsulated a system of knowledge which was based on *doing* rather than *being*.[11] In the context of the latter half of the nineteenth century when many curricula were dominated by the classics, technical education became almost synonymous with 'modern' education. Llewellyn-Smith's report on technical education for the T.E.B. in 1893, for example, defined it as including the whole field of education apart from ancient languages and literature.[12] On this basis anything from French to mechanical engineering could be defined as technical.

More specifically the term denoted one which prepared individuals for work and consequently assisted industry and commerce. Accordingly, there was no real difference between technical education *per se* and training. It was only those who were opposed to technical education, who believed the best place to learn vocational skills was by experience in the work place itself, who insisted on a distinction between the two terms.[13]

Commercial education thus had a very elastic application. It could mean on the one hand learning specific skills such as bookkeeping, shorthand or typewriting while on the other it could stretch to more 'academic subjects' such as English, foreign languages, geography or history. As the subject matured into a discipline in its own right towards the end of the nineteenth century its definition became more finely tuned. This was assisted by the growth of higher institutions of commercial learning, particularly the founding of the London School of Economics in 1895.[14] Consequently, an important distinction came to be made between 'ordinary' and 'higher' commercial education. While the former focussed on the basic skills needed for office work such as shorthand, type-writing and correspondence, the latter was concerned with more specialized areas.[15] At the LSE, for example, this included subjects such as the organization of the modern business world at home and abroad, commercial history and geography, railway administration, banking and currency, and commercial law.[16] In addition, an important further development, which enabled the discipline to distinguish itself partially from technical education, was the observation that commercial education was chiefly concerned with the exchange rather than the production of goods. Commercial education became effectively the teaching of skills and subjects which facilitated this process. This came to encompass a whole range of disciplines from French to the laws regulating bills of exchange.[17]

Structural Shifts

While a perceived crisis in Britain had a very real effect in galvanizing support for commercial education, this was not enough to explain the incredible burst of energy and money that in thirty years provided a comprehensive system that yearly educated and trained tens of thousands of individuals. Such a crisis may have provided the fuel that powered the drive for a more formalized means of transferring business skills and knowledge to achieve critical mass, but it was deeper structural shifts in the business world itself that laid the foundation and ultimately success of commercial education between 1880 and 1914. These changes can be briefly summarized as the need to acquire more technical skills, the impersonalization of office work and breakdown of the apprenticeship system and the professionalization of office work.

The Need for a More Technical Education

On 13 October 1888, an article appeared in the *Office* entitled, 'Qualifications for Office Work'. Following a criticism of the English education system, in which it was argued that present-day youths were not being adequately prepared for office work, it went on to observe,

> The qualifications for office work must, in many details, depend upon the particular office in which a youth is engaged. But there are certain general qualifications without which no man can hope to succeed in this calling. Some of these are comparatively new to clerks of an older generation, and are not yet sufficiently recognized as essential by those who have charge of our schools.[18]

The qualifications which the author had in mind were listed as bookkeeping, shorthand, foreign languages and typewriting.

Clearly the technical advances and new skills that had been introduced into the office in the second half of the nineteenth century had to be learnt. Whether learning bookkeeping or exchange rates was better in the office or the classroom was for some a hotly contested area of debate.[19] For subjects such as shorthand, typing and languages, however, there was a clear consensus that these were best learnt outside of work and under some guise of formal instruction.

Parallel to these developments, London's leading financial and commercial position and the growth of world trade accentuated the need for commercial education. The physical boundaries of trade, the number of transactions which had to be recorded and accounted, the number of products, languages, buyers, sellers and middlemen that had to be dealt with on a daily basis had progressively become wider. Such a change in the spatial-temporal matrix of trade meant that a growing need for commercial education was imperative.

This point was clearly made by the T.E.B.'s report on technical education. Whereas, it argued twenty or thirty years ago a lad could enter business at the age of 14 direct from school and not suffer in his career, this was no longer the case. This was said to be due to three reasons; firstly improvements in general education meant that many more pupils were staying on at school until 14. The boy who left school for work at this age had nothing to differentiate himself from others. In addition, the extension of secondary and higher education on the continent 'for the needs of modern life' meant that this individual would be seriously disadvantaged when coming into direct contact with his European rivals. Finally, the report referred to the growth of world trade and the internationalization of British commerce. All three factors led to the inevitable conclusion that under modern conditions further education for those destined for commerce was essential.[20]

The emergence of new skills which were required in the office, and the heightened atmosphere of more fierce competition and internationalism of the late nineteenth and early twentieth century meant that the entire environment and fabric of the office world demanded more commercial education. There was simply too much to learn which could not be done during office hours.

The Breakdown of the Apprenticeship System

In the second half of the nineteenth century the old apprenticeship system, whereby a youth worked in an office for nothing and in return learned the skills of the trade, sometimes living with his employer, sometimes having to pay a premium for the privilege, was steadily breaking down.[21] Writing on the subject, *Business Life* commented that a youth on leaving school would now instead receive one or two years special training before commencing work. He would then, unlike his predecessor fifty years ago, be able to start business trained in the routine of the business office and able to command a salary.[22]

While the article may have been slightly optimistic, there does seem to be some truth in the contention that older systems of training in the office were no longer as exclusive as they had previously been. As seen in Chapter 2 in relation to the banking sector, the habit of premiums and living-in had broken down completely in the second half of the nineteenth century. In addition, as has been seen in the last chapter, the average starting age of clerks was becoming higher. Finally, there is strong evidence to suggest that the apprenticeship system as a whole across all industries was in decline. The *Office* in 1888 reported on an article from the *Quarterly Review* in which it was argued that the apprenticeship system had collapsed.[23] This was argued as being due to the introduction of a division of labour and machinery in many trades. The emergence of Trade Schools in London at the turn of the twentieth century, established by the L.C.C. in order to provide boys and girls with practical skills, which it was felt employers were no longer doing, is further evidence of this. As the Report said, '… modern industrial conditions are altering and eliminating the old methods and trade education, and … are providing no adequate substitute'.[24]

One should not infer from this that the office had ceased to be a site of learning for young recruits. Equally as much in the nineteenth century as today, Britain distinguished itself from its continental neighbours by the amount of informal learning that went on in the workplace, be it workshop, factory or office. Evidence from employers in interviews conducted by the Technical Education Board confirm this. At the offices of the Orient line of steamers, for example, junior clerks at the age of 16 rose up through the several departments. According to Mr John Bell who was connected with the company, they began by copying and then proceeded, '… step by step until they become familiar with voyage accounts, bills of lading, measuring, &c'.[25] At the London County and Westminster Bank the system was virtually identical. Discussing how his father acquired his work skills, Jim Hancock stated,

> You picked up your work by experience. You literally were told that you were going to move to another section within the building and you were then shown what your tasks were to be, and you then had to learn them extremely rapidly to make certain you were competent.[26]

While this may still have been the case, the growth of some companies could have made this increasingly difficult. It is here, in the breakdown of the apprenticeship system and the increase in the size of some offices, that a more formalized system of learning became more necessary. London railway companies, for example, sent their promising clerks and assistant managers to the LSE.[27] *Business Life* reported in 1902 that banks and insurance offices in London had for some time made use of the Situation Bureau at Pitman's Metropolitan School.[28]

In an earlier edition it also referred to the training of twenty or thirty clerks and assistants from one of the biggest firms in London.[29]

More impersonal relations between employers, management and clerks also contributed to establishing a more formalized style of learning. An important change in relations in the office was that employers and senior officials performed far less clerical duties than earlier and far more executive functions.[30] Face-to-face relations between them and their clerks would consequently have been less and chances to learn from one's senior correspondingly fewer. An article in the *Office* in 1891 bemoaned the fact that relations between clerks and their superiors was no longer as close as they had previously been and admonished employers to be more sympathetic and show more interest in their clerks.[31] The failure of many of them to do this may well have contributed to a greater need for a more formal commercial education.

The Professionalization of Office Work

In his work, *The Rise of Professional Society: England Since 1880*, Harold Perkin has argued that towards the end of the nineteenth century, British society began to change into one based on professionalism rather than structured around land or industrial capital. This entailed several fundamental structural shifts. The social ideal now became the professional – the doctor, the lawyer, the accountant, the trained business manager – rather than the landlord or the industrial entrepreneur. Social ideals themselves became dominated by notions of expertise, efficiency and selection by merit rather than older concepts of property and patronage or active capital, production and competition. In addition, concepts of capital increasingly centred around human capital – what an individual knew, what services he could perform, his level of expertise – rather than ones based on land or industrial production.[32] Hand in hand with these structural shifts was the rapid rise of professional organizations, groups which were able to restrict entry into certain occupations. Between 1800 and 1914 fifty-nine new professional associations appeared. These included solicitors, pharmacists, chartered accountants, auctioneers and estate agents. In addition, a number of non-qualifying associations were established, such as the National Union of Teachers and the Institute of Directors.[33]

For virtually all clerical workers professional status remained no more than a distant dream. Clerks were unable, despite attempts, to limit entry into their occupations by establishing a stringent series of examinations and qualifying conditions. Nevertheless, one must make a distinction between achieving professional status and professionalization: the recognition that a certain occupation had particular skills and knowledge requirements, and that these could be proven by examined qualifications. For some it also meant the establishment of non-qualifying associations. While not being able to restrict entry, these bodies nevertheless conferred status on their members, had links with employers and were usually active in establishing and administering examinations which contributed to controlling the flow of new recruits and salary levels.

In this sense, professionalization certainly took place among many clerical workers from 1880 to 1914. A number of associations such as the Institute of Bankers, the National Association of Local Government Officers and the United Law Clerks Society were established.[34] These bodies established stringent examinations for their members. The Institute of Bankers introduced preliminary and senior certificates from its very inception, the first examinations being held in May 1880. The examinations were a combination of papers in arithmetic and algebra, bookkeeping, commercial law, political economy and practical banking.[35] By 1906 the examinations were being taken in 376 centres across Britain and even overseas in cities such as Bombay, Cape Town, Hong Kong and Yokohama.[36]

In addition, the growth of public commercial examinations assisted this process. In 1902 there were 276 centres of examination for the Society of Arts with nearly 10,000 papers taken.[37] Such examinations were symptomatic of the professionalization of society and the increased value attached to knowledge and ability. As such, they were proof of merit which could be used as symbols of human capital and exchanged for professional positions. According to *Business Life*, 'Certificates of efficiency, when gained from a recognized public examining body, are certainly very valuable documents to possess as evidence of capacity proved by undergoing definite tests'.[38] Those for shorthand and typing were singled out as being particularly valuable.

In the context of professionalization, the growth of formal commercial education is clearly discernable. In London institutions such as Birkbeck College, City of London College, King's College and the Young Men's Christian Institute set up classes for the Institute of Bankers examinations as recognized centres. At the Birkbeck Institute, for example, students for the session 1896–7 took examinations from the following bodies; University Extension society (Political Economy), University Extension Society, (Commercial Geography), Institute of Bankers, Institute of Actuaries, Institute of Chartered Accountants, The London Chamber of Commerce, The Society of Arts, Higher Civil Service appointments and London County Council appointments.[39] Formal Institutes of commercial education and examining bodies were symptomatic of a shift in society which placed increasing importance on knowledge. This had marked effects for clerical workers and all those involved in the business world and public administration. It is partially in this development that growth in these institutions and the rise of commercial education can be located.

The Development of Commercial Education In London

Just as commercial education developed out of technical education, the evolution of institutions where the two could be learnt were closely related. Throughout the nineteenth century progress was haphazard, uneven and sometimes opportunistic rather than systematically thought out and implemented.[40] In London where no one industry dominated, but rather a cacophony of industrial, commercial, financial, professional, transport, service and other activities characterized its economy, the situation was even more fluid. What made the situation still more complex were the several economic, social and political faces of London. Industrial centre, global metropole, hub of empire, transport interface, political and administrative axis; all of these were London. Educational provision was also varied both in terms of source and character. Voluntary societies, philanthropic individuals, private companies, and local and central government were all involved in building up its structure. It was not until the end of the nineteenth century that systematization and coordination began to take place, and not until the establishment of the London Education Authority in 1903 that one can begin to talk in any real sense of an education system in the capital.[41]

Gregory Anderson has commented on the relative backwardness of Britain in this field compared to its principal competitors. Victorian Britain was said to have had, '... no institution worthy of comparison with the Paris School of Commerce founded in 1820, the Superior Institute of Commerce in Antwerp or America's chain of thirty commercial colleges'.[42] These were certainly sentiments echoed at the time. The T.E.B.'s report on commercial education eulogized the Leipzig and Antwerp commercial institutes on the continent, comparing them to the backwardness of the Capital.[43] The 'backward looking' tendency of British firms to train their workers 'on the job' was seen as damaging to both individual and nation.

From the 1880s to the 1900s, however, this situation had radically improved. In his section on commercial education in London, Sidney Webb made three important comments concerning the state of the subject in the capital in the years running up to the outbreak of war in 1914.[44] There was a lot more of it available than was fully appreciated at the time. Furthermore, from the 1880s great progress had been made in the provision of this type of education. Finally, the supply and content of commercial education had been systematically laid out. Between 1880 and 1914 commercial education had transformed itself from a haphazard collection of subjects taught in predominantly voluntary organizations such as the Mechanics Institutes and the YMCA to a systematic discipline taught in a number of well-funded educational institutions catering for all needs and levels. By 1914 the subject had very much come into its own right as a field of learning.

A key player in the development of commercial education was the London Chamber of Commerce.[45] As a result of repeated complaints concerning the poor standards of clerks in London offices, the Chamber launched a full inquiry into the matter in the 1880s. It was found that offices frequently had to employ a number of foreign clerks due to what was seen as the poor education of native clerical workers, particularly in languages. The conclusion of the investigation was that British clerks were inefficient, particularly in the linguistic field, due to a lack of systematic training in contrast to their overseas peers.[46]

As a consequence, a conference of schoolmasters and businessmen was held by the LCC at the Canon Street Hotel in 1887. Subsequent conferences followed, a committee was formed, and the end product was the establishment by the London School of Commerce of formal commercial examinations and certificates which would test candidates in a range of commercial subjects including, of course, languages. As an incentive to take up the examinations it was agreed by all the member businesses who made up the Chamber, over 200 firms, to give priority to applicants who passed these examinations.[47]

The creation of the London Chamber of Commerce qualifications was accompanied by formal commercial qualifications by other bodies such as the Society of Arts and the National Union of Teachers. Alongside this, the rise of formal commercial qualifications was complemented by the rapid increase of institutions providing commercial education in London, particularly at night school for clerks already in employment. This process was assisted by the establishment of the City and Guilds of London Institute in 1878, the 1883 City Parochial Charities Act and the establishment of the Technical Education Board at the London County Council in 1893, each of which released substantial resources into technical and commercial education in London.[48]

Chief among the institutes which supplied commercial education were the Polytechnics, the evening schools of the London School Board and later the London Education Authority, the London School of Economics, and private commercial academies, in particular the Pitman's Metropolitan School on Southampton Row in Holborn. In all of these bodies unprecedented numbers of clerks participated in an endeavour to improve their education and practical commercial skills. While there were other important centres in London where one could take courses in commercial education such as the YMCA and the Birkbeck Institute,[49] these four have been selected because of the extent of their operations, to show the diversity of institutes which provided commercial education, and to demonstrate the different types and levels of commercial education available in London. Each will now be looked at individually.

The Polytechnics

The history of the polytechnic movement has received some attention from historians.[50] What began as a ragged school in the 1860s in Charing Cross established by the merchant and philanthropist Quintin Hogg developed into a group of ten educational establishments by 1910–11, educating over 26,000 students.[51] Regent Street Polytechnic alone, the original polytechnic and blueprint of all the others had a membership of 15,000 for the session 1902–3.[52] While, however, research has tended to concentrate on the industrial technical side of the polys, their important contribution to commercial education and clerks in general has been ignored.

Technical Education at these institutes followed in the tradition of practical training for professional life. Subsequently a very broad range of subjects could be taken, from Electrical and Mechanical Engineering to Breadmaking and Cookery.[53] Commercial Education was an important part of this. The Polytechnics became one of its principle suppliers in London. At Regent Street Polytechnic, for example, its Commercial and General Classes and Special Examination Preparatory Classes, which predominantly prepared individuals for civil service examinations, were two of the largest departments of the Polytechnic. University Extension Lectures were also frequently held on commercial subjects. In the 1910–11 session a course of thirteen lectures on Commercial Law were given by Percy W. Millard, LL.B. The prospectus for that year noted, 'The lectures will be found especially useful by Solicitors Clerks, Bank Clerks, Clerks in Insurance and Mercantile Houses, and by tradesmen generally.'[54] When the London Chamber of Commerce launched its commercial examinations in 1890 Regent Street organized special early morning classes to prepare for the examinations which were held each morning from 7:00 to 8:00.[55]

By 1910 these two commercial departments had evolved into two separate bodies. The Commercial and General Classes Department had become The Shorthand, Typewriting, Bookkeeping and Business Training School on Balderton Street, Oxford Street. Courses such as Bookkeeping, Languages, Business Practice and 'The Making and Sharing of Wealth' could be taken there. Course were held during the day and evening.[56] The Special Examination Preparatory Classes, or Civil Service Department, had become Clephane's College on Great Portland Street. The school prepared students for entrance examinations into banks, insurance offices, commerce and the professions, in addition to the Civil Service.[57] Both schools were affiliated to the Polytechnic.

The energy which Regent Street expended on commercial education was rewarded by the large number of clerks who made use of its facilities. Of its 8,700 members for 1888–9, 2,052 were clerical workers, by far the largest single occupational group.[58] Similarly Julie Stevenson has estimated that 28.7 per cent of female and 34.0 per cent of male members of Regent Street Polytechnic between 1905–13 were in white-collar clerical occupations. For men this compares to 15.3 per cent non-occupied, 5.3 per cent student, 6.7 per cent professional, 12 per cent retail and only 20.7 per cent manufacturing and 6 per cent unskilled.[59] At the other London Polytechnics, the situation was similar. Replies from Battersea Polytechnic, Birkbeck Institution, City of London Institute, and Goldsmiths' Institute to the T.E.B. concerning their provision of commercial education showed widespread and comprehensive activity in this area.[60] Webb wrote of commercial education being given in daytime classes at Northern Polytechnic, Goldsmiths' Institute and other polytechnics. At South Western Polytechnic in Chelsea a regular day college had been established which pro- vided systematic instruction for young men and women from sixteen upwards in all subjects needed by office workers. Describing it Webb wrote, 'It is not exactly a school, and it can scarcely aspire to be a university college. But it is much more than a congeries of isolated classes, and the extent to which it is taken advantage of proves that it fills a useful place in London's commercial education.'[61]

Similar developments took place in the City of London College where £25,000 from the Mitchell Trustees and City Companies was collected to build a new centre devoted to commercial subjects.[62] In many respects the demand from the Sub-Committee of the T.E.B. on Commercial Education in 1898 that more commercial education should be provided in first- and second-grade public secondary schools in London was actually met by the Polytechnics throughout this period.[63] It is from these institutions that a significant part of London's sup- ply of commercial education came to be provided. It is no surprise therefore that some of the leading business schools in the country today such as Westminster and Cass Business Schools originate from the commercial pedagogical endeav- ours of these polytechnics.

Evening Schools

The efforts which the Polytechnics went to in order to provide commercial edu- cation was matched by the work of the London School Board, the T.E.B. and later on the London Education Authority in its evening schools. In London the number of people attending these classes increased from 9,000 in 1882 when they began to 128,464 for 1910–11.[64] A significant number of these took com- mercial courses, including foreign languages. Of the six most popular subjects for 1910–11, for example, three; bookkeeping, shorthand and French, were in this group. A total number of 62,140 enrolled for these subjects out of 104,652 for all six subjects.[65]

The role of evening schools changed in London throughout this period. Orig- inally the schools had been intended as duplicating the work of the day schools for the many Londoners who had failed to obtain a basic elementary education. With the improvement in general education this function disappeared.[66] Increas- ingly the schools provided education for those who had entered work but wished to continue their education and enhance their occupational skills. By the turn of the century some of these had begun to provide distinctive higher grade education in commercial subjects, science and art and became known as commercial centres. By 1912, according to Mr W. J. Chalk, responsible master of Barnsbury Park commercial centre, with higher-grade science and art being taught at the polytechnics, technical institutes and art schools, nearly all of these commercial centres were concentrating on teaching commercial education.[67]

In 1909–10 there were thirty-two commercial centres in London with an average of 953 students. The combined number of students in the centres for the session 1910–11 was 31,814. According to W. J. Chalk, 'In a centre containing over 1,000 students, there may be from 50 to 150 separate classes in from 20 to 50 subjects with a staff of 30 to 70 instructors'. The subjects in these centres were divided into ordinary commercial including shorthand, bookkeeping, arithmetic and typewriting, higher commercial such as commercial law, economics, banking and accountancy, languages and miscellaneous Subjects which included literature, domestic subjects, physical exercises and technical subjects. Demand for higher commercial subjects and languages were said to be rising while the other two remained stationary. In addition, courses comprising several subjects had been developed which students were encouraged to take.[68] Chalk wrote in relation to this of the need to create specialized courses for specific groups of clerks. 'Under ideal conditions', he stated, 'there might be preliminary courses for junior clerks, but afterwards there would be courses for accounting clerks, for warehouse and invoice clerks, for bank clerks, for insurance clerks, for municipal clerks, for civil servants, for railway clerks, and for others'.[69]

These developments were seen as partially due to a change in the students attending the courses and their respective requirements. Chalk saw the development of higher commercial education and foreign languages resulting from students no longer wanting to learn mechanical subjects for work but rather those which would give them a grasp of the principles underlying their work. Clerks in senior positions were noted to be taking more advantage of the schools. Importantly, Chalk also wrote that prejudice against the schools from the middle classes was decreasing.[70]

Such a trend led to schools being increasingly monopolized by clerks and other members of the business community or those wishing to enter commercial and professional work. Mr S. E. Bray, for example, district inspector of schools noted in his section on the ordinary evening schools that, 'There have been no marked changes either in methods or organization, but there is generally an upward tendency, the chief aim being preparation for commercial life'.[71] Evening schools reacted to this shift by providing more commercial education. As Cloudesley Breton, M.A., divisional inspector for modern languages observed, '... it is obvious that the vast majority of the students take up modern languages in order to improve their command of them for business purposes. We cannot therefore ignore the professional and technical side of the subject; we have in fact no right to ignore it for the sake of giving instruction on more liberal lines'.[72] The high demand by clerical workers and those desirous of clerical work, and the upgrading and specialization of certain schools into commercial centres bears in many respects striking resemblances to what was happening in other areas of higher and further education in London, including the polytechnics.

The London School of Economics – 'Our Commercial University'[73]

The LSE was established in 1895 partially as a result of Lord Cowper's Commission on the reorganization of London University which regretted in 1894 the absence in London of a higher commercial and administrative college which would equal continental institutions such as the Ecole des Hautes Etudes Commercialles in Paris.[74] In this respect the development of the LSE was akin to the establishment of the London Chamber of Commerce Examinations and the Polytechnics in that all three were reactions to reports showing weaknesses in English commercial education. The fact that it was set up at the suggestion of the London Chamber and with financial assistance from this body makes the similarities more striking. In 1900 Cowper's regret was mollified by the establishment in the reconstituted University of London of a faculty of Economics and Political Science and the admittance of the LSE as a school of the University.

While the LSE was conceived as an academic institution, it was equally seen to provide practical instruction to those already in business. As was spelt out by the Education Officer of the L.C.C., 'The objects of this school are to promote the study of economics and allied subjects, and to provide courses adapted to the needs of persons engaged in public service or in the higher branches of commerce and industry'.[75] This point was earlier echoed by the Report of the Sub Committee on Technical Education at the LSE. While it recommended that the studies of the school should concentrate on the economic laws which governed commercial and industrial life, it also suggested that the School should provide practical education for its students. As the report recommended, 'It would also have the direct training of the future leaders of commerce and industry, and of the national and municipal civil servants and consular attaches, who it is hoped, do much to guide the commercial policy of the empire'.[76] Just as Imperial College, established in the 1900s, was built to safeguard the technical supremacy of the British Empire, so the LSE was meant to protect its commerce.

Most of the initial students were working and studying part-time in the evening. These were engaged predominantly in business and worked as both principles and clerks.[77] In 1898, only twelve students studied there full time, all university graduates engaged in research. Discussing its students, the T.E.B.'s report commented, 'The school in the session of 1897–8 had 378 students, drawn mainly from the class of young men designed for or already engaged in commercial life, especially banking, shipping and foreign trading, together with railway administration and the national and municipal civil service'.[78] The affiliation of the School with the University of London in 1900, and the power to work for B.Sc's and D.Sc's in the new Faculty of Economics and Political Science did increase it number of full time students. In the 1911–12 session it had 194 students taking full courses. These were overshadowed, however, by 682 students taking separate lectures, who most probably were already in work, and 459 railway students. There were also 621 teachers studying at the school.[79]

The heavy emphasis in the LSE on practical training was reflected by Hewins comments on what commercial education should mean,

> Judging from the experience we have had at the school, it is most important not to launch any general commercial programme framed to meet the needs of some hypothetical 'clerk' or 'businessman'. The students should be split into different groups, classified according to the trades or professions in which they are engaged, and after consultation with employers or heads of departments, who may be presumed to know what their assistants require, special curricula, suitable for different groups should be arranged. The organization of commercial education therefore involves the organization of the public, the clerks, businessmen, &c., for whom it is intended, and then the arrangements of curricula suitable for each group.[80]

These sentiments and the system of commercial education at the LSE was very much in line with other developments in educational institutes in London of which it was seen to be an integral part. It was clerks, managers, businessmen, railway officials, civil servants and others involved in the business world attending part-time courses who were the chief beneficiaries of the School in its early years, and not full-time students. What differentiated the LSE from the polytechnics, evening schools and other learning centres was simply that its level of learning was somewhat higher. Clerks and assistant managers from railway companies, for example, could take courses in railway law and railway accountancy, the application of economics to specialist problems such as railway rates and railway electrification, railway statistics, a comparative study of administration or relations to the state of the railway systems of other countries.[81] Such specialization led Webb, one of the leading pioneers of the School, to comment, 'The new 'commercial' faculty of the University of London … fitly crowns the organization of commercial education in London'.[82]

Pitman's Metropolitan School: 'Learning and Earning'[83]

While the polytechnics, evening schools and LSE were public bodies receiving significant aid from the government, the L.C.C., and private commercial and individual donations, there existed also a significant private sector in commercial education in London. A glance at *Kelly's London Suburban Directory* for 1902, for example, reveals on the High Street in Lewisham, Blackheath Commercial College.[84] Similarly *Kelly's London County Suburbs Directory* for 1904 show shorthand schools in Peckham and Forest Hill.[85] Many of these schools had only brief existences. Others, however, turned into solid educational establishments. Chief amongst these in London was Pitman's with its principal school, the Pitman's Metropolitan School on Southampton Row in Holborn.

The Pitman's Metropolitan School was big. Indeed, in its monthly journal *Business Life* the school often referred to itself as the largest commercial school in the world. Another epithet it liked to give itself was 'London's Business University'.[86] In 1904, for example, the School recorded a record simultaneous attendance in its school of 1,500 to 1,600 students. In that year between 1,500 and 2,000 positions in the business world had been 'placed at the disposal of the school'.[87] With students attending full-time courses during the day, part-time courses during the evening, and individuals from overseas leaning 'English for Foreigners' its total number of yearly students must have run into many thousands. The young Winston Churchill may not have exaggerated in the annual prize giving ceremony at Queen's Hall, Regent Street in 1904 when he declared that the school was, '... without an equal in the world'.[88]

What had begun as a school established to teach shorthand was by the turn of the twentieth century a major provider of commercial education in London. During the day many of its students took courses for two or three years depending on age. Those joining at ages of between twelve and fourteen required three years and those starting at a later age generally finished after two years. The subjects were strictly practical and were designed to equip individuals with all the skills they would need for a career in an office. Students learned business composition, which included grammar, spelling and style, arithmetic, shorthand, typewriting, bookkeeping, commercial geography and foreign languages. In addition there was a Business Training Hall where students would roleplay commercial transactions, such as writing out Bills of Exchange, and office procedure. Letter writing in both English and foreign languages was also taught.[89] The school, like Regent Street Polytechnic, taught English to non-native speakers, many of whom subsequently went on to do commercial courses at the school.[90] In the evening students already in work would take these classes individually. Exam preparation for the civil service, the L.C.C. and other public professional examinations was also taught.

The success of the school was partly due to the appeal that it made to its students' and parents' financial sensitivities. Articles in its journal such as 'Education as an Investment' and 'Educating the Parents' advocated the simple message that it made financial sense in the long term to spend money on commercial education. As was argued in the former article in 1904, 'Parents having a numerous family to bring up, educate and get out in the world, have too often but little scope for accumulating money to leave to their children, and realize that the best thing they can do for them is to help them to help themselves, and if necessary to make some little sacrifice in order that their sons and daughters may start with the advantage of a good and useful education.'[91] This message, loaded with such middle-class concepts as self-help, self-sacrifice, the value of education and the need to prepare for the future was bound to appeal to what was chiefly a predominantly lower-middle class audience that desired a secure, respectable future for their children but lacked the financial means to guarantee this. With fees at £5 5*s*. for shorthand lessons, £2 2*s*. for type-writing and £3 3*s*. for bookkeeping learning was not cheap, but just about affordable for this group. Payment was softened by the existence of instalment systems such as £1 1*s*. a month or 5*s*. weekly for shorthand which spread the cost over a period of time.[92]

As a result of this, the school's journal was extremely frank, almost to the extent of being mercenary, in its exposition of education. 'Learning and Earning' was both a motto of the school and the name of a regular column that appeared in the magazine. The salaries that could be earned in the City or in the Civil Service were regularly discussed, examples of students who had passed through the school and were in well-paid positions were routinely paraded through the magazine. The argument of Pitman's was simple; education should be about acquiring practical skills which could then be translated in the workplace into accumulating money. Education in the country was argued to be old and out of date, hopelessly wedded to a love of the classics which in a modern business environment that demanded practical skills such as shorthand, typing, book-keeping and a knowledge of foreign languages was useless.[93] To guarantee future success in the business world, a course of training at a school such as Pitman's was imperative. This argument was in turn linked to the dictum that changes in the business world meant that the old apprenticeship system was dead, employers no longer had the time to teach their juniors office skills, and that this role had been effectively transferred to business schools.[94]

The appeal of Pitman's message was further cemented by the claim that teaching was based on individual need and that following completion of a course the school would help individuals find work via its Situation Bureau. The latter was effectively an employment office where companies placed vacancies. This was a principle recruitment practice of the time for clerical workers and was only available to members of institutions where positions were advertised. Such a system clearly worked to the advantage of all parties; the students received work at the end of their courses, the school attracted students via the bureau and companies attracted applicants from an institution with which it enjoyed a working relationship, and which to some extent had already trained and screened hopeful candidates. By 1907 Pitman's claimed that its Situation Bureau had secured 40,000 appointments for its students. This was said to be not only a result of the great influence that the school wielded in business circles, but also because of its system of registering tests passed by students in its files which would be matched with positions that became available.[95]

Pitman's Metropolitan School had some differences to the other commercial educational institutes which have already been discussed. It was private, it put a heavy emphasis on the pecuniary advantages of the education which it offered, and it only taught 'ordinary' commercial subjects with no provision for subjects such as commercial law, statistics or economics. Yet despite this, there were many similarities between them. All were based on a common interpretation of commercial education which juxtaposed the practical advantages of their systems with what Pitman's had called, '... the trammels of an old effete system'.[96] Here it was not simply the content – i.e. shorthand as compared to Shakespeare, but also the methodologies of these systems. Commercial education was based on a direct, student-centred method of teaching which was argued to have direct relevance to daily life. It emphasized the active skills of speaking and writing rather than the passive ones of reading and listening. As Professor Hewins had earlier said, it did not create an artificial universal clerk or manager but rather organized its teaching and schemes of work around individual classes and students. In addition, much of what these institutions taught such as languages and shorthand was similar, as was the fact that there were close relationships between these schools and businesses. Regent Street Polytechnic, for example, had a Situation Bureau like Pitman's.[97] Finally, all schools laid the same emphasis on the advantages of commercial education to individual, nation and empire. Commercial education was seen as not only benefiting the individual but also the commercial supremacy of Britain's Empire.[98] The polytechnics, the London School of Economics, the evening schools and Pitman's were all to some degree or other responses to the same crisis outlined at the beginning of this chapter. It is therefore no surprise that they shared many things in common.

Employers' Attitude to Commercial Education

What were the attitudes of employers' of clerical workers to commercial education? Whilst it is true that British employers were cynical about the management schools which were being established across the United States and in parts of Europe during this period, where cadres of young men were trained in commerce and business, this chapter has demonstrated a positive and pro-active attitude towards commercial education, particularly in London. Many of the polytechnics, for example, were founded or supported by businessmen such as Regent Street Polytechnic, City Polytechnic and Woolwich Polytechnic, or were established by business associations such as Goldsmiths' Institute (the Goldsmiths' Company) and the Northern Polytechnic (the Clothworkers' Company).[99] The

London Chamber of Commerce, founded in 1882 by London businesses, was a major supplier of commercial education.[100] Its qualifications being recognized by all of its members. By 1913 its examinations were being sat in 800 schools and institutions across Britain and as far as India, Trinidad, Istanbul and Tasmania.[101] The organization was also a leading body in the establishment of The London School of Economics in 1895.[102] A similar association to the London Chamber of Commerce was the Institute of Bankers established in London in 1879 by Britain's major banks.[103] Like the London Chamber of Commerce, the organization was an important supplier of commercial education to its members, and similarly had been partly established to provide what was felt to be a long standing pedagogical vocational need within the banking sector.[104] By 1914 the Institute had 10,542 members (mainly clerks) with 4,366 of these sitting its examinations in that year.[105] Thus we can see that London business and London businessmen were important contributors towards the supply of commercial education in London from 1880 to 1914.

An important document which provides remarkable insights into the attitude of London businessmen to commercial education was the aforementioned report by London County Council's Technical Education Board on Commercial Education in London published in 1897.[106] During the course of its enquiry the T.E.B. interviewed a wide range of London businessmen and employers of clerks, probing them on their attitudes towards commercial education. Whilst the full-time, vocational model of commercial education found in the US and Europe was rejected by the vast majority, there was strong support for part-time commercial education for the clerical worker whilst in work. The office was seen as the most important site of commercial learning, but it was opined by many businessmen who were interviewed that large tranches of business skills and knowledge could and should be learnt by the clerk in evening schools. Such areas included typewriting, shorthand and foreign languages. Other more advanced areas such as statistics and commercial geography were also mentioned.[107] Whilst employers realized that evening education was not ideal, many clerks being physically and mentally worn out by a full day's work, the motivation and drive demonstrated by the clerk in attending such courses was seen to reflect well on their commercial character and attitude towards work. In addition, the model of the internal labour market and clerical career paths outlined in previous chapters was clearly evident in many of the comments of London businessmen in the Report. Clerks slowly worked their way up through the company during their period of employment and gradually specialized. Commercial education had a role to play in this vocational process. Such a blending of part-time commercial education and career path, encouraged by employers, can be clearly seen in the comments of Mr Bradgate, representative of the Hon. Sydney Holland, Chairman of the London and India Docks Joint Committee,

... The best kind of training for those entering the Joint Committee's service was a good secondary education, followed up by evening classes. Evening work was encouraged in various ways. Thus, on entering, the junior clerks were advised not to consider their education at an end, but to take up shorthand and bookkeeping as likely to give them a start. It was a condition of employment in the secretarial and managerial offices that a clerk should be able to write shorthand at the rate of 80 words a minute, and where a clerk was unsuccessful in the test, he was given three months to learn, and if not then successful would be sent to the docks. Prizes were given to junior clerks after three, and to messenger after four years' service for passing an examination of secondary character. Clerks after two years in the fourth class may pass an examination on the lines of the Civil Service second grade, in shorthand, book-keeping, précis writing, commercial geography, knowledge of terms used in dock documents, compositions, and digesting returns; and notice had been given that clerks who had passed this examination, other things being equal, would have a preference for vacancies in the chief executive offices.[108]

The growing use and encouragement of commercial qualifications and skills acquired from commercial education can be detected in other sectors of clerical employment and clearly indicate that, particularly in larger concerns, these were being integrated into internal labour markets. At the London County and Westminster banks clerks were offered £5 and £10 bonuses for passing stage one and stage two in the Institute of Bankers examinations and were told that such qualifications would stand them in good stead for promotion.[109] At the Great Western Railway clerks, like at the London and Indian Docks, were expected to acquire shorthand. Classes to teach the skill were established within the company.[110] The railway companies in London also sent clerks intended for progress to management to train at the London School of Economics where they took courses in railway rates, railway electrification, railway statistics, railway history and geography and comparative administrative studies with other countries.[111] The curriculum at the LSE was devised with the help of senior railway managers from the Great Western Railway and North-Eastern railways.[112] Other sections of the business world such as general merchanting, shipping, insurance and those involved in foreign exchange were also said to send their employees to the LSE.[113] In sectors such as insurance and accountancy, where clerks could fully professionalize as actuaries and chartered accountants, commercial and formal education whilst at work was fully integrated into career paths.[114] Overall the integration and acceptance of commercial education into internal labour markets and career structures, combined with financial and organization support for providers of commercial education, evident across all sectors of London's clerical sectors, is clear evidence for its support by many of London's employers.

The Attitude of Clerks towards Commercial Education

No fact more clearly shows the dedication and respect that London clerks had for commercial education than the 29,569 male clerks attending evening classes for the session 1908–9 in the capital out of a total of 92,944.[115] No other occupational group came anywhere near this figure. If one adds the 592 builders clerks and 560 civil service clerks and officials the figure rises to 30,721, one third of the total participants. The figure was correspondingly high for female clerks at 7,741 out of a total of 68,920. If one considers that around one in ten men were clerks in the County of London the magnitude of this figure becomes clear. Additionally, the figure represented around 25 per cent of the estimated 130,000 male clerks in London.[116] If one bears in mind that the majority of individuals would stay in evening education for limited periods, concentrated in their earlier years, this figure would suggest that a large majority of clerks at some point in their lives would have attended evening schools, with most of them doing commercial subjects.

These figures are borne out by the qualitative evidence. Education was taken seriously by the diarists. Of the five, three attended evening school at one point or another, and a further one, Daniel McEwen, was an autodidact, who read constantly, wrote a book on his work, regularly published articles, and lectured.[117] Out of the Paul Thompson and Thea Vigne interviews a striking example of commercial education is Mr Frederick Henry Taylor. Though from Hanley in the Black Country, near Stoke-on-Trent, and not London, Taylor is interesting in that he was an invoicing clerk who worked in manufacturing – the pottery industry – rather than the commercial or financial sector which dominated London. Taylor ended his career as a cashier. During his fifty-two year career, however, he had had several supervisory and managerial positions and had also been responsible for buying supplies. At Johnsons, the pottery works where Taylor worked for thirty-two years, he was responsible for a period for the decorating shops where the pottery was gilded and lithographed. He consequently not only learnt shorthand and French at evening school but also chemistry and pottery.[118] Taylor's example suggests that for those clerks in the manufacturing sector, which had a significant presence in London, who aspired for promotion to a managerial or commercial traveller position, technical education was as important as commercial education. Mr John Brigg, MP and vice-chairman of the Technical Instruction Committee of the County Council of West Riding, for example, stated to the T.E.B.'s commission that technical classes were vital for those wishing to become commercial travellers in the woollen industry, a position to which many clerks aspired.[119]

The question remains, however, of why commercial education was so important to clerks? Julie Stevenson's explanation for the preponderance of clerks at Regent Street Polytechnic being due to their higher earnings cannot be accepted.[120] Clerks at the Polytechnic were young and would therefore have been on low incomes. With their incremental salary structures it was not until their late twenties that male clerks began to pull ahead of artisans, for example, who they outnumbered heavily. One occupational advantage that clerks may have had over skilled workers and the working class in general was that they worked shorter hours, finished work earlier and had steadier jobs which would enable them to plan and carry out a course of education. This certainly may have been a factor.

The above, however, does not adequately help us understand fully why clerks themselves were so wedded to the idea of continuing education after taking up work. One important factor here, in line with structural explanations for the emergence of commercial education at the beginning of the chapter, was that it was felt to have concrete effects in improving one's chances of promotion. Further occupational education did make sense in the long term. Clerks tended to semi-specialize in office duties. They would become ledger clerks, bookkeepers, or correspondence clerks. Promotion in many cases meant further specialization. Learning shorthand or French enhanced a clerks chance of promotion by equipping him or her with skills that would give comparative advantage when situations in the workplace became vacant. There is certainly evidence of this professional strategic outlook in the many advice books that were written for clerical workers. Haslehurst Greaves, for example, advised the correspondence clerk to learn at least one foreign language to gain promotion.[121] The bookkeeper was urged to learn statistics and all the most up-to-date methods for similar purposes.[122] John B. Carrington argued that, 'Every clerk, who is prepared to devote the necessary amount of time to the work, should be provided with means by which he could prove his capacity for more important duties than those in which he is at present engaged'.[123] Evidence from the T.E.B.'s Report clearly showed that the main reason why clerical workers attended evening courses was to better their chance of promotion. As G. Armitage Smith from the Birkbeck Institute wrote when discussing the feasibility of introducing new commercial subjects, 'As a rule young men are induced to make a special study of a subject when they see some monetary advantage will arise from it'.[124]

To talk, however, merely about financial gain would be to put too prosaic a light on the topic. Commercial education as a means of bettering oneself lay at the heart of the clerical worker's world view because it was the reification of one of his most sacred doctrines – the belief in self-improvement. The bettering of the individual through his own endeavour was at the epicentre of the conceptual framework of the clerk and the larger lower-middle class to which he belonged. It was an ethos which was preached from the pulpit, broadcast from books, newspapers and magazines, seen in the weekly potted biographies of 'successful men' who shone like beacons from this literature, and propagated by organizations such as the YMCA. The fact that many clerks, or their parents, had managed to climb socially out of the working classes made its basic tenets seem even more pertinent. In taking evening courses clerical workers were being more than simply mercenary, they were conforming to a social type.

Finally, commercial and further education for many clerks was never simply a question of classrooms and learning. Many people who take evening courses do so for the social as much as educational amenities that this offers them. In addition to the social contact which the lessons provided, many of these educational institutions had social and sporting sides as was the case at Regent Street Polytechnic. At Merton Hall near Wimbledon, for example, it boasted a twenty-seven-acre sports ground and pavilion with the largest athletics club in the kingdom.[125] At its site in Regents Street it had one of the grandest indoor swimming pools in central London with heated baths and later showers. In addition, it had at this site a gymnasium, a theatre (later part converted into a cinema), dining facilities, social rooms and its own magazine. In 1890 it had twenty-seven clubs and societies which ranged from a boxing club, to a polytechnic parliament to various volunteer companies.[126] The poly also had a strong religious dimension with prayer meetings, bible readings and talks on religious topics being an important part of its life. Finally it was also a major organizer of holidays for its members to both Britain and abroad, and can be seen as one of the principal harbingers in the UK of the cheap package holiday.[127]

For the young clerical worker, barred from the public house and music hall by social prejudice, often living in restrictive lodgings, and unable to marry until he could afford to provide a home, such institutions must have appeared very appealing, particularly given the opportunities it offered them to meet the opposite sex! On Saturday, 7 October 1905, for example, George Rose walked to Langham Place and decided to join Regent Street Polytechnic's Art School. The rest of Rose's subsequent day by day careful diary entries were dominated by the institution, the education it offered him, the social amenities he derived from it, such as the concerts held at the Queen's Hall, and the people he met there. The Polytechnic for this period became a part of Rose's life, identity and in many respects his hopes and dreams for the future.[128]

Conclusions

By the time the Education Officer of the London County Council had come to compile *Eight Years of Technical Education* the capital had developed a system of commercial education which was comprehensive in its scope, and served the needs of London and Londoners. Commercial education in 1912 spanned all levels, from the secondary to the postgraduate. A set of institutions had been established where the subjects that comprised this body of practical knowledge could be learned. A syllabus, a body of literature, and a system of examinations had been created. An acceptance by the business community of its worth had been achieved. Equally as crucial, it had received the support of London's clerical workers who attended it in their tens of thousands. The need for such a system of education and training which was expressed at the beginning of this chapter had been largely met.[129]

Sean Glynn in his essay on the establishment of higher education in London has argued that the subject should be seen in the context of a city made up of a large upwardly mobile working class which blended at imperceptible points into a newly emergent lower-middle class.[130] It was also one where, 'burgeoning commerce, retailing, finance and services created growing employment opportunities. As did the growth in land transport, navigation and the Port of London'.[131] It was these groups, high with aspirations for a better life, egged on by ideas of self-improvement, that the growing polytechnics, technical institutes, evening colleges, and other educational establishments chiefly catered to. Foremost amongst these were clerical workers. Clerks attended these institutes because they knew that in the context of a growing economy which offered more and more opportunities, they provided skills which could result in promotion, more money and more security. On 15 January 1902, for example, George Rose's employer, much to the consternation of the diarist, told his father that his son and his colleagues could be getting £50 a year more if they knew shorthand. He wondered why they were not able to see this for themselves.[132] Under such circumstances Pitman's Metropolitan School was right, learning really was earning, and not, as has been argued, some last-ditch desperate attempt to stave off social collapse.

Finally the rise in commercial education and higher education in general in London can be seen as a forerunner to what Peter F. Drucker has called the rise of a knowledge economy, i.e. one where knowledge rather than land, labour or capital becomes a primary economic resource.[133] Clearly it would be premature to say that London and Britain's economy was based on knowledge. It was not. It would not be, however, wrong to say that what one knew rather than what one simply could do was becoming of increasing importance. This point was underlined by the veteran technical education campaigner Lord Lyon Playfair in 1895,

> Formerly the possession of iron, the source of strength, and of coal, the source of power, gave to England its character as an industrial nation. But gradually iron and coal were found as cheap in other countries, or they could be acquired as cheaply by other nations through improvements in means of transport by sea and land. Industrial competition then becomes converted into a competition of intellect. The nation which becomes the most educated nation will become the greatest nation – if not today, certainly tomorrow.[134]

As self-styled 'brain workers' this point had deep implications for clerical workers. More education could only result in an improvement in their status. This explains why the establishment of commercial education as a recognized academic discipline, crowned by its inclusion in the syllabus of London University in 1900, was of such importance to clerks and all those involved in the business community. By association, its establishment as a recognized discipline gave respect to the entire profession. As Sidney Webb wrote, 'Such university recognition is essential in our view both to give *status* [his italics] to the higher branches of commercial education and to increase their attractiveness to students of the highest mental capacity. But it is also of the utmost importance to commercial education itself, as tending to ensure a high intellectual standard, and to counteract a tendency to an unduly utilitarianism'.[135]

Michel Foucault, based on the diktats of Nietzsche, argued that in a modern society knowledge is power. Such 'knowledge', however, was seen as something that was produced, validated and reproduced by society itself. The chief engine for this process was, and is, modern science and academic institutions. In his writings Foucault showed how over the course of modern history knowledge was institutionalized, turned into disciplines and professional discourses, and monopolized by select groups.[136] Something similar to this process was taking place in the business world towards the end of the nineteenth century. The T.E.B.'s report on commercial education, for example, noted when discussing instruction at university level that, '... The organization of those studies should be framed under the idea that commercial and industrial life rest upon a complex series of laws, which it is the duty of the trained student to investigate'.[137] As part of its process of professionalization, commerce, business, finance, administration, etc., like medicine in seventeenth- and eighteenth- century France, were becoming codified into blocs of knowledge, dispersed and reproduced by the institutions which provided commercial education and validated by the various examining bodies that have been outlined in this chapter. As such, commercial education began to act as a gatekeeper into the business world. It both included and excluded. At such a basic, but also fundamental level, it can clearly be seen why commercial education was of such importance to clerical workers and why it came to have such an important hold on them.

8 CLERICAL TRADE UNIONS, ASSOCIATIONS AND COLLECTIVE ORGANIZATIONS

Of all subjects relating to clerical workers, no area has attracted more historical attention than clerical trade unions. All of the principal organizations, the Railway Clerks Association (RCA), the National Union of Clerks (NUC), the National and Local Government Officers Association (NALGO), the postal unions and the civil service associations have received comprehensive historical coverage.[1] These studies have tended to be descriptive in their scope, mapping the growth of these various unions and charting their activities and achievements rather than providing much in the way of analysis. It is perhaps ironic that so much research has gone into an area where there is a relatively broad consensus that clerks had little interest.

David Lockwood and Gregory Anderson have approached the subject in their studies on clerical workers.[2] Both noted that clerical unionization was starkly uneven before the First World War. While there was strong growth amongst railway clerks, post-office clerical and manipulative workers, local government officers and civil servants, many clerical workers, particularly in the commercial and financial sectors, were almost untouched by it. It is this phenomenon which has interested commentators most. The fact that growth was sectional suggests that structural factors may have been chief determinants in deciding whether unionization took place amongst clerks or not. Both Lockwood and Anderson have argued that unionization was dependent on capital concentration and bureaucratization. Where offices became large, where relations between owners, management and employees became governed by impersonal regulations and codes of procedure rather than by personal relations, unions were able to flourish.[3] Such an explanation, however, while valid, is too simplistic and requires deeper analysis. In addition, both Lockwood and Anderson have tended to take a very one-dimensional approach to clerical unions, and consequently overlooked the diversity of their structures and organization. At the same time, little has been said about the aims and strategies of these unions, in what ways they were similar to manual unions and how they were different.

This chapter will attempt to fill these gaps in the research on clerical unions. It will begin by outlining the different varieties of clerical organizations, of which trade unions were in fact only one manifestation. Following this it will ask to what extent these organizations reflected the 'new unionism' which was said to have been a phenomenon of this period. It will then detail the demands of clerical trade unions and associations, and examine the strategies these organizations selected to realize their goals. Following this, it will examine the question of whether there was any inherent contradiction between collective action and clerical workers, and will end by re-examining the question of why some unions succeeded and others failed.

Overall the chapter will argue that many clerical workers were in fact organized in this period, and that the distinction between trade union organizations and associations should not be overstated. There were differing degrees of collective action, with some far less radical than others. Such action was often used by clerks to reinforce individualist, traditional demands such as the rule of merit and self-help.

In addition, trade unionism appealed to a significant number of clerks with progressive ideas in London, providing entry for them into the political life of the capital. In relation to the unions themselves, it will be argued that while these organizations reflected the general characteristics of the 'new unionism' of the period, clerical unions differed in some respects from other groups. One chief difference was their rejection of the strike weapon and their exclusive adoption of parliamentary pressure and propaganda. It is here that the success of clerical trade unions lay. While the extent of bureaucratization and standardization was certainly a *sine qua non* for collective action and development, it was this combined with their ease of access to parliament and other state agencies that determined their success. In addition, it will be argued that low income was certainly a factor determining unionization amongst clerical workers despite Anderson's claims to the contrary.

Clerical Organization – Its Extent and Variety

By 1914 a significant number of clerks had become organized. The RCA for example had a membership of almost 30,000 members in 1914, and the NUC 12,500.[4] In 1912, the National Amalgamated Union of Shop Assistants, Warehousemen and Clerks had almost 65,000 members.[5] In addition, most civil servants and post offices workers belonged to an organization, chief amongst which were the Assistant Clerks Association (ACA), the Second Division Clerks Association, the Inland Revenue Staff Federation, the Postal Clerks Association and the Postal Telegraph Clerks Association.[6] While a significant minority of clerks were unionized before 1914, a very large number, both in London and across the nation, were not.

Such a picture, however, is too simplistic, and does not illustrate the complexity of clerical organizations. It fails to do so for two reasons. Firstly, clerks belonged to a plethora of professional and work organizations, some of which functioned in ways similar to trade unions. Secondly, there were several types of unions, all of which varied in the intensity of their collective action. Some of these were more radical than others. Some were similar to professional associations which have not been branded by previous commentators as unions. Consequently, it can be argued that clerical organization was more comprehensive than has been previously assumed. In addition, one cannot simply dismiss professional associations and other clerical organizations as irrelevant.[7] These two areas will be looked at in turn.

The extent and range of clerical organizations can be seen in the Booth Collection in the archives of the London School of Economics.[8] This collection contains in it pamphlets, rule books and other material of clerical organizations in London around 1900. This material was used by Booth for his seminal social and economic survey of the capital, *London Life and Labour*, and by the Webbs in their work on trade unions. The collection contains material from a number of organizations which include unions such as the NUC and RCA, and in addition from non-union organizations such as the London Clerks Association, a registered friendly society, the Association of Foremen and Clerks of the Docks, Wharves and Warehouses of London, and even the Ibis Society, the sports and social club of Holborn Bars, the headquarters of the Prudential Life Assurance Company. The inclusion of such material in one collection suggests that for Booth such diverse groups were part of a common phenomenon, the collective organizations of clerical workers whose aim was to improve, in different ways, the professional lives of their members.

Alongside these groups were a large number of other non-union clerical organizations in London from a wide range of sectors. These included the London County Council Staff Association, the Staff Association of the London Metropolitan Water Board, The Institute of Bankers, and the Law Clerks Association.[9] While these bodies were not registered as official trade unions they nevertheless collectively represented their individual members in order to improve their professional positions. When in 1909, for example, the London County Council imposed a £200 barrier on its officials, the L.C.C. Staff Association was created, and was able by lobbying members of the Council, organizing petitions, collectively representing its members before management, to raise the £200 barrier by £45.[10] Similarly, the Institute of Bankers, an organization that was created as a result of agitation from bankers clerks, created a series of professional banking examinations which aimed at improving the status of those working in the banking industry. In addition, the Institute ran and financed a Sanatorium for those suffering from Tuberculosis and established a widows and orphans fund. Via the Institution, bank clerks were thus able to collectively wring important concessions from their employers which would have been impossible if attempted individually.[11] This is not to argue that the Institute of Bankers was a trade union, a claim which would probably have turned its founders in their graves, but to emphasize that there were other mediums of clerical professional collective action which did not necessitate having to taking the path of trade unionism.

In addition, one should not lump all clerical unions into one uniform organization which had common characteristics and goals. There was wide variety within these organizations. Whether an organization was registered as a union or not, whether it was affiliated to the Trades Union Congress and/or the Labour Party, and whether it endorsed strike action were all important factors in a body's makeup. The National Union of Clerks by 1914, for example, had all of these characteristics, the Railway Clerks Association was affiliated to the TUC and Labour Party, though only in 1910 in relation to the latter, and not without considerable acrimony within the movement,[12] insisting on non-militant action to achieve its goals. Clerical Associations within the Civil Service were neither registered as unions nor had links to the Labour Party. Yet even here the radical Assistant Clerks Association affiliated to Labour in 1916. In contrast the Post Office Unions were registered and active supporters of the TUC and Labour Party. Similarly, some of these unions, such as the NUC, offered members a full range of social benefits and services such as pensions, unemployment benefits and assistance with illness, some, such as the RCA offered limited benefits, and others offered none at all.

It is thus clear that the dichotomy between unionized and non-unionized, or organized and non-organized clerks is wrong. Instead it would be more accurate to speak in terms of a spectrum of organization and militancy. On this basis, at one extreme would be the National Union of Clerks, unionized, politically radical and militant and at the other end were groups such as The Institute of Bankers. Such a system of analysis would incorporate the key Weberian concept of 'Party', the idea that along with one's class position and social status, the groups to which a person belongs, particularly those that are specifically concerned with influencing policies and making decisions in the interests of their members, are key determiners in an individual's social position.[13] The advantage of this would be that it would include a broader range of London's clerical workers than has been previously permissible.

Clerical Unions and 'New Unionism'

The rise in collective action amongst clerks from the 1890s was part of a wider growth in trade unionism across Britain in this period. Trade Union membership in Britain and Ireland grew from 1.5 million members in 1890 to 4,145,000 in 1914.[14] Much of this has been attributed to the rise of 'New Unionism'. The term, most renowned from its usage by the Webbs in their history of British Trade Unions in 1920, denoted, as its name suggests, a change in the nature of collective action. It has been argued that it was a shift in the nature of trade unions which was responsible for their numerical growth after 1890.[15]

The Webbs saw the chief characteristics of 'New Unionism' as an inclusion in the ranks of organized labour of large groups of workers who had traditionally remained outside of the pale of Trade Unionism. These covered, in particular, semi-skilled and unskilled workers. Other characteristics included a new assertiveness on the part of trade unionism. This was reflected, for example, in demands for a minimum wage, an eight-hour working day and a willingness to engage in the political sphere, both on a local and national level, which saw eventual fruition in the establishment of the Labour Party. Finally, the growth of national, general unions which covered all grades and, in some cases, types of labour was seen as another characteristic. This was typified in the establishment of unions such as the Transport and General Workers and the General and Municipal Workers Unions. In sum, 'New Unionism' was said to be inclusive rather than exclusive, pro-active rather than reactive, and national rather than local. While the concept has undergone revision by historians its core ideas have, for all intents and purposes, remained relatively unscathed.[16]

In the confines of the above definition, the new 'black-coated' unions were prime examples of this new trend in collective action. Clerks, like dockers, gas-workers and municipal employees were workers who had previously shown no real history of collective action began, in varying degrees, to unionize after 1890.[17] Additionally, many clerical unions were as assertive in their demands for a minimum wage, shorter working hours and better working conditions as their manual counterparts.[18] They were also equally prepared to use political means, particularly through lobbying, as a means of realizing their aims.

Where clerical unions differed from other manual unions was in their demands and strategies. Organized clerical workers, while wanting more money and having to work fewer hours to obtain this, also wanted other things such as improved career opportunities. They also rejected the strike weapon and tended to put more emphasis on two other weapons; publicity and politics. Both these areas will be examined in turn.

The Demands of Clerical Unions

The demands of clerical unions concentrated on ameliorating working conditions. Improvements of salaries were foremost amongst their demands. The National Union of Clerks, for example, stipulated a minimum wage at 21 of 35s. a week.[19] Since clerical incomes were gradual and incremental, much energy was also devoted to standardizing and improving pay scales and maxima. The R.C.A., for example, tirelessly petitioned railway companies via memorials with demands for pay increases and the implementation of new salary scales.[20] Such action, for example, was mirrored by the Association of Assistant Clerks before and during the MacDonnell Commission, established in 1912 to enquire into recruitment and salaries in the Civil Service.[21]

Demands for pay increases, however, only reveal part of the activities of the clerical unions. Clerical associations fully appreciated the fact that office work required a fragmented hierarchical structure with disparate levels of income. Improving incomes for its members, consequently, meant not only attempting to improve overall pay, but also, over the course of their careers, facilitating access to these more prestigious and highly paid positions. In this respect, demands such as the institutionalization of systems of recruitment and promotion based on merit rather than patronage, the establishment of modern training systems, and a system of professional examinations were all advocated to varying degrees by these organizations. In this respect, we can see that clerical unions fully endorsed the new system of internal labour markets and their standardized systems, which were being introduced by larger employers. Dispute revolved around the structures of these markets rather than around clerical work and income *per se*. Unions clearly understood that without the reform of these employment structures in the interests of their members, general pay increases would be meaningless.

Merit *versus* Patronage

Clerical trade unions were *both* defensive and aggressive. As has been argued in the opening chapters of this study, clerical work underwent many a transformation in the second half of the nineteenth century with the introduction of internal labour markets. Within this overall context, methods of recruitment and promotion gradually changed. Patronage systems became replaced by merit. What one knew and was capable of doing in many spheres of clerical work gradually began to take the place of who one knew and how much wealth one had. Merit opened doors to thousands of young men and women who under the older system would have been prescribed to more menial positions as a result of their parents' social strata. It became, in many respects, the leading ideology of the newly emerging lower-middle class, a group rich in ambition but relatively poor in financial resources. Clerical unions consequently strongly pushed the ideology of meritocracy and fiercely resisted any challenge to its onward march.

A good example of this was the campaign by the Assistant Clerks Association against what they saw as the reintroduction of patronage in the Civil Service. The foundations of meritocracy in the office can be seen as being laid by the report of Sir Stafford Northcote and Sir Charles Trevelyan (1853), prepared for Gladstone, then Chancellor of the Exchequer, outlining recommendations for the reform of the Civil Service. Their two proposals, recruitment by competitive examination and the establishment of a central board to oversee such examinations became the defining features of the modern Service.[22] While recruitment by competition became gradually established throughout all the government departments, this system was felt to be challenged at the turn of the twentieth century by the increasing use of direct recruitment. This was particularly so in the new Labour Exchange Centres and National Insurance Offices. While the government argued that these new positions needed men with experience and practical knowledge who could only be properly selected by limited competition and/or interview, the civil service clerical associations only saw in this a covert attempt to re-introduce patronage.[23]

The result of such changes was a sustained campaign by the A.C.A. (as well as the Second Division Clerks Association), which from the evidence of their monthly journal, *Red Tape*, appears to have absorbed much of their time and energy. It was rewarded by the establishment of the MacDonnell Commission in 1912. Memoranda were sent to Members of Parliament, Ministers were questioned in parliament by supporters of the associations, a memorial was sent to the prime minister protesting the issue, and article after article was written on the subject.[24]

The A.C.A.'s attack on patronage did not simply stop at protest against the increasing failure to use the competitive examination for government appointments, but evolved into an all-out attack on the entire constitution of the Civil Service itself. The Service by 1910 had evolved into a highly complex structure. Following the recommendations of the Playfair Commission, 1874–5, two grades of civil servants had been created, the Lower Division (later called the Second Division) who were responsible for clerical work, and the First Division who were responsible for administrative work. Thirty years later these grades were joined by an Intermediate Class, located somewhere between the other two classes, an Assistant Clerk grade, who carried out more menial clerical work, and female clerks and boy clerks who were responsible for mechanical office work such as copying and filing.[25] Each grade had their own entrance examination which for many locked them into one particular grade for their entire career. This was condemned by the A.C.A. as being socially divisive, biased towards the rich who were able to dominate the higher clerical positions due to their superior education, completely antithetical to the efficiency of the Service and opposed to the principle of merit. As the Association argued in 1912, the current Civil Service competitive examinations consisted of the '...judicious use of a system of Patronage, and the manipulation of the examination scheme in such a way as to secure that ability shall only have chances of success when it has received a particular type of education at a particular type of school'.[26]

The A.C.A. ultimately failed in their efforts to establish a common entrance examination for the Civil Service. The MacDonnell Report recommended a simplification of the clerical grades, but insisted on the maintenance of the distinction between Administrative and Clerical work, and distinctions within the latter. Despite this, however, the Commission reconfirmed its overall commitment and support to the competitive system and selection based on merit.[27] The struggle by the A.C.A. and other civil service associations for the cause and protection of merit was indicative of the deep commitment that clerical workers had towards this ideology. It was one which was fully articulated by their associations, and one which reverberated loudly among the other white-collar unions.

Training and Professional Examinations

Whilst the growing acceptance of merit within businesses and government offices was welcomed by clerical trade unions, the large increase in the number of individuals entering the clerical profession was not. Clerical unions believed that an uncontrolled influx of new recruits into offices, due to an extension of education, had resulted in the lowering of the income and status of the average clerical worker. As the President of the Railway Clerks Association argued in a speech to the Seventeenth Annual Conference of the union in Edinburgh, 1914, '...The economic position of clerks as a class has been encroached upon very seriously indeed since the supply of clerical labour was increased to an almost unlimited extent by the institution of free education in this country...'[28] The response of the unions to this was twofold. On the one hand, they argued that better opportunities in the way of education and training should be furnished to clerks to make them more efficient and thus better remunerated. On the other, they argued for a restriction of the supply of clerical workers by the introduction of a system of professional examinations.

The demand for better education and training chimed with the general clerical commitment to self-improvement. Vocational education took centre stage in the policies and agendas of many white-collar trade unions. The second rule, for example, of the National Union of Clerks (c. 1894) was, 'To provide (when funds permit) educational facilities for members and for the issue of certificates of clerical efficiency.'[29] Similarly, at the annual conference of the Railway Clerks Association in 1894 in London, three key subjects were discussed by delegates: Labour Representation, Nationalization and Technical Education. Indeed, it was argued by *The Railway Clerk* that the latter should be first among their objectives.[30]

While clerical unions attempted to improve their members' education collectively through organized lectures, educational groups and articles in their publications,[31] some unions went further in arguing that it was the responsibility of the companies, rather than their workers, to educate and train their staff. This argument was foremost in the Railway Clerks Association where a tradition of company training had already been well established in the railway industry. One of the chief arguments of the R.C.A. was that while the companies were prepared to invest money in educating other grades such as drivers, engineers and signal men, little had been done for the clerks. Such education was needed to ensure that clerks had an equal opportunity for promotion and because many of the managers of the companies were recruited from the clerical grades of the railway companies.[32] It was an area where the union to some extent gained concrete results. Railway Clerks were able to push for the establishment of classes provided by the firms in many railway companies, including, for example, the formation of classes on the Metropolitan Railway in 1911 at the Neasden works to study the principles of electric train working and other railway subjects.[33]

The argument for more education and training was complemented by the demands of the unions for the establishment of professional examinations. Such demands were voiced, to varying degrees, by virtually all the clerical associations, both unions and non-unions alike. Via such examinations it was hoped that the flow of recruits into clerical positions could be stemmed, overall recruitment controlled, and subsequently wages improved. In addition, such examinations were seen as a way of diminishing nepotism and enhancing promotion by merit. Finally, it was hoped that such examinations would professionalize clerical work and thus raise its status. In this respect, clerical unions and associations hardly differed, at least in terms of their goals, from other contemporary professional organizations such as the Chartered Institute of Accountants or the National Union of Teachers.

While grandiose plans such as those of the N.U.C. for a comprehensive system of clerical examinations for all grades and sectors ultimately failed, other groups with more moderate schemes were more successful.[34] The Institute of Bankers' qualifications became gradually more widespread and accepted.[35] The N.A.L.G.O. introduced its own professional examinations in 1905, which soon became popular across the country.[36] The railway companies too extended their support for technical and commercial education for their clerical workers. As was seen in the previous chapter, several companies even introduced management training programmes in the years running up to the First World War, with the co-operation of educational institutes such as the LSE.[37] Such programmes provided railway clerks with a more structured path into management positions, opening for some the possibility of a career. While such programmes may not have been the sole result of union pressure, they are evidence of important structural shifts in the clerical labour market. It was these shifts which clerical unions and associations encouraged and strove for, and which, in addition to demands for pay increases and better conditions, represented one of the major goals of these organizations.

Strategies of Clerical Unions and Associations

How did clerical unions operate? What strategies did they develop in which to try and realize their goals? The strike or direct action was certainly not one of them. An article in the *Clerk*, for example, commented in 1908 that, '...Strikes are barbarous, should already be obsolete, are particularly unsuitable for clerks, and the handle of the weapon cuts worse than the blade. We can therefore dismiss it.'[38] Evidence of the limited industrial action that clerks took against their employers in this period confirms this view. A refusal to perform overtime by 282 clerks at the Post Office Savings Bank in January 1891, led to a lock-out by management who demanded written apologies from all clerks concerned. Within a week all clerks were back at their desks, having complied with the wishes of management.[39] Similarly strikes by the N.U.C., despite the above protestation, at the Port of London authority 1912–13, and at Rees Roturbo Co. Ltd. at Wolverhampton in 1914 both ended in complete failure.[40] The latter, indeed, descended almost into farce, with two of the striking clerks having a summons taken out against them by a blackleg, ex-commercial traveller from Walsall, for 'persistently following him from place to place'.[41]

Instead of resorting to strike action, clerical unions turned to two other areas of action. The first of these was publicity. By the dissemination of information directly aimed at their grievances, these organizations hoped to win over public support and also convince colleagues and employers of the legitimacy of their claims. The second was politics. In many respects, clerical unions and associations were lobby groups. They regularly put pressure on and formed alliances with individual MPs, and later on the Labour Party, to push their demands onto centre stage in the political arena. Both these strategies were used to varying degrees by all the white-collar organizations of this period, and can be said to be defining features of these bodies.

The Use of Publicity

The article in the *Clerk* which rejected strike action, advocated the use of N.U.C. employment bureaus and the demand for a national minimum wage as two alternatives. In addition it argued, '... There remains yet another weapon, and that, perhaps, the strongest, if properly used – public opinion. This we must create'.[42] Rather than directly force issues, clerical unions attempted to win hearts and minds. This was felt to be doubly important as many unions argued they laboured under the disadvantage of being widely stereotyped by a relatively unsympathetic public. 'At present', argued the *Clerk*, 'public opinion re clerks is that they will let themselves be trampled upon. Stiff collar, cuffs, and a penny in his pocket is the mental picture conjured up in many minds at present when 'clerk' is mentioned. The phrase 'Pound a week Clerks' is one of contempt, and we shall deserve the contempt until we have killed the phrase'.[43] It was also argued that many believed clerks to be in well paid, secure and undemanding jobs where promotion was guaranteed. The opening edition of *Red Tape* in October, 1911, for example, spoke of the civil servant of popular mythology who was dignified, leisurely, well-paid, worked in luxurious surroundings, and performed work which while light in amount, was profound in content. This was said to be a far cry from the working lives of many of the low-paid, routine clerks of the Service.[44] Similarly, an article in the *Railway Clerk*, in 1911 entitled, 'Facts and Fiction re Railway Clerks' Salaries' lambasted the popular press for exaggerating the salaries and opportunities open to railway clerks.[45]

The principal propaganda weapon which the unions put to work was the written word. Unions often used national and local newspapers to broadcast their message to a wider audience. The *Clerk*, for example, wrote in 1910 that one result of a deputation of the Union in the previous year to the then Prime Minister Asquith and his Chancellor, Lloyd George, was a conversion of the Daily Express to the N.U.C.'s cause.[46] In the same year the Second Division Clerks Association compiled a memorandum against patronage appointments in the civil service. The text was issued to Members of Parliament *and* sent to the Press.[47] In addition, all the major unions had journals in which their grievances were clearly and repeatedly stated. These papers were intended equally for non-union members who these organizations wanted to attract as well as those who had already joined. Union policy and arguments were disseminated in articles, short essays and letters. Fiction, usually in the form of short stories, and poems, were also used to hammer home the message of these organizations. This was brilliantly done, for example, in *Red Tape*, where a series of entertaining short stories, entitled 'Civil Service Sketches' depicted civil servants in harrowing positions, from out-of-work clerks hanging around outside pubs on Tottenham Court Road to tormented young husbands with expectant wives living in sub-urban flats in Wandsworth.[48] Such journals often had readerships in excess of their association's numbers, showing that they were widely read by members and non-members alike, and thus assisted in spreading their message. *Red Tape*, the journal of the A.C.A., for example, had sales of over 5,000, despite the fact that membership of the association was just over 2,000.[49]

Clerical unions often collected, collated and published statistics and other facts which they used in their war of words with their employers. This was either done in pamphlet form, which was distributed to the wider public and employ-ers, or, as seen, inserted in petitions when clerical workers made direct appeals to their superiors. In relation to the former, one of the best examples of these was a publication by the R.C.A. in 1911 entitled, *The Life of a Railway Clerk, Some Interesting Facts and Figures*.[50] This thirty-two-page document was a com-prehensive collection of facts and figures which presented the average income of railway clerks, compared their incomes with clerical workers in other sectors, and showed that railway officials were being adversely affected by increases in the cost of living. The booklet was distributed across the country to the public, parents, and management in the railways. It was advertised in the press and even sent to schools.[51] One of its aims was to discourage parents from selecting careers in the railways for their offspring. For an industry which was having difficulty in finding adequate recruits, the publication must have been highly effective, and certainly played a role in the pay increases that were awarded to clerks across the railway industry in 1911.[52]

The Use of Politics

Alongside the use of media, publicity and propaganda, clerical unions used formal political channels to further their ends. The two were clearly related. If unions were able to muster public support, politicians and parliament would have to respond by assisting these organizations in realizing their goals. The R.C.A. made this connection in 1906 when it observed that, 'Nothing but publicity of the shortcomings of the management, the drawing of attention to the ordinary citizens of the fearful wrongs under which the rank and file of the service lay, will bring about the desired reforms, and to this end we hope and believe we shall receive the attention of Parliament itself'.[53] Additionally, some demands such as the maintenance of a minimum standard of hygiene in offices or compensation for injuries incurred during working hours expressly needed parliamentary action. The inclusion of office workers in the Workmen's Compensation Act, 1906 was a case in point. The original bill which was introduced to parliament excluded clerical workers. Intense lobbying by the Parliamentary Committee of the Trades Union Congress and the newly formed Labour Party with support from the R.C.A. and N.U.C. was successful in persuading the Home Secretary, Herbert Gladstone, to include clerks within the remit of the bill.[54]

Clerical unions and associations made sure that they had a coterie of MP's whose support they could rely on. The opening editions of the *Railway Clerk*, for example, proudly introduced Members who supported the R.C.A.'s cause to its readers by providing potted biographies of each one. These men, all back-benchers, came from a variety of parties including the Conservative Party. All had interests in trade unionism. The ties between the men and the union were formalized by each of them being vice-presidents of the organization, with Sir Fortescue Flannery, a radical/progressive, and MP since 1895, President of the Association.[55] Similar ties existed with other clerical associations including the N.U.C., Postal Unions and Civil Service Associations.[56] Over time, particularly within the R.C.A., the bonds between the Labour Party and the unions became stronger, and the party became the principal engine of parliamentary action. In many respects, these affiliations and formal ties simply institutionalized relations that had existed between clerical unions and politicians since the inception of these organizations.[57]

One MP who was active in white-collar unions was the future Labour Chancellor Philip Snowden. Snowden was among a group of well-wishers reported in the opening edition of the *Clerk* in 1908. 'I am very glad to hear that there is a move of an encouraging character among clerks in the direction of organization', he wrote, 'No other class stands more in need of it.'[58] Snowden was the principle parliamentary supporter of the A.C.A. He regularly asked questions on its behalf in parliament and was persistent in his support of meritocracy in the Civil Service.[59] His composition of a memorial outlining the problems of promotion and appointment in the Service, which received 403 signatures from MPs, played an important role in the appointment of the Macdonald Commission in 1912.[60] Snowden sat on the Commission, and used his questions to articulate the claims and grievances of the Civil Service Associations.

Such support for the establishment of parliamentary enquiries into conditions of office work was a key strategy of the clerical unions and associations. This was extremely important for civil servants, local government officers and postal clerks, since these were state employees. Such enquiries were the only legal means by which these associations could put their grievances and claims directly before the government and parliament.[61]

A parliamentary strategy was also central to the R.C.A. In this period railway companies were not strictly speaking purely private concerns. They were private companies in that they were owned by private shareholders, eligible for a share of their profits. They were public, however, in that their charters were granted by parliament. If the companies wanted to make any major structural alterations such as mergers, take-overs or even altering the makeup of their pension schemes, this could only be done with prior parliamentary permission. As the railway companies expanded in the second half of the nineteenth century their public face became more pronounced. Their growing use by the public and business world, and the resultant increased dependency that came from this, made the railway industry an area of national concern. This point was fully emphasized by Sam Fay in his Presidential speech as head of the Railway Students Union at the L.S.E.,

> ... Time was when railways were looked upon as private properties run for private gain only, but I doubt if any railwayman to-day ... regards railways as private in the sense that a shopkeeper's business is private. The railways are private on the financial side alone. The shareholders who have found the capital expect their dividends in the same way as holders of Consols would expect interest if the Government took over the railways and issued Consols on account of the purchase, but even on the financial side they are controlled by specific Acts of Parliament. They are public in that everybody has a right to use them upon terms not exceeding charges fixed by legislation. They are common carriers. They assume serious public responsibilities, and their acts and duties are regulated by the legislature. The work of their officers and servants is public work in precisely the same sense as is the work of officers and servants in the Post Office.[62]

Due to the railway's growing public prominence, the R.S.A., sometimes in conjunction with other rail unions, was able to have its representatives appear as witnesses in important parliamentary inquiries into the railway industry which directly affected their interests. The two most important of these before the First World War were a government inquiry into superannuations in the railway companies in 1907, and another to enquire into Railway Agreements and Amalgamations, appointed in 1909. Both, especially the first, resulted in important concessions for railway clerks.[63]

The R.S.A. was also able to use its power in parliament to block railway bills in order to push forward its demands and gain concessions from the rail companies. This was a very effective weapon of the union in the years running up to the First World War. One particular reason for this was because of over-competition amongst the railway companies which led to costly price wars and reduced profits. The answer to this was mergers and operating agreements amongst the companies, and increases in charges. All needed parliamentary approval, and it was here, where the companies were most vulnerable, that the R.C.A. repeatedly struck. Parliamentary bills were 'blocked' in 1909 against the North-Eastern Railway Company, and in 1913 against the Midland Company. In both cases, the railway companies were intimidating clerks who became members of the R.C.A., and in both cases the union was successful in opposing this.[64]

Parliamentary action lay at the centre of the operational strategy of the Railway Clerks Association as it did amongst the other clerical unions. For a sector of workers for whom the strike weapon was unsuitable, both in terms of the unwillingness of many clerks to strike and the relative ease of 'blacklegging' striking clerical work, the use of politicians and parliament was the perfect answer. It was both respectable and effective. It was this political tool, along with propaganda and an attempt to foster public opinion that clerical unions used, to varying degrees of success, between 1890 and 1914.

Collective Action and Clerical Values

Was there an inherent contradiction between being a clerk and being a member of a trade union or association? Did one exclude the other? On 18 August 1912, for example, the correspondence was read to the Executive Committee of the National Union of Clerk's London Central Branch. A Miss E. S. Nunn had returned her Insurance Card, Book, and other items (the N.U.C. offered social insurance, and had recently insisted that those subscribing to these facilities should become a member of the union), and stated that she could not join the organization on account of it being a trade union. Five other members had written to the union in the same strain.[65] Fifteen years later, the R.S.A. wrote that when the union was founded in 1897, '...All the traditions of clerical employees were against the idea of trade unionism'.[66] Frequent references were found in the *Clerk* to the snobbishness and disdain of the average clerk for trade unionism. The failure of the majority of clerks to join the union was put down to the incompatibility of collective action with the individualism of the clerk, his overriding desire to be respectable and his abhorrence of anything that smacked of the working classes.[67]

The main problem with this argument is that a significant minority of clerks did belong to some type of collective professional organization, some unions, some not, and an even larger minority would do so during and after the First World War with no essential re-structuring of clerical social values. In addition, the dichotomy between a unionized working class and a non-unionized clerical or even lower-middle-class group is far too simple. Most working people in Britain throughout this period did not belong to a union, and within the union movement there was considerable diversity.[68] In addition, as Harold Perkin has shown, many middle-class groups were organizing themselves in the second half of the nineteenth century.[69] Finally failure to unionize probably had as much to do with structural factors within work itself, as it had to do with class prejudice.

In relation to clerks, it is important to point out that social organization can be argued to be one of their defining features, as it was amongst the broader middle class to which they belonged.[70] Their commitment to individualism can be easily exaggerated. Clerks, as an important segment of the lower-middle class, wanted to lead a lifestyle that was beginning to emerge among the more established middle classes in this period, one based on consumption, leisure, sport, holidays, education, etc. They lacked, however, the financial means to do this. They subsequently tended to club together to subsidize each other collectively in their quest for this way of life. The sporting clubs, social organizations, holiday associations and night classes that have been evidenced throughout this study are all examples of the collective spirit of clerical workers and their families. An examination of the *Ilford Guardian* between 1898 and 1901 has revealed fifty-three different associations in a thriving London suburb which contained a large proportion of clerical workers and their families. An additional eleven societies appeared in the Town Council's promotional brochure in 1911.[71] Such private, voluntary bodies included sports clubs, recreational societies, self-help groups, church clubs and political organizations.

Another example of this spirit of co-operation amongst clerical workers was the establishment of the Public Servant Association in June 1914. The Association opened a co-operative store at 210 Westminster Bridge Road later that year for the capital's estimated 80,000 public servants. The Association was inaugurated by representatives from a large number of public bodies, including the local government and the Civil Service, and was founded to, '... promote the economic and social well-being of its members'.[72] From the perspective of collective action there was not much difference between joining the above association and being a member of a clerical union. Both, whilst having different aims, attempted collectively to achieve what the individual could not.

The aims of most of these organizations also conformed with general clerical values. There was no real contradiction between what many clerks wanted individually, and what these bodies sought to achieve. Clerical unions and associations attempted collectively to enhance the power of the individual at work. Their demand for the acceptance and full integration of the principal of merit at work is an excellent example of this. Clerical unions repeatedly emphasized that their goal was to enforce this sacred principle for the benefit of the individual and for the organization they worked for. Discussing this in late 1911, for example, the *Railway Clerk* wrote,

> We all like to think of Merit as being synonymous with Success, but of course as abstract terms they do not exist ... As railway clerks cease to hibernate, so they become alive to the fact that their employers choose to make much of the term merit. And when those same employer are asked to define 'merit', there is either great ambiguity, or no answer at all. There is then the feeling of distrust on the part of the enquirer and a prescience is formed that merit will be a mysterious something to conjure up as occasion requires.[73]

The message here was clear. The railway companies liked to talk merit but failed to deliver. As a result, bad faith and distrust plagued the industry. The R.C.A. as a collective body would therefore become the custodian of the principle, force the issue and create a working environment, as the article later argued, that was congenial for railway clerk and company alike.[74]

Another key clerical value which the unions supported was the clerk's commitment to the domestic sphere. This included his desire to marry, establish a home, and to maintain it at an adequate level. Both of these were fundamental to a clerk's sense of masculinity. Promotion was not longed for simply as an end in itself, but also as a means of obtaining more money which was seen as essential in terms of setting up a marital home. As *Red Tape* wrote in 1911, tying together the two themes of a gradually increasing income and the eventual domestic responsibilities of the clerk, '... If manhood means anything at all, it means progressive development and fulfilment. Does anyone really believe that self-realization is possible on £45 a year, paid monthly, or that the duties and responsibilities of later years can be properly discharged on £150?'[75] Money was crucial to a clerk's concept of manhood. Without it he could not marry, establish a decent home, rear a family, and thus, in his own terms of reference, become a man in the true sense of the word.

This link between work and the domestic sphere was one which was central to clerks and was supported by clerical unions. Clerks, as members of a larger middle class worked with the primary goal in mind of establishing and maintaining a house which pertained to certain levels of consumption and standards crystallized in the Victorian concept of respectability.[76] This is clearly evidenced in the 'Civil Service Sketches', referred to earlier in *Red Tape* where the desire to establish and maintain a respectable home was continuously juxtaposed to the impossibility of doing so on the income the Assistant Clerk in the Civil Service actually obtained. It was a point which was made when Mr. David Milne gave evidence to the MacDonnell Commission as a representative of the A.S.A. Questioned whether economists would agree with the A.S.A. in their claims of increases in the cost of living, Milne told the Commission that assistant clerks came from a group of boys who had received a secondary education and came from comfortable and decent homes. A living wage calculated for a working class family living in Whitechapel was hardly appropriate for one of his colleagues.[77] The A.S.A.'s and other clerical unions' demands for a living wage was one which related specifically to the class background of the individuals concerned. It was a demand which in no way conflicted with a clerk's sense of masculinity, and indeed may have assisted in the growth of some white-collar unions.

This emphasis by the clerical unions on supporting accepted gender roles was mirrored in their antipathy to female clerks, both in terms of entering the clerical profession and the unions themselves. While the unions admitted female clerks from their inception and claimed to want to ameliorate working conditions for both sexes their action did not often match their rhetoric.[78] From the actions and comments of the male majority members in these unions (the N.U.C. had 12 per cent female members in 1914), it is clear that women clerks were viewed as being one of the principle causes of the perceived decline in clerical incomes and working conditions, and were thus viewed by many with hostility.

On 4 October 1908, for example, the National Union of Clerks held a public meeting in Brockwell Park, Brixton, to protest against the employment of cheap female labour. A crowd of over 2,000 people were reported to have assembled around a wagon, over which a prominent banner bore the words, 'Are you a Clerk?'[79] In the same edition of the journal a letter from the female clerical trade unionist activist, Mary E. Taplin was published. The letter bitterly complained about an article written in the same magazine by the General Secretary of the N.U.C., in which he wrote of his hope, whilst discussing the unhygienic conditions of offices, of the ideal time when female-labour would not be known in factory, workshop or office.[80] Taplin vigorously protested the right of women at work to be treated on an equal basis as men, and hoped that the majority of members of the Union did not share the same sentiments as the General Secretary. Despite this, articles and letters still continued to be published in the *Clerk* complaining and warning about the increased use of women in the office. Similar hostilities were also evident in the R.C.A.[81]

The Progressive Clerk

Finally, in discussing the issue of collective action and clerical workers it is important not to conflate clerks into one homogenous mass. Within the whole there were various sub-sectors. One group of clerical workers who were certainly drawn to trade unionism were progressive clerks. The concept of a 'progressive London' as a sub-sector of the capital drawing together individuals, clubs, societies, political and economic movements, and constituting an important element of its civil society, is a very useful tool for the purposes of this particular discussion. The collection itself was composed of a heterogeneous number of groups who were linked, often tenuously, in their opposition to the hegemonic contemporary discourses of liberal economics, utilitarianism, imperialism and the growing influence of corporate capitalism. Many of these groups and individuals were influenced in their critique of state and society by the English nineteenth-century counter-discourses of radicalism and idealism, the latter heavily influenced in this period by the writings of T. H. Green and F. H. Bradley, which led to calls for social and political reform.[82] Such groups covered a wide range of organizations, some political, some not, within the capital. They included political groups, co-operative organizations, religious bodies, women's groups, educational bodies and unions.[83]

Within this movement clerks played a part. Susan Pennybacker, for example, in her study of the L.C.C. has located a number of progressive officials within the Council.[84] One such individual was Daniel McEwen. McEwen was a clerk in the Office of the Official Receivers in Bankruptcy attached to the High Court. He was an active member of the co-operative movement, was for a period a committee member of the Tenants Co-operation Co., and even lived with his wife in two of their properties. He lectured at one point on socialism in a University Extension Class, wrote articles on Trade Unions and had connections with the Fabians. McEwen was an active member of progressive society in Camberwell where he lived, and his diaries, which cover the period 1887 to 1909, are full of detail of his activities within this world.[85]

A number of individuals such as McEwen, and those L.C.C. officials described by Pennybacker, became members of clerical unions, and found no problem in doing so. A significant number of these unions were highly political. Membership of them provided a gateway into the vibrant socialist, radical and progressive life of the capital. This was particularly so in relation to the National Union of Clerks. An examination, for example, of the Minute Book of the London Central Branch of the N.U.C. reveals a group of individuals who were very political. The Branch sent delegates to the Women's Trade Union League. It had connections with the Independent Labour Party and the Fabians with whom it co-operated in a movement in 1912 called 'The War Against Poverty'. It participated with the Independent Labour Party and another group, the L&S.C.D.C., in a conference protesting against an increase in armaments. It also, via the London Trades Council, had connections to the Labour Party and other socialist and labour bodies in London. In the interwar period, the N.U.C. as a whole continued its political activities, devoting much energy, for example, to the League of Nations Union.[86]

It can, therefore, be argued that there was no inherent obstacle preventing clerks from becoming members of a trade union or association. This is not to deny that many clerks in this period did not become members of such groups, because they thought it was socially beneath them, or that they were committed to individual rather than collective approaches. This phenomenon, however, was not exclusive to clerks. Clerks were equally happy to organize in many areas, created organizations that were specifically sensitive to their needs, and to some degree did unionize. The question that this chapter will end with is therefore why did some sectors of clerical workers unionize and others not?

Structural Pre-Conditions of Clerical Collective Action

Some sectors of clerical work were organized, some were left untouched. Railway clerks and civil servants were far more amenable to trade unionism than bank clerks or commercial clerical workers. Such distinctions have led commentators to the conclusion that there must have been structural factors at work affecting collective action. Office environments which had become concentrated, centralized and bureaucratized, where internal labour markets had developed, and where pay structure and staff policy were determined by impersonal codes and procedures, rather than on a personal and individual basis, were those where organization was most likely to take place. Under these conditions, it made sense for clerks to negotiate collectively with management rather than do so individually as senior decisions affected everybody. Since this was a feature of large-scale concerns it appears to explain why clerks in the Post Office, the Civil Service and the Railway Companies began to unionize.[87] While there is much strength in this argument, there are also weaknesses. If concentration was the chief factor there should have been unionization in the banks and insurance offices where such conditions held sway. Both these sectors, however, failed to unionize. In addition, railway clerks at head office, where centralization and bureaucratic conditions were most advanced, tended not to unionize.[88] Concentration on its own is thus not an adequate explanation.

The answer lies in concentration, and two other factors which have been addressed in this chapter, politics and level of income. The first area is relatively straightforward. White-collar unions and associations were effective where there was an opportunity to use politics and parliament. All the collective bodies that were successful in attracting significant numbers in this period, the Railway Clerks Association, the post office clerks' unions, the civil service associations and the local government organizations, were in public or semi-public sectors where the use of the parliamentary weapon was feasible. All won pay increases and other concessions in the years running up to 1914 and beyond with the assistance of political action. Political support often protected these unions during their initial years and enabled them to attract members. Without the chance to exercise this system of attack and defence, fledgling unions were often unable to exist in hostile environments in which superiors were frequently opposed to their development.

The second area of income is more problematic. Low income levels as a cause of clerical unionization has previously been rejected on the basis of figures published by the British Association in 1910 which showed the percentage of salaried employees earning over £160. These figures showed insurance clerks and banking clerks being the top earners, 46 per cent and 44 per cent of them respectively earning over this figure, with only 23 per cent of commercial clerk doing so. Civil Service clerks also appear to be a relatively affluent group with 37 per cent of them earning over £160.[89] Gregory Anderson has argued that since Civil Servants unionized, pay did not appear to be an important factor in determining the formation of clerical unions. He also argued that bank clerks became rapidly unionized in the 1920s, thus further weakening the significance of income.[90]

There are, however, several major problems with this argument. The first concerns bank clerks. While it is true that a significant proportion of this group unionized in the 1920s, this was the result of the failure of the banks to increase salaries sufficiently in the years during and immediately after the First World War when there was heavy inflation. Bank clerks went from being one of the highest-paid sectors of clerical workers to one of the worst paid. As a result, while there was no unionization in this group during their heyday in the years covered in this study, significant segments did organize when bank clerks suffered severe economic decline. Here is clear proof of the existence of a correlation between income and degrees of unionization among clerical workers.[91]

Additionally, the statistic of 37 per cent civil servants earning over £160 should also be treated with extreme caution. The term 'civil servant' is an extremely difficult term to define in this period. Did this figure simply refer to those working in government departments, or did it also include the Post Office, and other areas such as the British Museum, for example? The question is extremely pertinent as government employees were among the first to unionize.

It would appear that this figure did not include post office clerks as their salary scales were far too low for this figure to have any real relevance. Statistics provided by the R.C.A. showed post office clerks in London receiving 18s. a week at age seventeen and rising gradually to 65s. (£169 p.a.), and less in other cities and provincial areas.[92] While there would have been better paid senior positions beyond this, these figures do not appear to suggest that more than a third of this group were earning £160 p.a. and over. This is particularly so as the workforce of the postal service, which had expanded rapidly in this period, would have been relatively young. If postal clerks, telegraphists and other manipulative workers had been included, it is arguable that the figure would have been lower. Even if, in the unlikely event, this was the case, it is clear that this figure does not reveal very much about post office incomes in 1910. In relation to this later point, the same can be said in relation to the Assistant Clerks of the Civil Service whose salary scale in 1910 ranged from only £45 to £150 p.a.[93]

From the immediate evidence it appears that low income was a factor in unionization before 1914. All the successful clerical unions which continued to maintain their momentum after 1918 were in low paid sectors. The Railway Clerks, Post Office Clerks and more mechanical grades of the Civil Service were all low-paid and organized. The Second Division Clerks Association is a case in point. The organization failed to maintain a continuous existence between 1890 and 1914, and it is unlikely that it attracted as many members as its more radical counterpart, the Assistant Clerks Association.[94] In addition, the association neither developed a journal, developed contacts with the Labour Party, or succeeded in its demands to the MacDonnell Commission. In contrast to the Assistant Clerks Association, its members were much higher paid, with scales ranging between £70 and £300 p.a.[95]

Concentration, access to politicians and formal political procedures and level of income were the three key factors in determining clerical unionization between 1890 and 1914. All were found in the sectors where clerks were able to organize. It is these factors which explain why such collective action began in the public sector and has remained so strong there. It also helps to explain the failure of the National Union of Clerks to develop as a trade union. Those areas which were most amenable to trade unionism had already been usurped by other organizations. The N.U.C. found itself in a terrain which proved, in many cases, simply unresponsive to its solicitations.

Conclusion

Trade Unionism and other forms of clerical professional collective organizations provide a fascinating avenue from which to observe clerks in London and Britain between 1890 and 1914. While their development was uneven within the group as a whole, it certainly took place, and should be included in any analysis of this sector of workers. This chapter has argued that one should take a much more flexible approach when discussing clerical unions and other collective bodies. Rather than adopt an exclusive view of such bodies based on some ideal-type of trade union organization, analysis should take account of the diversity of these organizations, both unions and non-unions alike. In addition, while it is correct to see clerical unions proper as a manifestation of the 'new unionism' of the period, these unions had their own particular characteristics. A rejection of the strike weapon, an overwhelming emphasis on the institutionalization of merit in the workplace, sufficient training and professional examinations, and the demand for a living salary tailored to the requirements of a lower-middle class family made these bodies distinct. The singularity of these organizations, and the negotiating structures they developed, were clearly related to the office workers they represented, a group who were different from other manipulative workers who similarly organized themselves.

Within this context, it is also important to note that the idea that the clerical workers were somehow essentially antithetical to collective action should be rejected. The large numbers of clerks who did organize themselves, both inside unions and other associations, the compatibility of many of these organizations' aims with clerical values, and the difficulty in trying to treat such a diverse group as a homogeneous whole should preclude this. Structural conditions in the workplace were the principle factors in deciding whether clerks became organized or not. In this respect, concentration, the opportunity for politics to be used effectively, *and* prevailing low incomes were the most important predeterminants. It is this which explains why clerical unions first appeared in the railways and public sector.

Nevertheless, one should not see structural factors, or even ideological constraints for that matter, as the sole grounds for collective action. Workers generally organize, both now and in the past, if they feel under pressure at work. The failure of many clerks to unionize in this period was probably as much to do with the lack of such pressure as it had to do with any positive factors. With salaries increasing, with office work expanding, and with openings and opportunities growing year by year, unions and similar bodies for many clerks in the Metropolis simply held no appeal. It is here, in this lack of unionization amongst a significant proportion of clerical workers in the capital, in the failure of the National Union of Clerks to attract more than 12,500 individuals out of a potential membership nationwide of 600,000, that one see a major refutation of the declinist argument, that working conditions were deteriorating for clerks in the thirty or so years running up to the First World War.

CONCLUSION

In May 1913 an article was published in *Red Tape* by W. J. Sheriff of the Civil Service Federation (an organization which attempted to link all the unions and associations of the service) entitled, 'Civil Service Agitation – How Not to Do It'.[1] The article aimed at providing friendly advice to the Assistant Clerks Association and other kindred bodies whose agitation for reform in the civil service at the time, as a result of the ongoing MacDonnell Commission, was reaching a peak. Sheriff advised civil servants against wasting their energy on in-fighting amongst the differing grades. In addition, the article criticized the grades and associations for not presenting a common front to the Commission. It was, however, in his advice to civil servants not to exaggerate their grievances that the most pertinent points in relation to this conclusion were made. While Sheriff congratulated the various associations and their members on the high quality of their literary output he warned against hyperbole,

> The overstatement, however, to which I am complaining is seen more in the journalistic side of agitation. Editors – and, even more, correspondents – in Service and other journals do not always remember that these are the only source from which the public and the hierarchy are likely to cull any fresh information about State employees. Led on by righteous indignation they don't always play the game. The result is that the average Service paper presents an unbroken vista of long hours, low pay, and sweating conditions. It is not suggested that the facts stated are not the truth; it is only too true that many Civil Servants are working longer hours than they were originally intended to, or that they are ever paid for, and that there are many scales of salary where the shoe pinches at certain ages, and even some where it never ceases to pinch; that conditions often arise where a self-respecting man cannot possibly do his work in the time officially allotted. But that isn't the whole truth, and the fact remains that, taken all round, as general labour conditions go, it isn't such a bad old Service after all. And that's just where the mischief arises, for the higher official knows this, and the great British public thinks it knows it too.[2]

It should be remembered that the basic historic argument of decline and crisis amongst British clerical workers between 1880 and 1914, first formulated by Klingender and later reproduced in Britain, amongst other writers, by Anderson and more recently Wilson, first saw light in clerical trade union journals in the

1900s similar to those Sheriff was criticizing for not stating the whole truth and being prone to embellishment. While all may not have been perfect for clerks in the years running up to 1914, and for many in the lower echelons of clerical grades there may certainly have been some hardship, to argue that the profession was in terminal decline was quite simply exaggeration. The problem, however, is that while many of the 'great British public' may have recognized this at the time, as the years went by this became less and less the case. Contemporary trade union polemics, mixed with a dose of ideological dogma, imperceptibly became historical truths.

This book rejects this argument. It is impressionistic and not sustained by any substantial evidence. As B. G. Orchard argued in the first study of British clerks written 130 years ago, 'Too much has been said and written of the disadvantages connected with this branch of employment; for inquiry does not corroborate the angry complaints which are often heard'.[3] The evidence unearthed by this research, both quantitative and qualitative, from organizations, associations and from clerical workers themselves, supports this evaluation.

The argument for the decline of clerical workers was based on the premise that the increase in the scale of operations in offices in the second half of the nineteenth century and the sheer increase in the number of clerical workers changed a group of workers from an affluent and exclusive profession to one which was increasingly impoverished and destitute. This argument was grounded on the supposed pernicious effects of the rise of mass education, the oversupply of clerical workers in the labour market, the application of technology and the entry of women into the clerical profession. This study has looked at each of these arguments and found all to be unconvincing. The increasing importance of secondary, higher and further education mitigated the effects of mass elementary education. Technology facilitated rather than decimated clerical labour. Women mainly replaced boys and youths, and were overwhelmingly concentrated in secondary clerical markets, often to the benefit of male clerks.

Arguments over the increase in the size of operations should also be treated with caution. Many offices up until 1914 remained small, and those that grew, principally concentrated in certain sectors such as rail, banking, government and utilities, attempted to mitigate the pernicious effects of expansion such as anonymity and the breakdown in personal working relations by the provision of social welfare and sporting and social facilities. At the same time growth in size of some operations often meant that clerks were able to meet men and women of a similar age and form, in many cases, close friendships. Growth in the number of clerks also had no overall negative effect. In general, as seen in Chapter 4, clerical incomes in London rose, in some cases quite considerably, and opportunities for promotion in no way diminished. Clerical work continued to be stable. Unemployment, though ever-present, remained a relatively rare experience.

How was this the case? How were most clerks able to maintain or even improve their standard of living and social position in the face of large increases in clerical numbers and such seismic structural changes to their profession? One explanation, as maintained in Chapter 1, is that the rise in numbers of male clerical workers in London was more than compensated by the expansion in its overall economy. Developments in finance, transport, commerce, retailing, distribution, government and other service industries meant that growth in clerical recruitment was accompanied by increases in income and mobility. In simple economic terms demand outstripped supply. In addition, much of this upturn can be seen as the proliferation of a global economy with London at its centre. Many of the sectors studied in this thesis such as banking, insurance and transport witnessed growth as a result of this. Domestic and international factors thus exerted positive synergies which led to structural changes in London's economy and resulted in a sharp increase in the demand for clerical labour. The more intensive application of women and technology to office work was one consequence of this in an effort by organizations to keep costs down. Far from having harmful effects on the majority of male clerks, the consequences were benign. They kept costs down, were chiefly employed in routine and mechanical work, and thus provided leeway for increases in male clerical salaries and opportunities for promotion and career chances. Finally, as Chapter 4 has argued, the development of internal labour markets were also a factor in boosting clerical income. The extension of job security, which these markets entailed, combined with regular, semi-structured increments and career pathways, meant that for those clerks working in these internal markets total income increased over the entire course of their working lives.

It must be borne in mind, however, that the distribution and extent of these benefits were not uniform in London in the thirty-five years covered in this study. Some benefited more than others, and these benefits were more abundant in the first half of the period than they were in the latter. While this does not compromise the overall arguments put forward in this book, it does present limitations, and prevent one from constructing too rosy a picture of the London office and clerk.

In relation to the first, the growth of secondary labour markets should not be forgotten. While this was certainly an uneven process, with some sectors such as banking being unaffected, and others such as insurance and the post office being transformed, the bifurcation of the London clerical market was a constant feature of the period, and was one which continued and accelerated during the First World War and throughout the interwar period. It is interesting to note, for example, that Booth did not comment on this division of labour of clerical work in his study of London life and labour in the 1890s, whereas during the 30s this division had plainly been observed by the teams of investigators from the London School of Economics, and was subsequently highlighted in their section on London clerks.[4]

While the existent of a dual market predated this study, its growth was accompanied by a structural transformation between 1880 and 1914, as argued in Chapter 5, of a body made up predominantly of youths, to one comprised chiefly of women. Despite this, however, there were considerable numbers of men in these secondary markets. While this in itself was no inherent evil, the growth of these sectors allowed segments of society, particularly members of the working classes such as William Evans and his brothers, to enter white-collar work and achieve in their eyes social mobility,[5] this growing split invariably resulted in increasing inequalities in the clerical sector. Clerks in secondary positions did share in the benefits which issued from the growth in clerical work, they did not do so, however, equally, and it was this, as evidenced in the growth of clerical unions and associations, which galled and harrowed many clerical workers. The officers of the Assistant Clerks grade of the Civil Service, for instance, despised the fact that despite their secondary education and abilities, their ambitions for promotion, more demanding and responsible work, and increases in salaries were all denied to them because of a hierarchical structure which appeared to be based more on class rather than inherent merit.[6]

In relation to the extent of the increasing rewards of clerical work, there is evidence which strongly suggests that to some extent there was a contraction following 1900.

The growth of the Railway Clerks Association (R.C.A.) and the Assistant Clerks Association, and to a lesser extent the National Union of Clerks, the £200 Barrier Campaign amongst the officers of the L.C.C., the inauguration of the MacDonnell and the Holt Commissions by the government to investigate working conditions in the Civil Service and Post Office, and the increase in prices following the turn of the century all point to this. Much of the heady growth of the 1880s and 90s began to tailor off by 1900. The 1911 census, for example, while showing an overall small increase for male clerks in London, did actually reveal a reduction in male commercial clerks from 84,317 in 1901 to 82,027 in 1911.[7] Since these were by far the largest group of London clerks this fall was significant. While this did not invariably lead to lay-offs, pay cuts or cutbacks, it did mean that the rate of improvements which many clerks may have begun to have grown accustomed to began to slow down. Amongst the larger corporate employers, for instance, there was evidence of this. The R.C.A. argument that a diminishing of organic growth in the railways had led to a slowdown of promotion opportunities was an indication of how this adversely affected clerks.[8] For many of the larger organizations merger appeared to be the most logical solution. The marriage of the London and County Bank with the London and Westminster Bank in 1909, for example, was a sign of things to come. Following the First World War, for instance, there were major amalgamations across British businesses, including the Banking and Railway sectors.[9] These were often greeted with apprehension by clerks, fearful of the rationalizing tendencies which followed, often mixed with heavy doses of feminization.

A major argument of this book is that from the late nineteenth century, employers in large-scale bureaucratic organizations developed internal labour markets. In many of these concerns, both in the public and private sector, industrial welfare in the guise of pensions, provident funds, holiday pay, company magazines and leisure facilities such as sport and social clubs were introduced and encouraged in an effort to integrate staff into these bodies. At the sports club dinner of the London County and Westminster Bank in 1913, for instance, the chairman of the bank, Lord Goschen, gave a speech. Commenting on the enlargement of the pavilion on the bank's Norbury sports ground he observed,

> ... I should like to say that the directors, as I have said, think this is an object to which the bank can well contribute, because we believe that in furthering the interests of the Sports Club we are at the same time furthering the interests of the bank. Owing to the prosperity of the Sports Club we have a happier and healthier staff.[10]

Industrial welfare was a strategic response by these bodies to structural changes in their staffing operations and relations. Their aim was to build up a core of loyal, contented and productive staff. This was vital in relation to the heavy investment many had made in response to market (and political) conditions, and to the development of a new style of management which was evolving at the time in these new bureaucratic businesses and government bodies.

In addition, in relation to the growth of internal labour markets, there were important developments in the work that clerks performed for companies over the space of their entire working lives. Many employers assisted in the development of career structures for their clerical workers. This was still very much at a rudimentary stage and was in no way universal. In the pay structures devised by some, however, as seen in Chapter 2, and in the hierarchies and job titles that this entailed, one sees evidence of this. It is also disclosed in the tendency for companies to recruit more senior positions internally. In addition, the support that employers gave to commercial education, examined in Chapter 7, further facilitated this process. This support came in several guises; in direct provision such as by the railways, in collective support such as by the London Chamber of Commerce or the Institute of bankers or by the recognition and rewards that individual organizations gave to their employees for holding these qualifications. The establishment of career paths was another means by which companies and governmental offices hoped to integrate their clerks into their organizations. Such structures meant that for many, especially the more ambitious, clerical work was not a mindless repetition of tasks which individuals performed throughout their working lives in anonymous institutions. Instead, it was increasingly a pathway with goals and fixed agendas. By 1914 clerical labour markets, both internal and external, had been established in London and across the country. Their impact transformed the nature of office work.

This last point is extremely important for the final major question of this research, the reaction of clerical workers themselves to changes in their working environment. In 1998 the sociologist Richard Sennett brought out a book entitled, *The Corrosion of Character: The Personal Consequences of Work in the New Capitalism*.[11] The study was essentially an examination of office workers and professionals in the new working environment of the 1990s. Characterized by aspects such as 'discontinuous reinvention of institutions', 'flexible specialization' and 'concentration without centralization', terms one might add which are fully endorsed and used by modern corporations today, Sennett sharply contrasted the new working environment of instability, short-termism and insecurity with the system which had been in place for over 100 years before this. The latter was one defined by stability, order and continuity and can be broadly argued to reflect the system outlined in this research. The title of Sennett's fourth chapter was 'Illegible – Why Modern Forms of Labor are Difficult to Understand'.[12] Its importance for this study is clear. Clerical work in the period covered by this study was legible. It could clearly be understood as long as one played by the rules over the course of one's working life. It had clearly defined parameters, goals and signifiers. It could be mapped out from the ages of 16–65. Such 'legibility' can be seen in the poem 'The Seven Ages' written by a clerk at the London County Council in 1912. The poem was a parody of Jaques's soliloquy in Shakespeare's *As You Like It*, where the different phases of a man's life from birth to death are substituted by the different stages of a clerk's professional career from the junior (or novice) to retirement,

> The County Hall's a Stage
> And all the Staff are kept behind the scenes:
> They have their exits and their entrances.
> And some clerks do the work of two and three,
> For one man's wages. At first, the novice
> Thinking of home and school and prone to talk
> And shining morning face (for he at last
> Has won promotion). Then the Benedict
> Who runs the gauntlet with his office friends
> And settles down. And then the husband
> Full of fierce oaths and choking gall
> Because his Chief reveals no sympathy,
> With growing calls upon his beggared purse
> From year to year. And then the rebel who,
> With fiery mien and pallid brow

With eyes severe, suggests a flight abroad,
Where men breathe air and net a tidy hoard
And so he chucks his crib. The sixth age shifts
Into the lean and docile senior
With spectacles on nose and pipe in mouth,
His soul, subdued by sore philosophy
No longer soaring with ambitious spur
Resting content with what the gods bestow
And leaving youth to work. Last scene of all
That ends this strange eventful history
Is sad retirement and last farewell
Sans work, sans colleagues, and sans screw![13]

It was the realization and willingness of many clerical workers to accept these seven ages, to see one's job in the long-term in which one slowly edged up the organization which can explain much of their behaviour. This became the principal strategy which many took in relation to their work and which provided legibility and ontological coherence and stability.

Within this paradigm came values of loyalty (both to and from the company), service, professionalism, hierarchy, order, mobility, seniority, individualism and merit. From this was derived a strange mixture of conservatism and radicalism. Clerks were conservative because they played a long game. Because they saw their careers in terms of thirty or forty years, where income was regulated by scales and promotion was often dictated by seniority, they were opposed to any changes to the structures which shaped their working lives. Clerical workers were extremely sensitive towards any attempts by employers to change the goalposts such as altering recruitment policy, changing pay scales or attempting to bring in outsiders for senior positions. At the same time clerks were radical in their support for meritocracy and individualism and their almost visceral antipathy to anything that smacked of cronyism, patronage or nepotism. As seen in Chapters 7 and 8, meritocratic principles were crucial to clerks because they offered to a group low in economic capital but high in aspiration the opportunity for advancement in hierarchical working environments. The extent of their support has been seen in the support of some, when opportunities permitted, for white-collar unions and associations whose principal aims were often to protect and extend meritocratic principles at work. The campaign of the Assistant Clerks Association with support from the Second Division Clerks Association against the monopoly by privileged groups of First Division positions is an extremely good example of this.

On a more personal level, another key strategy of clerical workers was the development of the self, or in more contemporary terms, 'self-improvement'. This chiefly articulated itself in a commitment to education, which as has been argued was a defining feature of many clerical workers. This commitment, as has been seen in Chapter 7, was evidenced in the extent of participation in and support for higher and further education, particularly in the commercial sphere, by London clerks. It can also be evinced in their private study and reading, participation in sport, debating societies and other self-improvement and cultural groups, and the high literary and academic standards of the work which they produced and published in their journals which ranged in topic from rail electrification to paths and temples in Celtic Britain.[14]

In relation to work, the centrality of self-improvement articulated itself through the clerk's concept of professionalism. As argued in Chapter 3, clerks took great pride in the skills that they need to carry out their duties: accuracy, tidiness, detail, etc. The craft-based nature of clerical work was encouraged and enhanced by the developments outlined in this study. With the growth in complexity of business operations and office duties came new demands. To their basic skills, were added secondary proficiencies: typewriting and shorthand, indexing, languages, commercial geography, law, statistics. Further reinforcement of this process was provided by the growth of comprehensive structures of commercial education in London, recognition and reward by employees, and the gradual evolution of system of professional examinations, many of which were organized by the emerging clerical associations of this period. The degree of commitment to professionalism by the clerical workers in London can be seen in the extent of their participation in commercial education, as witnessed in Chapter 7.

This commitment also interlaced with their long-term approach. One important element here was their strong attachment to education for their offspring. Improvement and advancement was not just personal, it was also intergenerational. Reminiscent of what Bourdieu has termed 'social trajectory', the tendency of some social groups to project themselves over periods of time, a central strategy of clerks was investment in their children's education so as to guarantee them better opportunities and chances than they themselves enjoyed.[15] This is apparent in the examples of Mr Frank Lee and Mr Alfred Pyle. Both individuals were sons of clerks, both attended grammar schools at some sacrifice to their parents, and both went onto clerical careers which were improvements on what their fathers had achieved. Mr Frank Lee, whose father was a confectioner's clerk, became Principal Assistant to the Chief Accountant at the London Electricity Board, Mr Alfred Pyle, whose father was a railway clerk, went onto a career in the Civil Service. In this context, the expansion of secondary education and grammar schools in London was a great boost both psychologically and practically to its clerical workers.[16]

Finally, it should be noted that all these strategies which clerks developed and practised were aimed principally at one key goal, stability. While self-improvement and promotion certainly resulted in more money, that was not its chief aim. Of overriding importance to London clerical workers was their search for stability. Clerical workers were not, in the main, concerned with earning large sums of money or grandiose schemes of consumption. The principle aim of those married and with families (and for the majority of those single who aimed to become married and rear families) was to support and maintain a home at a decent level which was free of financial anxiety. Following the growing-up and departure of their children it was to prepare for a retirement which allowed a certain degree of independence. It is because of this that attempts to estimate clerical incomes and compare these with those of the working class are unhelpful. It was not the amount that clerks earned that was important. Charles Booth was probably right when he said that the majority of London clerks earned no more than artisans. It was the fact, however, that this income was stable, rose incrementally, and provided security thus enabling clerical workers to develop discursive strategies that emphasized education and long-term planning, and enabled a degree of consumption that allowed for a modicum of middle-class status and lifestyle, that was important. For many it may not have been a very glamorous or exciting life, but at least it was a safe one, which allowed for happiness within the confines of home and the community. As Frank Lee said in his later years,

> My parents always stressed the value of less money for a secure job, and apart from a very short period in my life I have always been fully employed and I've been very grateful for it. And looking back I suppose there are moments when I would have very much liked to have a more adventuresome and more colourful sort of life, but of course, I'm reaping the fruits of the … shall we say the years of monotony by the things that a secure job has.[17]

It is a sentiment that many of the clerks who have appeared in this book would have agreed with.

NOTES

Introduction

1. C. F. G. Masterman, *The Condition of England* (London: Methuen & Co., 1909), pp. 69–70.
2. *Census of England and Wales, Vol. III, Conditions as to Marriage, Occupations and Birthplaces of the People* (London: Her Majesty's Stationary Office, 1881), pp. 12–13, *Census of England and Wales, 1911, Volume X: Occupations and Industries Part 2* (London: His Majesty's Stationary Office, 1911), p. 293.
3. *Census of England and Wales, 1911, Volume X*, p. 383, p. 137, p. 432, p. 556, p. 191.
4. S. Webb, *London Education* (London: Longman, Green and Co.), pp. 99–100.
5. A. A. Jackson, *Semi-Detached London; suburban life, development and transport, 1900–1939* (London: Allen & Unwin, 1973), R. B. Pugh (ed.), *The Victoria History of the Counties of England: A History of the County of Essex Volume V* (London: The Institute of Historical Research, 1994), pp. 249–66, W. R. Powell (ed.), *The Victoria History of the Counties of England: A History of the County of Essex Vol VI* (London: The Institute of Historical Research, 1973), pp. 174–205.
6. H. J. Dyos, *Victorian Suburb A Study of the Growth of Camberwell* (Leicester: Leicester University Press, 1966), D. J. Olsen, *The Growth of Victorian London* (London: Batsford, 1976), J. White, *London in the 19th Century* (London: Vintage, 2008), pp. 67–98.
7. Masterman, *The Condition of England*, p. 70.
8. J. P. Cornford, 'The Transformation of Conservatism in the Late Nineteenth Century', *Victorian Studies*, 7 (1963), pp. 35–77.
9. S. Laurence, 'Moderates, Municipal Reformers and the Issue of Tariff Reform, 1889–1934', in A Saint (ed.), *Politics and the People of London: The London County Council, 1895–1965* (London: The Hambledon Press, 1989), pp. 93–102.
10. Masterman, *The Condition of England*, p. 74.
11. S. Szreter, *Fertility, Class and Gender in Britain, 1860–1940* (Cambridge: Cambridge University Press, 1996), for discussion of working conditions in textile industry in London's East End see D. Feldman, *Englishmen and Jews, Social Relations and Political Culture, 1840–1914* (New Haven, CT and London: Yale University Press, 1994), p. 206, See also T. Hunt, *Building Jerusalem The Rise & Fall of the Victorian City* (London: Wiedenfeld & Nicolson, 2004), ch. 9.
12. For a general historical discussion of leisure and popular culture see J. Hill, *Sport, Leisure and Culture in Twentieth Century Britain* (Basingstoke: Palgrave, 2002).
13. J. K. Chalaby, *The Invention of Journalism* (London: Macmillan, 1998), M. Hampton, *Visions of the Press in Britain, 1850–1950* (Urbana, IL: Illinois Press, 2005), J. Wild, *The*

Rise of the Office Clerk in Literary Culture, 1880–1939 (Basingstoke: Palgrave Macmillan, 2006).

14. F. Sheppard, *London A History* (Oxford: Oxford University Press, 1998), pp. 305–6. See also P. Hosgood, '"Doing the Shops" at Christmas: Women, Men and the Department Store in England, *c.* 1880–1914', in G. Crossick and J. Jaumain (eds), *Cathedrals of Consumption: the European Department Store, 1850–1939* (Aldershot: Ashgate, 1999), pp. 97–115.

15. J. Lowerson, *Sport and the English Middle Classes, 1870–1914* (Manchester: M.U.P., 1993).

16. S. Farrant, 'London by the Sea: Resort Development on the South Coast of England 1880–1939', *Journal of Contemporary History*, 22:1 (1987), pp. 137–62.

17. M. Weber, *Economy and Society, Volume 2* (Berkeley, CA: University of California Press, 1978), pp. 956–1005.

18. Ibid., p. 987.

19. Ibid., pp. 973–4.

20. B. G. Orchard, *The Clerks of Liverpool* (Liverpool: J. Collinson, 1871).

21. G. Anderson, *Victorian Clerks* (Manchester: Manchester University Press, 1976).

22. Orchard, *The Clerks of Liverpool*, p. 26.

23. F. D. Klingender, *The Condition of Clerical Labour in Britain* (London: Martin Lawrence, 1935).

24. For a discussion on Marx's writings on clerks see Ibid., pp. 105–7.

25. D. Lockwood, *The Blackcoated Worker: A Study in Class Conciousness* (Oxford: Clarendon, 1958).

26. Ibid., p. 35.

27. See J. H. Goldthorpe, D. Lockwood, F. Bechhofer, and J. Platt, *The Affluent Worker: Industrial Attitudes and Behaviour* (Cambridge: Cambridge University Press, 1968), A. Stewart, K. Prandy, and R. M. Blackburn, *Social Stratification and Occupations* (London: Macmillan, 1980), R. Crompton and G. Jones, *White-Collar Proletariat: Deskilling and Gender in Clerical Work* (London: Macmillan, 1984). See also H. Braverman, *Labor and Monopoly Capitalism* (New York: Monthly Review, 1974).

28. Ibid.

29. Anderson, *Victorian Clerks*.

30. R. G Wilson, *Disillusionment or New Opportunities? The Changing Nature of Work in Offices, Glasgow 1880–1914* (Aldershot: Ashgate Publishing Limited, 1998).

31. L. Holcombe, *Victorian Ladies at Work: Middle Class Working Women in England and Wales 1850–1914* (Newton Abbott: David & Charles, 1973).

32. G. Anderson (ed.), *The White-Blouse Revolution* (Manchester: Manchester University Press, 1988).

33. S. Cohn, *The Process of Occupational Sex-Typing: the Feminization of Clerical Labor in Great Britain* (Philadelphia, PA: Temple University Press, 1985).

34. E. Jordan, 'The Lady Clerks at the Prudential: The Beginning of Vertical Segregation by Sex in Clerical Work in Nineteenth-Century Britain', *Gender and History*, 8:1 (April 1996), pp. 65–81.

35. Cohn, *The Process of Occupational Sex-Typing*, ch. 3.

36. See S. Pennybacker, *A Vision for London 1889–1914: Labour Everyday Life and the L.C.C. Experiment* (London: Routledge, 1995), J. Pellew, *The Home Office 1848–1914 From Clerks to Bureaucrats* (London: Heinemann Educational Books, 1982) and D. King, *The History of the Hongkong and Shanghai Banking Corporation Volumes I and II* (Cambridge: Cambridge University Press, 1987).

37. P. Attewell, 'The Clerk Deskilled: A Study in False Nostalgia', *Journal of Historical Sociology*, 2:4 (1989), pp. 357–87.
38. See, for example, M. Savage, 'Career Mobility and Class Formation: British Banking Workers and the Lower Middle Classes', in A. Miles and D. Vincent (eds), *Building European Society Occupational Change and Social Mobility in Europe 1840–1940* (Manchester: Manchester University Press, 1993), pp. 196–216.
39. M. Savage, 'Discipline, Surveillance and the "Career": Employment in the Great Western Railway 1833–1914', in A. McKinlay and K. Starkey (eds), *Foucault, Management and Organisational Theory* (London: Sage, 1998), pp. 65–92, A. McKinlay, '"Dead Selves": The Birth of the Modern Career', *Organization*, 9:4 (2002), pp. 595–614.
40. Savage, 'Discipline, Surveillance and the "Career"', p. 67.
41. McKinlay, '"Dead Selves"', pp. 598–600.
42. Savage, 'Discipline, Surveillance and the "Career"', pp. 84–7, McKinlay, '"Dead Selves"', pp. 605–7, pp. 610–11.
43. Wild, *The Rise of the Office Clerk in Literary Culture, 1880–1939*.
44. Ibid., pp. 2–3.
45. In addition to Wild see K. Flint, 'Fictional Suburbia', in P. Humm, P. Stigant and P. Widdowson (eds), *Popular Fictions: Essays in Literature and History* (London: Methuen, 1986), pp. 111–26, P. Keating, *The Haunted Study: A Social History of the English Novel 1875–1914* (London: Secker & Warburg, 1989), pp. 303–18.
46. Ibid., ch. 5.
47. British Library, QD1/FLWE/183, P. Thompson and T. Vigne, *Family Life and Work Experience before 1918*, 'Mr. Frederick Henry Taylor'.
48. Interview with Jim Hancock at his home, 26 November 2001.
49. Essex Records Office, D/DU418/1, 'The Diaries of George Rose, 1900–14'.
50. London Borough of Southwark Archives, MS-1982/117, 'The Diary of Daniel McEwen, 1887–1910'.
51. London Guildhall Archives, MS-20382, 'The Diary of Andrew Carlyle Tait, 1893–94'.
52. London Borough of Hackney Archives Department, DS/EVA/1–3, 'The Diaries of William Evans, 1881–84, 1889–1900'.
53. S. Moseley, *The Private Diaries of Sydney Moseley* (London: Max Parish, 1960).
54. For a discussion of discourse theory in history see G. S. Jones, 'The Determinist Fix: Some Obstacles to the Further Development of the Linguistic Approach to History in the 1990s', *History Workshop Journal*, 42 (Autumn, 1996), pp. 19–35.
55. For an overview of Foucault see L. McNay, *Foucault A Critical Introduction* (Cambridge: Polity Press, 1994).
56. M. Foucault, *The Archaeology of Knowledge* (London: Tavistock, 1972).
57. See H. H. Gerth and C. W. Mills (eds), *From Max Weber: Essays in Sociology* (London: Routledge, 1991), pp. 180–95.
58. P. Bordieu, *Distinction A Social Critique of the Judgement of Taste* (London: Routledge, 1986).
59. See G. Crossick, 'The Emergence of the Lower Middle Class in Britain', in G. Crossick (ed.), *The Lower Middle Class in Britain 1870–1914* (London: Croom Helm, 1977).
60. *Fifty-Sixth Report of the Civil Service Commission on the Civil Service*; 1912–13, Cd. 6332, Vol. XV, 17 May 1912, p. 147.
61. See, for example, A. L. Bowley, *Wages and Income in the United Kingdom Since 1860* (Cambridge: Cambridge University Press, 1937), p. 127.

1 Changing Worlds and Changing People: A Definition of the Late Victorian and Edwardian London Clerk

1. *Clerk*, 1 August 1890, p. 58.
2. London Metropolitan Archives B/THB/F 3, 'Messers Truman, Hanbury, Buxton and Co., Brewer's Clerks Salaries and Rest Expenses, 1898–1920'.
3. T. R. Gourvish and R. G. Wilson, *The British Brewing Industry, 1830–1980* (Cambridge: Cambridge University Press, 1994), p. 238.
4. S. Mosley, *The Private Diaries of Sydney Moseley* (London: Max Parrish, 1960).
5. Archives of Prudential Plc, MS – 1292, 'Life Claim Department papers'.
6. E. A. Cope, *Clerks Their Rights and Obligations* (London: Sir Isaac Pitman and Sons, Ltd, 1909).
7. Ibid., p. 2.
8. Ibid., pp. 3–4.
9. Ibid., pp. 4–5.
10. Ibid., p. 5.
11. See T. E. Headrick, *The Town Clerk in English Local Government* (London: George Allen & Unwin Ltd., 1962), pp. 198–9.
12. *Office*, October 1889, p. 259.
13. London School of Economics and Political Science, *New Survey of London Life and Labour, Vol. VII* (London: P. S. King and Son Ltd, 1934), p. 272.
14. Ibid., p. 273.
15. British Library, *Millennium Memory Bank*, C900/07507, 'Arthur Whitlock'.
16. *The Private Diaries of Sydney Moseley*, p. 16.
17. H. Gospel, *Markets, Firms and the Management of Labour in Modern Britain* (Cambridge: Cambridge University Press, 1992).
18. See Orchard, *The Clerks of Liverpool*, ch. X.
19. Savage, 'Discipline, Surveillance and the "Career"', p. 81.
20. Cohn, *The Process of Occupational Sex-Typing*. E. Jordan, 'The Lady Clerks at the Prudential: The Beginning of Vertical Segregation by Sex in Clerical Work in Nineteenth-Century Britain', *Gender and History*, 8:1 (1996), pp. 65–81.
21. *Fourth Report of the Royal Commission on the Civil Service*, 1914, Cd 7378 Vol. XVI, p.12.
22. Ibid., p. 28.
23. Ibid., pp. 19–22.
24. *Clerk*, February 1912, p. 24.
25. See P. Attewell, 'The Clerk Deskilled: A Study in False Nostalgia', *Journal of Historical Sociology*, 2:4 (1989), pp. 357–87.
26. *The Private Diaries of Sydney Moseley*, p. 38.
27. For changes in company structure and organization see J. F. Wilson, *British Business History, 1720–1994* (Manchester: Manchester University Press, 1995), ch. 4.
28. R. C. Michie, *The City of London* (London: Macmillan Academic and Professional Ltd., 1992), p. 14.
29. Ibid., p. 17.
30. London Guildhall Library, *The City of London Day Census, 1911 Report*, p. 41.
31. See Michie, *The City of London*, ch. 1.

32. A. Lewis, 'The Rate of Growth of World Trade, 1830–1973', in S. Grassman and E. Lundberg (eds), *The World Economic Order: Past and Prospects* (London: The Macmillan Press Ltd, 1981), pp. 49–50.

33. Michie, *The City of London* . D. Kynaston, *The City of London Volume II Golden Years 1890–1914* (London: Pimlico, 1995).

34. Michie, p. 34.

35. Ibid.

36. Kynaston, *The City of London*, p. 17.

37. Michie, p. 39.

38. See J. Harris, *Private Lives, Public Spirit: A Social History of Britain, 1870–1914* (Oxford: Oxford University Press, 1993), ch. 7–8.

39. B. V. Humphreys, *Clerical Unions in the Civil Service* (London: Blackwell and Mott, 1958), p. 229.

40. J. Pellew, p. 77.

41. Ibid., p. 95.

42. For the growth of Ilford in this period see A. A. Jackson, *Semi-Detached London Suburban Development, Life and Transport, 1900–39* (London: George Allen & Unwin Ltd., 1973), ch. 4.

43. T. Byrne, *Local Government in Britain* (London: Penguin, 2000), p. 21.

44. See P. L. Payne, 'The Emergence of the Large Scale Company in Great Britain, 1870–1914', *Economic History Review*, 20:3 (1967), pp. 519–42. See also Wilson, *British Business History*, ch. 4.

45. Chandler, *Scale and Scope*.

46. J. F. Davis, *Bank Organisation, Management and Accounts* (London: Sir Isaac Pitman and Sons, 1910), p. 5.

47. E. Green, *Debtors to their Profession: A History of The Institute of Bankers 1879–1979* (London: Methuen & Co. Ltd., 1979), p.87 and p. 89.

48. See The Royal Bank of Scotland Group (hereafter RBSG) Archives GB 1502/WES/125/12 'London, County and Westminster Bank Staff Register 1911–12'.

49. W. S. Chevalier, *London's Water Supply, 1903–53: A Review of the Works of the Metropolitan Water Board* (London: Staple Press Ltd, 1953), p. 331.

50. See Sir J. G. Broadbank, *History of the Port of London* (London: Daniel O'Connor, 1921), ch. XXXI.

51. L. Dennett, *A Sense of Security: 150 Years of Prudential* (Cambridge: Granta Editions, 1998), p.155.

52. National Archives, RAIL 253/140, 'Great Western Railway Classification of Station Masters, Goods Agents and Clerks, 1922'.

53. See P. Bagwell, *The Railway Clearing House in the British Economy, 1842–1922* (London: George Allen and Unwin, 1968), p. 139.

54. London Guildhall Library, *The City of London Day Census, 1911*, p. 41.

55. See J. E. Martin, *Greater London: An industrial geography* (London: G. Bell and Sons, 1966).

56. Michie, *The City of London* p. 21.

57. London Guildhall Library, MS-11,069D, 'Antony Gibbs and Sons Ltd, Liverpool House: papers relating to the closure of Liverpool House in 1908'.

58. British Library, *Millennium Mind Bank*, C900/07507, 'Arthur Whitlock'.

59. F. B. Crouch, *From School to Office, Written for Boys* (London: Effingham Wilson & Co., 1890), p. 13.

60. H. Greaves, *The Commercial Clerk and His Success* (London: Cassell & Co., 1909), p. 7.
61. Ibid., particularly chapters 1–3.
62. *Report from the Royal Commission on the Civil Service 1914*, p. 28.
63. Ibid.
64. J. Pellew, *The Home Office 1848–1914*, p. 88.
65. Ibid., ch. 5.
66. G. Clifton, 'Members and Officers of the L.C.C., 1889–1965', in A. Saint (ed.), *Politics and the People of London: The London County Council, 1889–1965* (London: The Hambeldon Press, 1989), pp. 9–10.
67. London Metropolitan Archives, CL/ESTAB/1/393, 'Report of the Establishment Committee, 20ᵗʰ July, 1905, Officials of the Central Office on Yearly Salaries'.
68. London Metropolitan Archives, CL/ESTAB/1/393, 'Report of the Establishment Committee, 20ᵗʰ July, 1905,Temporary and Other Assistants at Weekly Salaries'.
69. London Metropolitan Archives, CL/ESTAB/1/393, 'L.C.C. Establishment Committee Papers, 21ˢᵗ July 1898'.
70. See the evidence of Mr. E. Phipps, Principal Assistant Secretary of the Elementary Education Branch of the Board of Education, *Fifty-Sixth Report of the Civil Service Commission*; 1912–13 Cd. 6332, Vol. XV, 26 April 1912.
71. J. Simmons and G. Biddle (eds), *The Oxford Companion to British Railway History* (Oxford: Oxford University Press, 1997), p. 431.
72. P. Wardley, 'The Emergence of Big Business: The Largest Corporate Employers of Labour in the United Kingdom, Germany and the United States, c. 1907', *Business History*, 41:4 (1999), pp. 88–116.
73. *The Railway Clerk*, June 1911, p. 119.
74. See A. A. Jackson, *Semi-detached London*, ch. 4.
75. *The Great Eastern Magazine*, 1914, p. 43.
76. Ibid., 1911, p. 110.
77. Railway Clerks Association, *The Life of a Railway Clerk, Some Interesting Facts and Figures*, London: The Railway Clerks Association, 1911), p. 31.
78. *The Railway News*, 'Education and Advancement of the Railway Clerk', 1910.
79. Ibid.
80. *The Great Eastern Railway Magazine*, September 1912 to May 1914.
81. *Sydney Moseley*, p. xi.
82. See Humphreys, *Clerical Unions in the Civil Service*, pp. 54–8. See also E. Phipp's evidence in *Fifty-Sixth Report of the Civil Service Commission*, 26 April 1912.
83. Ibid. See also *Red Tape*, 1911–14, journal of the Assistant Clerks Association.
84. See M. Wallace, *Single or Return? The History of the Transport Salaried Staffs' Association* (London: Transport Salaried Staffs' Association, 1996), ch. 1–6.
85. *Clerk*, August 1890, p. 3.

2 The Clerk, the Office and Work: Changing Horizons

1. H. Braverman, *Labor and Monopoly Capitalism* (New York: Monthly Review Press, 1974), Anderson, *Victorian Clerks*, R. Guerriero, *Disillusionment or New Opportunities? The Changing Nature of Work in Offices, Glasgow 1880–1914* (Aldershot: Ashgate, 1999).
2. P. Attewell, 'The Clerk Deskilled: A Study in False Nostalgia', *Journal of Historical Sociology*, 2:4 (1989), pp. 357–87.

3. R. Fulford, *Glyn's: 1753–1953* (London: Macmillan and Co Ltd, 1953), p. 168.
4. See E. A. Cope, *Clerks Their Rights and Obligations* (London: Sir Isaac Pitman and Sons, Ltd, 1909), p. 6.
5. RBSG Archives GB 1502/LWB/113, 'London & Westminster rules and regulations, 1909'.
6. F. H. H. King, *The History of the Hongkong and Shanghai Banking Corporation, Vol. I* (Cambridge: Cambridge University Press, 1987), p. 597.
7. E. A. Cope, *Clerks Their Rights and Obligations*.
8. RBSG Archives GB 1502/GM/339/1, 'Glyn's Bank, Clerk's Register, 1864–1918'.
9. Ibid., GB 1502/GM/710/1 'Glyn's Bank Town Office Annual Reports, 1896–1911'.
10. R. Fitzgerald, *British Industrial Management and Industrial Welfare 1846–1975* (London: Croom Helm, 1988), H. Jones, 'Employer's Welfare Schemes and Industrial Relations in Interwar-Britain', *Business History*, 25:1 (1983), pp. 61–75, N. Mandell, *The Corporation as Family: The Gendering of Corporate Welfare 1890–1930* (Chapel Hill, NC: University of North Carolina Press, 2002).
11. Fitzgerald, *British Industrial Management and Industrial Welfare 1846–1975*.
12. Ibid. See also GB 1502/LWB/113, 'London and Westminster Rules and Regulations, 1909'. For an overall discussion of the development of pensions see L. Hannah, *Inventing Retirement: the development of occupational pensions in Britain* (Cambridge: Cambridge University Press, 1986).
13. See G. S. Layard, 'A Lower Middle Class Budget', in *Cornhill Magazine*, 10 (1901), p. 666.
14. Interview with Jim Hancock at his home, 26 November 2001.
15. M. Heller, 'Sports, Bureaucracies and London Clerks 1880–1939', *International Journal of the History of Sport*, 25:5 (2008), pp. 579–614.
16. See R. Holt, *Sport and the British: A Modern History* (Oxford: Oxford University Press, 1989), J. Lowerson, *Sport and the English Middle Classes 1870–1914* (Manchester: Manchester University Press, 1993). See also R. J. Morris, 'Clubs, Societies and Associations', in F. M. L. Thompson (ed.), *The Cambridge Social History of Britain 1750–1950 Vol. 3* (Cambridge: Cambridge University Press, 1990), pp. 395–443.
17. National Arhvies RAIL 258/237 'Great Western Railway (London) Athletic Association, 1900–47'.
18. Ibid.
19. *The County and Westminster Magazine*, 1911, p. 6.
20. Ibid.
21. L. Dennet, *A Sense of Security: 150 Years of Prudential* (Cambridge: Granta Editions, 1998), p. 87.
22. Ibid., pp. 156–61. See also *The Ibis Magazine*, 1878–1914.
23. *County Magazine* (1908), p. 107.
24. Ibid., p. 87.
25. Ibid., 1913, p. 173.
26. See advert for L.C.C. Cricket Club Colours in *The London County Council Gazette*, April 1904.
27. Ibid., 1911, p. 108.
28. See 'Sport, Matrimony and Domestic Bliss', in *County Magazine* (1909), pp. 6–8.
29. Heller, 'Sports, Bureaucracies and London Clerks 1880–1939'.
30. E. H. Schein, *Organizational Culture and Leadership* (London: Jossey-Bass, 2004), M. Alvesson, *Cultural Perspectives on Organisations* (Cambridge: Cambridge University

Press, 1995), M. Rowlinson and S Procter, 'Organisational Culture and Business History', *Organisational Studies*, 20:3 (1999), pp. 369–96.

31. Heller, pp. 586–600.
32. Weber, *Economy and Society*, p. 959.
33. *London County Council Gazette*, December 1904, p. 172.
34. *Sports Club Review*, April 1923, pp. 122–3.
35. T. E. Young and R. Masters, *Insurance Office Organisation, Management and Accounts* (London: Sir Isaac Pitman & Sons, 1904), p. 10.
36. Ibid., p. 46.
37. See National Archives RAIL 258/237 'Great Western Railway (London) Athletic Association, 1900–47'. See also R. J. Morris, 'Clubs, Societies and Associations', pp. 412–3.
38. See L. Goschen's speech in *The County and Westminster Magazine*, 1913, p. 173.
39. Savage, 'Discipline, Surveillance and the "Career"', pp. 65–6.
40. McKinlay, '"Dead Selves": The Birth of the Modern Career', *Organization*, 9:4 (2002), pp. 595–614.
41. Savage, 'Discipline, Surveillance and the "Career"', pp. 66–7.
42. Weber, *Economy and Society*, p. 975.
43. Ibid., p. 968.
44. A. D. Chandler, Jr., *The Visible Hand: The Managerial Revolution in American Business* (Cambridge, Massachusetts: Harvard University Press, 1974).
45. H. Gospel, *Markets, Firms and the Management of Labour in Modern Britain* (Cambridge: Cambridge University Press, 1992).
46. Ibid., pp. 26–30.
47. Ibid., p. 30.
48. National Archives, RAIL 258/400, 'Great Western Railway Clerical Staff: recruiting, examination of, 1877–1914'.
49. Ibid., Letter 'Appointment of Clerical Staff', from G. K. Mill, 12 November 1900.
50. Ibid., Letter of M. F. Staines to The Secretary, 22 February 1901.
51. Ibid., Letter of A. W. Solten to G.K. Mills, 14 November 1900.
52. Savage, 'Discipline, Surveillance and the "Career"', McKinlay, '"Dead Selves"'.
53. Ibid., pp. 601–11.
54. Weber, *Economy and Society*, p. 968.
55. RBSGA GB 1502/NAT/174/1–46, 'Staff Record Cards of the National Provincial Bank Ltd'.
56. S. Smiles, *Self-Help* (London: Murray, 1859).
57. *Fourth Report of the Royal Commission on the Civil Service*, 1914 Cd 7338, Vol. XVI, p. 16 and p. 19.
58. RBSG Archives GB 1502/LWB/113, 'London and Westminster Rules and Regulations, 1909'.
59. W. S. Chevalier, *London's Water Supply, 1903–53: A Review of the Metropolitan Water Board* (London: Staple Press Ltd, 1953), p. 333.
60. London Metropolitan Archives B/THB/F/3 'Messers Truman, Hanbury, Buxton and Co., Brewers Clerks Salaries and Rest Expenses, 1898–1920'.
61. London Borough of Hackney Archives Department, DS/EVA/1–3, 'The Diaries of William Evans', 11 December 1897 and 10 December 1898.
62. See B. V. Humphreys, *Clerical Unions in the Civil Service* (London: Blackwell and Mott, 1958) and M. Wallace, *Single or Return The History of the Transport Salaried Staffs' Association* (London: Transport Salaried Staffs' Association, 1996).
63. P. Attewell, 'The Clerk Deskilled'.

64. R. C. Michie, *The City of London, Continuity and Change, 1850–1990* (London: Macmillan Academic and Professional Ltd., 1992), p. 42.
65. See *L. R. Dicksee,* Office Organisation and Management (London: Sir Isaac Pitman and Sons Ltd., 1910), *chapter V.*
66. *Clerk*, February 1908, p. 25.
67. Ibid., January 1908, p. 8.
68. National Archives, RAIL 264/8, 'Great Western Railway Register of Clerks, 1835–1911'.
69. Archives of Prudential Plc, MS–1292 'Life Claim Department Papers'
70. Guildhall Library, MS–20383, 'Diary of Andrew Carlyle Tait', 13 September 1894.
71. Ibid., no date given, last written entry.
72. See Young and Masters, *Insurance Office Organisation*, pp. 27–8.
73. RBSG Archives GB 1502/WES/20 'Clerk H Letters (London and County)'.
74. See R. R. Locke, *The End of the Practical Man, Entrepreneurship and Higher Education in Germany, France, and Great Britain, 1880–1940* (Greenwich, Connecticut: Jai Press Inc., 1984).
75. *The History of the Hongkong and Shanghai Banking Corporation, Vol. II*, pp. 182–3.
76. See J. F. Davis, *Bank Organisation and Accounts* (London: Sir Isaac Pitman and Sons, 1910), Ch. 8.
77. See Cohn, *The Process of Occupational Sex-Typing*, ch. 4.
78. Ibid., p. 24.
79. Ibid.
80. Ibid.
81. RBSG Archives GB 1502/GM/339/1,'Glyn's clerks register, 1864–1918'.
82. Ibid.
83. Ibid.
84. Ibid.
85. E. A. Cope, *Clerks Their Rights and Obligations*, p. 78.
86. Ibid.
87. F. H. H. King, *The History of the Hongkong and Shanghai Bank, Vol. I*, p. 574.
88. Ibid. Vol. II, p. 176.
89. See J. A. Mangan's, *Athleticism in the Edwardian Public School: The Emergence and Consolidation of an Educational Ideology* (Cambridge: Cambridge University Press, 1981).
90. RBSG Archives GB 1502/LWB/116/17 'London and Westminster establishment committee minute book 1903 to 1904'.
91. F. H. H. King, *Vol. II*, p. 178.
92. L. Dennet, *A Sense of Security: 150 Years of Prudential* (Cambridge: Granta Editions, 1998), p. 85.
93. D. King, *Vol. II*, p. 176.
94. Essex Records Office, D/DU4/8/1, 'Diaries of George Rose', 28 December 1902.
95. British Library, *Millennium Memory Bank*, C900/07507 'Arthur Whitlock'.
96. S. Moseley, *The Private Diaries of Sydney Moseley* (London: Max Parish, 1960), p. 11.
97. R. Fulford, *Glyn's: 1753–1953*, p. 184.
98. Ibid., p. 172.
99. G. Rose Diaries, 25 May 1910.
100. See Ibid., 7–21 January 1902.
101. S. Moseley, 6 June 1906.
102. RBSG Archives GB 1502/GM/339/1, 'Glyn's clerks register 1864–1918'.

3 Attitudes of the Clerk towards Work

1. See Anderson, *Victorian Clerks*, P. Attewell, 'The Clerk Deskilled: A Study in False Nostalgia', *Journal of Historical Sociology*, 2:4 (1989), pp. 357–87, R. Guerriero *Wilson, Disillusionment or New Opportunities? The Changing Nature of Work in Offices, Glasgow 1880–1914* (Aldershot: Ashgate, 1998).
2. J. Harris, *Private Lives, Public Spirits – A Social History of Britain 1870 to 1914* (Oxford: Oxford University Press, 1993), p. 124.
3. See Holcombe, *Victorian Ladies at Work*, p. 12.
4. *Office*, 13 October, p. 4.
5. See R. G. Acock's letter 'Machinery and Clerical Labour', in *Clerk*, March 1910, p. 38.
6. F. Mckenna, *The Railway Workers 1840–1970* (London: Faber, 1980), p. 105.
7. T. R. Gourvish and R. G. Wilson, *The British Brewing Industry 1830–1980* (Cambridge: Cambridge University Press), p. 197.
8. Crossick, 'The Emergence of the Lower Middle Class in Britain', p. 30.
9. Ibid.
10. See The Royal Bank of Scotland Group Archives GB 1502/00748, 'Rules and Regulations to be Observed by the Officers of the London and County Banking Company, Limited, 1908'.
11. See C. Breward, 'Sartorial Spectacle: clothing and masculine identities in the imperial city, 1860–1914', in F. Driver and D. Gilbert (eds), *Imperial Cities Landscape, Display and Identity* (Manchester: Manchester University Press, 1999), pp. 244–52.
12. See H, *Victorian Ladies at Work*, p. 149.
13. See R. N. Price, 'Society, Status and Jingoism: The Social Roots of Lower Middle Class Patriotism', in G. Crossick (ed.), *The Lower Middle Class in Britain 1870–1914* (London: Croom Helm, 1977).
14. See J. Schneer, *London 1900 The Imperial Metropolis* (New Haven, CT and London: Yale University Press, 1999), ch. 4.
15. See J. Davis, 'The Progressive Council, 1889–1907', in A. Saint (ed.), *The London County Council 1889–1965* (London: The Hambledon Press, 1989).
16. *The L.C.C. Staff Gazette*, February 1900, p. 13.
17. *The Great Eastern Railway Magazine*, July 1911, pp. 213–4.
18. *Office*, 15 May 1889, p. 101.
19. See H. Perkin, *The Rise of Professional Society: England Since 1880* (London: Routledge, 1989).
20. *The London County Council Staff Gazette*, January 1914, p. 7.
21. Interview with Jim Hancock at his home, 26 November 2001.
22. BANKER, *The Bankers Clerk* (London: Houlston and Sons, 1877), pp. 127–9.
23. See F. B. Crouch, *From School to Office* (London: Effingham Wilson & Co., 1890), ch. 1. See also H. Greaves, *The Commercial Clerk and His Success* (London: Cassell & Co., 1909), Chapter 1.
24. Archives of Prudential Plc MS – 1292, 'Life Claim Department papers'.
25. *The L.C.C. Staff Gazette*, January 1900, p. 4.
26. S. Moseley, *The Private Diaries of Sydney Moseley* (London: Max Parish, 1960) p. 3 and p. 9.
27. Essex Records Office, D/DU 4/8/1, 'The Diaries of George Rose', 1 December 1904,
28. London Borough of Southwark Archives, 'The Diary of Daniel McEwen', 2 January 1890.

29. *The L.C.C. Staff Gazette*, February 1900, p. 19.
30. T. E. Young and R. Masters, *Insurance Office Organisation, Management and Accounts* (London: Sir Isaac Pitman & Sons, Ltd, 1904), pp. 20–1.
31. Interview with Jim Hancock.
32. For a discussion of Victorian Manliness see J. Tosh, 'What Should Historians do with Masculinity? Reflections on Nineteenth Century Britain', in *History Workshop*, 1994, 38, pp. 179–202. See also Tosh, *A Man's Place. Masculinity and the Middle Class Home in Victorian England* (New Haven, CT and London: Yale University Press, 1999).
33. For a discussion of the importance of character to Victorian society and its morals see S. Collini, *Public Moralists, Political Thought and Intellectual Life in Britain 1850–1930* (Oxford: Clarendon Press, 1991), ch. 3.
34. Ibid.
35. See *Railway Clerk*, August 1904, p. 87.
36. See *Bankers Clerk*, p. 133.
37. 'The Diaries of George Rose', 12 January 1903.
38. T. E. Young and R. Masters, *Insurance Office Organisation, Management and Accounts*, p. 26.
39. London Metropolitan Archives, LCC/MIN/4633, 'LCC Establishment Committee Papers, 1898'.
40. *Office*, 15 May 1889, p. 101.
41. Young and Masters, *Insurance Office Organisation*, p. 10.
42. See speech of Mr. Dickenson, Chairman of the London County Council in *The London County Council Gazette*, July 1900, p. 77. See also J. A. Managan, *Athleticism in the Edwardian Public School: The Emergence and Consolidation of an Edwardian Ideology* (Cambridge: Cambridge University Press, 1981).
43. Young and Masters, p. 46.
44. 'George Rose Diaries', 6 January 1906.
45. See, for example ibid., 12 July 1902.
46. F. H. H. King, *The History of the Hongkong and Shanghai Banking Corporation Vol. I* (Cambridge: Cambridge University Press, 1987), p. 574.
47. British Libray, *Paul Thompson and Thea Vigne Interviews, Family Life and Work Experience before 1918*, QD1/FLWE/63, 'Alfred Henry Pyle'.
48. Interview with Jim Hancock.
49. W. Howarth, *Our Banking System and Clearing Houses* (London: Effingham Wilson, 1907), pp. 27–8.
50. *County Magazine* (1909), p. 5.
51. See Shneer, *London 1900*, ch. 4.
52. *Ilford Guardian*, 24 March 1900.
53. London Borough of Redbridge Library, *Ilford, Including Seven Kings and Goodmayes*, The Official Publication of the Urban District Council, 1911.
54. 'The Diary of George Rose', 28 February 1913.
55. See *County Magazine*, 1 (1907), p. 15.
56. National Archives RAIL 258/400 'Great Western Railway Clerical Staff: recruiting, examination of, 1877–1914'.
57. See 'George Rose', 3 January 1907. See also 'Civil Service Sketches No. 2 Promoted', in *Red Tape*, November 1911, pp. 4–5.
58. W. P. Ridge, *69 Birnam Road* (London: Hodder and Stroughton, 1908).
59. *The L.C.C. Staff Gazette*, February 1914, p. 31.

60. See Ridge, *69 Birnam Road*. See also Crossick, 'The Emergence of the Lower Middle Class in Britain', p. 31.
61. See 'Civil Service Sketches No. 5 – Marriage', in *Red Tape*, February 1912, pp. 6–7.
62. 'Diaries of George Rose', 18 December 1905.
63. Ibid. 3 January 1906.
64. L.C.C. Establishment Committee Papers, 14 July 1898.
65. RBSG Archives GB 1502/ GM/339/1 'Glyn's clerks register 1864–1918'
66. See London Metropolitan Archives, Andrews, C. D. and G. C. Burge, *Progress Report, 1909–1959: The First Fifty Years in the History of the L.C.C. Staff Association*, Privately Published.
67. Ibid., p. 15.
68. *The L.C.C. Staff Gazette*, February 1914, p. 32.
69. Ibid.
70. See *Red Tape*, July 1912, p. 6.
71. Anderson, *Victorian Clerks*.
72. P. Attewell, 'The Clerk Deskilled'.
73. *The County Magazine*, 1907, p. 15.
74. L.C.C. Establishment Committee Papers, 14 July 1898.
75. 'George Rose', 29 March 1909.
76. *Clerk*, March 1908, p. 35.
77. F. H. H. King, *The History of the Hongkong and Shanghai Banking Corporation Vol. II.*, p. 182.
78. *Clerk*, January 1908, p. 6.
79. National Archives RAIL 258/400, 'Great Western Railway Clerical Staff'.
80. J. Pellew, *The Home Office 1848–1914* (London: Heinemann, 1982), p. 117.
81. H. Greaves, *The Commercial Clerk and His Success*, p. 11.
82. P. Thompson and T. Vigne Interviews, QD1/FLWE/161, 'Geoffrey Rogers'.
83. See RBSG Archives GB 1502/GM/339/1, 'Glyn's Clerk's Register, 1864–1918'.
84. For a discussion of middle-class occupational masculinity see L. Davidoff and C. Hall, *Family Fortunes* (London: Century Hutchinson Ltd., 1987).
85. For the growth of a sensationalist form of journalism and press in this period see J. Chalaby, *The Invention of Journalism* (London: Macmillan, 1998).

4 Work, Income, Promotion and Stability: The Late Victorian and Edwardian London Clerk Revisited.

1. See for example Anderson, *Victorian Clerks*.
2. See especially *Clerk* and *Railway Clerk*.
3. See *Clerk*, in particular its first two editions.
4. F. D. Kilingender, *The Condition of Clerical Labour in Britain* (London: Martine Lawrence, 1935), H. Braverman, *Labor and Monopoly Capital: The Degradation of Work in the Twentieth Century* (New York: Monthly Review Press, 1974), Anderson, *Victorian Clerks*.
5. R. G. Wilson, *Disillusionment or New Opportunities? The Changing Nature of Work in Offices, Glasgow 1880–1914* (Aldershot: Ashgate Publishing Limited, 1998).
6. *Clerk*, January 1908, p. 2.
7. Ibid., "The Clerk and Trade Unionism," February, p. 26.

8. Crossick, 'The Emergence of the Lower Middle Class in Britain', p. 22.
9. Archives of the Prudential Plc, MS-7, 'Minutes Book, 29th December, 1870,' MS-11, 'Minutes Book, 17th January, 1880'.
10. The Royal Bank of Scotland Group Archives (hereafter RBSGA) GB 1502/GM/00748, 'Rules and Regulations to be Observed by the Officers of the London and County Banking Company Limited, 1908.' For the Prudential see L. Dennett, *A Sense of Security: 150 Years of Prudential* (Cambridge: Granta Editions, 1988), p. 85. See also E. Jordan, 'The Lady Clerks at the Prudential: The Beginning of Vertical Segregation by Sex in Clerical Work in Nineteenth-Century Britain', *Gender and History*, 8:1 (April 1996), pp. 65–81.
11. G. Clifton, 'Members and Officers of the L.C.C., 1889–1965', in A. Saint (ed.), *Politics and the People of London: The London County Council, 1889–1965* (London: The Hambeldon Press, 1989), p. 17.
12. L. R. Dicksee, *Office Organisation and Management* (London: Sir Isaac Pitman and Sons Ltd., 1910).
13. Essex Records Office, D/DU 4/8/1, 'The Diaries of George Rose', December – January 1900–1.
14. For the importance of contacts in obtaining good clerical positions see the magazine *Business Life*, June 1904, p. 280, held at the British Library.
15. London Metropolitan Archives, *L.C.C. Minutes of Proceeding*, 1908, pp. 1340–2.
16. RSBGA, GB 1502/WES/271, 'Report comparing the pay, holiday and pensions of staff of London and County Bank and London and Westminster Bank, compiled after the merger of the two banks, c. 1909.'
17. Crossick, 'The Emergence of the Lower Middle Class in Britain', p. 18.
18. Bowley, *Wages and Income in the United Kingdom*, p. 31.
19. Cohn, *The Process of Occupational Sex-Typing*, pp. 73–7.
20. E. Canaan, A. L. Bowley, F. Y. Edgeworth, H. B. L. Smitth, W. R. Scott, 'The Amount and Distribution of Income (other than wages) Below the Income Tax Exemption Limit in the United Kingdom', *Journal of the Royal Statistical Society*, LXXIV (1910–11), pp. 37–66.
21. Anderson, *Victorian Clerks*, pp. 24–5.
22. Jordan, 'The Lady Clerks at the Prudential'.
23. For the Civil Service see Parliamentary Papers, *Reports from the Royal Commission on the Civil Service*, 1914, Cd 7338, Vol. XVI. See also B. V. Humphreys, *Clerical Unions in the Civil Service* (London: Blackwell and Mott, 1958). For the L.C.C. see London Metropolitan Archives, L.C.C./MIN4666, London County Council Establishment Committee Papers, 8 May 1906, p. 1202. See also G. Clifton, "Members and Officers of the L.C.C., 1889–1965".
24. London Metropolitan Archives, ACC/3527/179, 'Lyons, Wages for Clerks at Cadby Hall and Olympia, 1895–1901'.
25. *Clerk*, November 1912, p. 5.
26. Cohn, *The Process of Occupational Sex-Typing*, and Jordan, 'The Lady Clerks at the Prudential'.
27. Cohn, *The Process of Occupational Sex-Typing*, p. 67.
28. Jordan, 'The Lady Clerks at the Prudential', p. 67.
29. See Railway Clerks Association, *The Life of a Railway Clerk Some Interesting Facts and Figures* (London: Privately Published by the Railway Clerks Association, 1911), p. 2. See also *Red Tape*, July 1912, 16, and February 1913, p. 69, held at the British Library.
30. Ibid. See also *The Railway Clerk*, August 1911, p. 162.

31. *Bank Officer*, "Cost of Living," May 1920, p. 7, held at the British Library.
32. Ibid., February, p. 25.
33. Ibid., and Anderson, *Victorian Clerks*.
34. T. Alborn, 'Quill Driving: British Life Insurance Clerks and Occupational Mobility, 1800–1914', *Business History Review*, 82 (Spring 2008), pp. 31–58.
35. For L.C.C. see S. Pennybacker, *A Vision for London 1889–1914: Labour Everyday Life and the L.C.C. Experiment* (London: Routledge, 1995).
36. *L.C.C. Staff Gazette*, April 1906, 46, held at the British Library.
37. London Metropolitan Archives, London County Council, 18.6 Minutes of Proceedings, p. 15 December 1908, 'General Purpose Committee Report', p. 1340.
38. Ibid., p. 1341.
39. Sir H. Howard, *The London County Council from Within: Forty Years' Official Recollections* (London: Chapman & Hall Ltd., 1932), p. 66.
40. Ibid., p. 68.
41. Ibid., p. 66.
42. *The L.C.C. Staff Gazette*, February 1902, 14.
43. G. Anderson, 'The Social Economy of Late-Victorian Clerks', in G. Crossick (ed.), *The Lower Middle Class in Britain*, p. 115.
44. A. D. Chandler, *Scale and Scope The Dynamics of Industrial Capitalism* (Cambridge. Massachusetts: Harvard University Press, 1994).
45. Clifton, 'Members and Officers of the L.C.C., 1889–1965'.
46. London Metropolitan Archives, CL/ESTAB/1/393, 'L.C.C. Establishment Committee Papers, 21st July, 1898'.
47. *The Railway News*, 8 October 1910.
48. Cohn, *The Process of Occupational Sex-Typing*, pp. 77–81,
49. Jordan, p. 67.
50. Savage, 'Career Mobility and Class Formation'.
51. Ibid., p. 203.
52. Ibid., p. 201.
53. J. F. Davis, *Bank Organisation, Management and Accounts* (London: Sir Isaac Pitman and Sons Ltd., 1910).
54. For evidence of this see the staff cards of the National Provincial Bank, RBSGA GB 1502/NAT/1–74. See also RSBGA, GB 1502/WES/125/14 for an overview of the central London offices of the London, County and Westminster Bank in 1914.
55. Savage, 'Career Mobility and Class Formation', p. 205.
56. E. Green, *Debtors to Their Profession: A History of the Institute of Bankers, 1879–1979* (London: Methuen & Co. Ltd., 1979), p. 104.
57. Ibid. See also *Bank Officer*, January 1920, 'The Guild's Origin Some Notes on its Formation', p. 5. In this account in the B.O.G.'s own journal the Bank Clerk's Association is never mentioned. See also Klingender, *The Condition of Clerical Labour in Britain*, pp. 32–46.
58. RBSGA GB 1502/NAT/174/1–74, 'Staff Record Cards of the National Provincial Bank Ltd'.
59. The British Library, *Millenium Memory Bank*, C900/07507, 'Arthur Whitlock'.
60. S. Moseley, *The Private Diaries of Sydney Moseley* (London: Max Parish, 1960).
61. 'Diaries of George Rose', 18 December 1906, 8 September 1913.
62. London Borough of Hackney Archives, DS/EVA/1–3, 'William Evan's Diaries', 19 October 1891.

63. Savage, 'Career Mobility and Class Formation' p. 197.
64. Anderson, 'The Social Economy of Late-Victorian Clerks', p. 117.
65. See J. F. Wilson, *British Business History 1720–1994* (Manchester: Manchester University Press, 1995), ch. 2, esp. pp. 27–9.
66. Ibid., p. 118.
67. Guildhall library, MS-24698, 'Messers Gillett Brothers, Staff, 1898, 1902 and 1949'.
68. D. Kynaston, *The City of London Volume II Golden Years* (London: Pimlico, 1995), p. 400.
69. British Library, Thompson and Vigne, *Family Life and Work Experience before 1918*, QD1/FLWE/216, 'Elsie Barralet'.
70. Ibid., p. 119.
71. Ibid., p. 122.
72. *The Railway Clerk,* January 1911, pp. 3–5.
73. Moseley, *The Private Diaries of Sydney Moseley*, p. 35 and p. 42.
74. 'Diaries of George Rose', 24 November 1906.
75. British Library, *Millennium Memory Bank*, C900/07507 'Arthur Whitlock'.
76. *Clerk*, April 1908, p. 41.
77. Anderson, *Victorian Clerks*, p. 120.
78. *Census Report for England and Wales, 1901, Lincoln-Radnor*, 'Metropolitan Borough Battersea' (London: His Majesty's Sationery Office, 1901), pp. 98–9.
79. L.C.C. Statistics 1896–7 (Vol. 7) p. xxv., 1901–2 (Vol. 12) p. xviii.
80. Ibid. Vol. IV., 1893–4, p.xxiii.
81. *Railway Clerk*, October 1904, p. 117.
82. *Clerk*, November 1910, p. 168.
83. *The Ilford Guardian*, 25 August 1900.
84. Ibid.
85. British Library, Thompson and Vigne, *Family Life and Work Experience before 1918*, QD1/FL WE/161, 'Geoffrey Rogers', p.3 and p. 31.
86. Ibid., QD1/FLWE/183, 'Frank David Charles Lee', pp. 1–3.
87. 'Diaries of George Rose', 26 November 1913.
88. W. J. Brown, *So Far* (London: George Allen & Unwin, 1943), p. 37.
89. Ibid.
90. D. Feldman, *Englishmen and Jews, Social Relations and Political Culture, 1840–1914* (New Haven, CT and London: Yale University Press, 1994), p. 206.
91. Ibid.
92. S. Blumenfeld, *Jew Boy* (London: Lawrence & Wishart, 1986).
93. British Library, Thompson and Vigne, *Family Life and Work Experience before 1918*, QD1/FLWE145/J1–2, 'Percival Chambers', p. 43.
94. Ibid., p. 5.
95. See London Guildhall Library, MS-20383, 'Diary of Andrew Carlyle Tait, 1893–4'.
96. Interview with Jim Hancock at his home, 26 November 2001.
97. *Clerk*, May 1914, p. 83.
98. See, for example, Anon., *The Story of a London Clerk: A Narrative Faithfully Told* (London: Leadenhall Press, 1896), J. Wild, *The Rise of the Office Clerk in Literary Culture, 1880–1939* (Basingstoke: Palgrave Macmillan, 2006), ch. 5.

5 The Mechanization and Feminization of the Office, 1870–1914: Threats or Opportunities?

1. J. E. Lewis, 'Women Clerical Workers in the Late Nineteenth and early Twentieth Centuries', in G. Anderson (ed.), *The White-Blouse Revolution – Female Office Workers Since 1870* (Manchester: Manchester University, 1988), p. 34.
2. P. Attewell, 'The Clerk Deskilled: A Study in False Nostalgia', *Journal of Historical Sociology*, 2:4 (1989), p. 357.
3. H. Braverman, *Labor and Monopoly Capitalism* (New York: Monthly Review Press, 1974).
4. Attewell, 'The Clerk Deskilled', p. 357.
5. G. Anderson, *Victorian Clerks* (Manchester: Manchester University Press, 1976), pp. 52–73.
6. For a summary of writings by feminist historians on the subject see the first part of Ellen Jordan's article, 'The Lady Clerks at the Prudential: The Beginnings of Vertical Segregation by Sex in Clerical Work in Nineteenth-Century Britain', *Gender and History*, 8:1 (1996), pp. 65–81.
7. Lewis, 'Women Clerical Workers', p. 35.
8. M. Zimmeck, 'Jobs for the Girls: the Expansion of Clerical Work for Women, 1850–1914', in A. V. John (ed.), *Unequal Opportunities – Women's Employment in England 1800–1918* (Oxford: Basil Blackwell Ltd., 1986), p. 156.
9. Attewell, 'The Clerk Deskilled'.
10. Cohn, *The Process of Occupational Sex-Typing*.
11. Jordan, 'The Lady Clerks at the Prudential'.
12. *Census of England and Wales, 1911, Volume X: Occupations and Industries Part 2* (London: His Majesty's Stationary Office, 1911), p. 293.
13. *Clerk*, February 1910, p. 20.
14. General Post Office Archives POST 30/1017A, 'Burroughs Adding Machine Use in Post Office (Papers 1900–1913)'.
15. M. J. Daunton, *Royal Mail The Post Office Since 1840* (London: The Athlone Press, 1985), p. 92.
16. See General Post Office Archives POST 30/ 4301–02, 'Labour Saving Appliances: use in relation to clerical work in Post Office, Parts 1 & 2'. See also above archive on Burroughs Adding Machine.
17. M. J. Daunton, *Royal Mail*, p. 194.
18. General Post Office Archives POST 30/1017A, 'Burroughs Adding Machine Use in Post Office (Papers 1900–1913) File XI'.
19. Cohn, *The Process of Occupational Sex-Typing*, p. 87.
20. Ibid.
21. J. Pellew, *The Home Office 1848–1914 – from Clerks to Bureaucrats* (London: Heinemann Educational Books Ltd., 1982), pp. 7–9.
22. See L. R. Dicksee, *Office Organisation and Management* (London: Sir Isaac Pitman and Sons Ltd., 1910), ch. V.
23. London Metropolitan Archives CL/ESTAB/4/59–62, 'Applications for Class II Typists, 1898–1915'.
24. Cohn, *The Process of Occupational Sex-Typing*, pp. 83–4.
25. *Clerk*, February 1910, p. 20.
26. Ibid., March 1910, p.38.

27. Ibid.
28. Attewell, 'The Clerk Deskilled', p. 377.
29. See Cohn, *The Process of Occupational Sex-Typing* ch. 3, and Attewell, 'The Clerk Deskilled'
30. The British Library, *Millennium Memory Bank Archive*, C900/04111, 'Felix Owen'.
31. The British Library, Paul Thompson and Thea Vigne Interviews, QD1/FLWE/300, 'Florence Johnson'.
32. General Post Office Archives POST 30/4301, 'Labour Saving Appliances'.
33. See J. F. Davis, *Bank Organisation, Management and Accounts* (London: Sir Isaac Pitman and Sons, 1910), p. 40.
34. RBSG Archives GB 1502/GM/710/1, 'Glyn's Town Office Annual Reports, 1896–1911'.
35. Cohn, *The Process of Occupational Sex-Typing*, pp. 81–90.
36. Ibid., p. 84.
37. Howarth, *Our Banking System and Clearing Houses*.
38. Ibid., p. 63.
39. Ibid., pp. 62–3.
40. Ibid., p. 69.
41. *Clerk*, March 1910, p. 38.
42. L. R. Dicksee, *Office Organisation and Management*, p. 43.
43. *Fifty-Sixth Report of the Civil Service Commission, 1912–13 Cd 6332, Vol. XV*, 16 May 1912, p. 116.
44. Ibid., 3 May 1912, p. 67.
45. Essex Records Office, D/DU418/1–15, 'The Diaries of George Rose'.
46. *Office*, 22 September 1888, p. 3.
47. Cohn, *The Process of Occupational Sex-Typing*, p. 85.
48. *County Magazine*, 6 (1909), p. 275.
49. Ibid.
50. Reports and announcements of such competitions regularly appeared in *Office*. See 10 November 1888, for example.
51. *Clerk*, February 1910, p. 20.
52. Ibid., January 1908, p. 9.
53. See Cohn, *The Process of Occupational Sex-Typing*, p. 105.
54. Ibid., ch. 8.
55. Ibid. ch. 4.
56. See Lewis, 'Women Clerical Workers', p. 37.
57. London Metropolitan Archives LCC/MIN/4644, 'L.C.C. Establishment Committee Papers, 1898'.
58. Ibid. Report of the Clerk, 27 April.
59. Cohn, *The Process of Occupational Sex-Typing*, p. 102.
60. London Metropolitan Archives, 'L.C.C. Establishment Committee Papers, 1898'
61. See evidence of Miss E. A. Charlesworth in *Fifty-Sixth Report of the Royal Commission*, 16 May 1912.
62. Jordan, 'The Lady Clerks at the Prudential', p. 74.
63. Zimmeck, 'Jobs for the Girls', p. 163.
64. British Library, Paul Thompson and Thea Vigne Interviews, QD1/FL WE/161, 'Geoffrey Rogers'.
65. Ibid. QD1/FL WE/63, 'Alfred Henry Pyle'.

66. For a discussion of pin-money clerks see G. Anderson, *Victorian Clerks*, pp. 57–8.
67. Zimmeck, 'Jobs for the Girls', p. 163.
68. See National Archives, '1891 Census, Street Index', RG 12/179–207 (for Hackney), RG12/1033–1038 (for Acton) and RG12/468 (for East Dulwich).
69. British Library, Paul Thompson and Thea Vigne Interviews QD1/FLWE/183, 'Geoffrey Rogers'.
70. British Library, *Millennium Memory Bank*, C900/07507, 'Arthur Whitlock'.
71. Ibid. C900/07509, 'Sylvia Ward'.
72. For a discussion of the changing nature of the private/public sphere for British middle class families in this period see J. Tosh, *A Man's Place, Masculinity and the Middle-Class Home in Victorian England* (New Haven, CT & London: Yale University Press, 1999).
73. Anderson, p. 59.
74. J. E. Lewis, p. 37.
75. Ibid., pp. 37–9.
76. *Fifty-Sixth Report of the Civil Service Commission on the Civil Service,* 26 March 1912, p. 12.
77. *Fourth Report of the Royal Commission on the Civil Service*, 1914 Cd 7338, Vol. XVI, pp. 6–9.
78. See J. E. Lewis, p. 42.
79. London Metropolitan Archives CL/ESTAB/4/59–62,'Applications for Class II Typists, 1898–1915'.
80. *Fifty Sixth Report of the Civil Service Commission*, Appendix II, p. 135.
81. G. Rogers, p. 45.
82. *Millenium Memory Bank*, C900/07509, 'Sylvia Warde'.
83. 'The Diaries of George Rose', 10 February 1910,
84. Ibid. 4 February 1910.
85. G. Anderson, p. 60.
86. See Cohn, *The Process of Occupational Sex-Typing*, pp. 142–52.
87. *Fifty-Sixth Report of the Civil Service Commission*, 26April 1912–13, p. 33.
88. See J. K. Chalaby, *The Invention of Journalism* (London: Macmillan Press Ltd., 1998), pp. 147–66.

6 Education, Merit and Patronag:The London Clerical Market

1. Webb, *London Education*, p. 101.
2. Ibid.
3. See *Clerk*, January 1908, p. 2.
4. Ibid., April 1910, p. 63.
5. See Holcombe, *Victorian Ladies at Work*, p. 157.
6. G. Anderson, *Victorian Clerks* (Manchester: Manchester University Press, 1976), p. 129.
7. For a discussion of the 1902 Balfour Education Act, and its 1903 version for London, see the conclusion of J. Roach, *Secondary Education in England 1870–1902* (London: Rouledge, 1991). See also S. Webb. The Fabian Society, *Fabian Tract No. 117. The London Education Act: How to Make the Best of it* (London: The Fabian Society, 1904).
8. Webb, *London Education*, passim.
9. Ibid., p. 6.
10. Ibid.

11. According to *London County Council London Statistics: Vol. XXIV: 1913–14*, pp. 409–11, there were 25,664 students in secondary schools recognized as efficient by the Board of Education, and 24,114 in secondary schools on the grant list of the Board of Education. This figure did not include private schools of which there were estimated to be at least 468 in London in December 1908 with an estimated 27,000 students. Most of these would have been young students however. Out of 158 of these schools with 8,995 students, 58 per cent were under 12, 22 per cent were aged 12–14 and 20 per cent were over 14.

12. Ibid., p. 29.

13. Sir H. Llewelyn-Smith and A. Acland, *Studies in Secondary Education* (London: Percival & Co., 1892) p. 147.

14. Webb, *London Education*, p. 30.

15. Roach, *Secondary Education in England*, ch. 1.

16. Ibid., p. 244.

17. Ibid., p. 3.

18. Ibid., p. 10.

19. London Metropolitan Archives 31.6, 'L.C.C. London Statistics Vol. XXIV. 1913–14', pp. 409–11.

20. Llewelyn-Smith, p. 161.

21. Roach, *Secondary Education in England*, p. 75.

22. Webb, *London Education*, pp. 109–10.

23. London Metropolitan Archives T.E.B. 80/4, 'Report of the Sub-Committee of the Technical Education Board, 1897'.

24. Ibid., p. 17.

25. Ibid., p. 70.

26. Acland and Llewellyn-Smith, p. 160.

27. 'Report of the Sub-Committee of the Technical Education Board, 1897' pp. 14–16.

28. Ibid., p. 71. See also, University of Westminster Archive (UWA) RSP 5/4/25 *Polytechnic Magazine* (advert), 7 August 1895, pp. vii–viii.

29. 'Report of the Sub-Committee of the Technical Education Board', pp. 16–17.

30. Ibid., p. 70.

31. Ibid., pp. 70–1.

32. Ibid., p. 3.

33. Ibid.

34. *Fourth Report of the Royal Commission on the Civil Service*, 1914 Cd 7338, Vol. XVI, pp. 29–30.

35. Webb, *London Education*, p. 111.

36. Roach, *Secondary Education in England*, p. 82 and p. 112. See also Acland and Llewellyn-Smith, pp. 161–3.

37. British Library, *Millennium Memory Bank*, C900/04111, 'Felix Owen'.

38. 'Report of the Special Sub-Committee', pp.iv–v.

39. Roach, *Secondary Education in England*, p. 166.

40. For an example of the integration of the public examinations into recruitment policies see the Great Western Railway Company, National Archives RAIL 258/400, 'Clerical Staff: recruiting, examination of, 1877–1914'.

41. RBSG Archives GB 1502/GM/2036, 'Regulations Concerning Applications to Clerkships, Glyn's Bank, *c*. 1875'.

42. See *Fourth Report of the Royal Commission on the Civil Service*, 1914 Cd 7338, Vol. XVI., pp. 6–8. For an examination of the effects of these reforms on the Home Office see J. Pellew, *The Home Office 1848–1914* (London: Heinemann Educational Books, 1982), ch. 2.

43. Roach, *Secondary Education in England*, pp. 157–8.

44. *Millennium Memory Bank*, 'Felix Owen'.

45. *Business Life*, July 1902, p. 13.

46. Essex Records Office D/DU4/8/1, 'The Diaries of George Rose'.

47. Ibid., 29 December 1900.

48. Ibid. 1 January 1901.

49. Ibid., 10 January 1902.

50. Felix Owen.

51. Guildhall Library, MS–20383, 'Diary of Andrew Carlyle Tait' (date not specified) July 1894.

52. Interview with James Hancock at his home, 26 November 2001.

53. London Borough of Hackney Archives Department, D/S/EVA/1–3, 'Diaries of William Evans', 21 October 1882.

54. RBSG GB 1502/GM/339/1, 'Glyn's Clerks Register, 1864–1918'.

55. E. G. Brown, *The History of the House of Glyn, Mills & Co* (Privately Printed, 1933), p. 178.

56. *Business Life*, June 1903, p. 139.

57. Ibid.

58. 'Report of the Special Sub-Committee', p. 16.

59. National Archives, RAIL 258/400, 'Great Western Railway, Clerical Staff: recruiting, examination of, 1877–1914'.

60. 'Report', p. 32.

61. Ibid., p. 33.

62. Ibid., p. 20.

63. Ibid., p. 16.

64. London Guildhall Library, Pamphlet-6841, The London Chamber of Commerce, *Commercial Education*, 1895, p. 5 and p. 10.

65. *Business Life*, June 1904, p. 280.

66. For the Home Office clerks see J. Pellew, *The Home Office 1848–1914*, ch. V. For Glyn's see R. Fulford, *Glyn's: 1753–1953* (London: Macmillan and Co. Ltd., 1953), pp. 168–84.

67. *Fourth Report of the Royal Commission on the Civil Service*, 1914, p. 16.

68. *Business Life*, July 1902, p. 12.

69. *Thirtieth Report of the Civil Service Commission*, 1886, Vol. XX., p. v.

70. *Business Life*, July 1902, p. 12.

71. *Fifty Sixth Report of the Royal Commission on the Civil Service*, Cd 6332 1912–13, Vol. XV., Appendix II, p. 130.

72. *Thirtieth Report of the Civil Service Commission*, Appendix, Table H, p. 36.

73. Ibid., p. v.

74. *Fifty-Sixth Report of the Royal Commission on the Civil Service*, Appendix II, p. 134.

75. RBSG Archives GB 1502/GM/2036, 'Regulations concerning admissions to clerkships, Glyn's Bank, c. 1875'.

76. From RBSG Archives GB 1502/GM/339/1, 'Glyn's Clerks Register 1864–1918'. Information on schools from Acland and Llewellyn-Smith, *Studies on Secondary Education*,

pp. 192–9, *The Annual Charities Register and Digest* (London: Longman, Green and Co., 1905), and *Kelly's Directories*

77. Ibid.
78. 'Great Western Railway, Clerical Staff: Recruiting, Examination of, 1877–1914'.
79. RBSG Archives GB 1502/GM/339/1, 'Clerks Register, Glyn's Bank, 1864–1918'.
80. See Acland and Llewellyn-Smith, p. 82.
81. *Fifty-Sixth Report of the Civil Service Commission, 1912–13*, Appendix II, p. 132.
82. Ibid., 2 May 1912, p. 56.
83. Ibid., p. 57.
84. RBSG Archives GB 1502/GM/339/1, 'Clerks Register, Glyn's Bank 1864–1918'.
85. *Fifty-Sixth Report*, 2 May 1912, p. 56.

7 Commercial Education and the Clerk

1. London Metropolitan Archives T.E.B. 80/4, 'Report of the Special Sub-Committee of the Technical Education Board of the L.C.C. on Commercial Education, 1897', p. ii.
2. *Business Life*, August 1902, p. 15.
3. For a comprehensive discussion of the National Efficiency Movement in Britain for this period see G.R. Searle, *The Quest for National Efficiency: a study in British Politics and Political Thought, 189901914* (Oxford: Blackwell, 1971).
4. See S. P. Keeble, *The Ability to Manage: A Study of British Management 1890–1990* (Manchester: Manchester University Press, 1992), pp. 2–4.
5. See M. D. Stephens and G. W. Roderick, 'Late Nineteenth Century Scientific and Technical Education. The Later Victorians and Scientific and Technical Education', *Annals of Science*, 28:4 (1972), pp. 385–400.
6. For the centrality of Empire to London's business outlook see J. Schneer, *London 1900 The Imperial Metropolis* (New Haven, CT and London: Yale University Press, 1999), ch. 4.
7. 'Report of the Special Sub-Committee of the Technical Education Board of the L.C.C., 1897', p. ii.
8. See for example E. P. Hennock, 'Technological Education in Britain 1850–1926: the uses of a German model', in *History of Education*, 19:4 (1990), pp. 299–331. See also A. Green, 'Technical Education', in *History of Education*, 24:2 (1995), pp. 123–39. For universities see M. Sanderson, *The Universities and British Industry, 1850–1970* (London: Routledge and Kegan Paul, 1972).
9. R. Floud and S. Glynn (eds), *London Higher The Establishment of Higher Education in London* (London: The Athlone Press, 1998).
10. G. Anderson, *Victorian Clerks* (Manchester: Manchester University Press, 1976), ch. 6. R. G. Wilson, *Disillusionment or New Opportunities? The Changing Nature of Work in Offices, Glasgow 1880–1914* (Aldershot: Ashgate, 1998), ch. 3.
11. See P. F. Drucker, *Post-Capitalist Society* (New York: HarperCollins Publishers, 1994), p. 19.
12. S. Glynn, 'The Establishment of Higher Education in London: A Survey', in R. Floud and S. Glynn (eds), *London Higher, the Establishment of Higher Education in London*, p. 27.
13. See *Office*, 24 November, 'Technical Education', p. 5.
14. See Webb, *London Education*, pp. 124–30.
15. See *Business Life*, 1902, p. 52.

16. 'Report of the Special Sub-Committee', p. xii.
17. Ibid., p. 16.
18. *Office*, 13 October 1888, p. 4.
19. See London Metropolitan Archives EO/HFE/9/37, 'Eight Years of Technical Education and Continuation Schools, 1912', p. 103.
20. 'Report', p. vii.
21. See 'Education for Business: The Old Way and the New', *Business Life*, May 1903, p. 125.
22. Ibid.
23. *Office*, 24 November 1888, p. 5.
24. 'Eight Years', p. 63.
25. 'Report', p. 18.
26. Interview with Jim Hancock at his home, 26 November 2001.
27. See Webb, *The Process of Occupational Sex-Typing*, p. 128.
28. *Business Life*, September 1902, p. 37.
29. Ibid., July, p. 4.
30. P. Attewell, 'The Clerk Deskilled: A Study in False Nostalgia', *Journal of Historical Sociology*, 2:4 (1989), pp. 364–5.
31. *Office*, 24 January 1891, p. 32.
32. Perkin, *The Rise of Professional Society*, pp. 2–9.
33. Ibid., pp. 85–6.
34. For the Institute of Bankers see E. Green, *A History of The Institute of Bankers, 1879–1979* (London: Methuen & Co. Ltd., 1979). For the United Law Clerks Society see London Metropolitan Archives, ACC/1559, 'United Law Clerks Society, 1832–1979'.
35. Ibid., pp. 56–7.
36. Ibid., p. 86.
37. *Business Life*, August 1902, p. 17.
38. Ibid., December 1902, p. 66. See also January 1903, p. 111.
39. 'Report', p. 74.
40. See 'Eight Years', p. 12, and S. Glynn, 'The Establishment of Higher Education in London', p. 4.
41. For an overall discussion of the development of technical education in nineteenth century London see E. P. Henlock, 'Technological Education in England, 1850–1926', and Glynn, 'The Establishment of Higher Education in London'. See also, 'Eight Years', pp. 1–11.
42. Anderson, , p. 90.
43. *Office*, 22 September 1888, p. 13.
44. Webb, *London Education*, p. 97.
45. For the background of the LCC see Steven R. B. Smith, 'The Centenary of the London Chamber of Commerce: Its Origins and Early Policy', in *London Journal*, 8:2 (1982), pp. 157–70.
46. London Guildhall Library, Pamphlet 6841, 'The London Chamber of Commerce, Commercial Education, 1895', pp. 1–2.
47. Ibid., pp. 5–6.
48. See Glynn, 'The Establishment of Higher Education in London', pp. 1–35.
49. For details of the educational work of the YMCA see 'Eight Years', p. 77.
50. See in particular Floud and Glynn (eds), *London Higher, The Establishment of Higher Education in London*.

51. London County Council, *London Statistics, Vol. 23 1912–13*, p. 395. See E. M. Wood, *A History of the Polytechnic* (London: Macdonald, 1965) for the development of Regent Street Polytechnic.
52. University of Westminster Archive (hereafter UWA), RSP/4/1/3, 'Regent Street Polytechnic Prospectus 1902–1903', p. 1. Regent Street had 8,886 students for the period 1911–13, *London Statistics, Vol. 23, 1912–13*, p. 395.
53. See *Polytechnic Magazine* for courses which were offered at Regent Streets Polytechnic.
54. UWA RSP/4/1/18, 'Regent Street Polytechnic Prospectus, 1910–11', p. 5.
55. UWA RSP/5/4/15, *Polytechnic Magazine*, 27 February 1890, p. 128.
56. Ibid., UWA RSP5/4/42 January 1905, Prospectus and Class Time Table 23rd Session 1904–5.
57. Ibid., UWA RSP5/4/48 May 1910, Advert.
58. Ibid., UWA RSP5/4/15 1 May 1890, p. 279.
59. J. Stevenson, 'Women and the Curriculum at the Polytechnic at Regent Street, 1888–1913', *History of Education*, 26:3 (1997), p. 284.
60. 'Report', pp. 72–7.
61. Webb, *The Process of Occupational Sex-Typing*, p. 121.
62. Ibid.
63. 'Report', p. xv.
64. 'Eight Years', p. 9 and p. 23. These figures peaked in 1904–5 at 150,605.
65. Ibid., p. 61. Note, however, that 46.4 per cent of those doing Bookkeeping, 48.7 per cent doing French and 39.5 per cent doing Shorthand made less than 14 hours.
66. Ibid., p. 9.
67. Ibid., p. 50.
68. Ibid., pp. 51–2.
69. Ibid., p. 52.
70. Ibid., p. 51.
71. Ibid., p. 53.
72. Ibid., p. 98.
73. Webb, *The Process of Occupational Sex-Typing*, p. 124.
74. Ibid., p. 124.
75. 'Eight Years', p. 74.
76. 'Report', p. xiii.
77. Ibid., p. 3.
78. Ibid., xii.
79. 'Eight Years', p. 74.
80. 'Report', p. 1,
81. Webb, *The Process of Occupational Sex-Typing*, p. 128.
82. Ibid., p. 131.
83. *Business Life,* July 1902, p. 13.
84. *Kelly's London Suburban Directory, Southern Suburbs, 1902* (London: Kelly's Directories Limited, 1902), p. 1440.
85. *Kelly's London County Suburbs Directory 1904* (London: Kelly's Directories Limited, 1904), p. 1145.
86. *Business Life*, August 1902, p. 17.
87. Ibid. February 1904, p. 239.
88. Ibid., February 1904, p. 238.
89. Ibid., December 1902, p. 66.

90. Ibid., April 1903, p. 113.
91. Ibid., April 1904, p. 255.
92. British Library of Political and Economic Science Archives Division, BOOTH F2/3/6, 'Pitman's School of Shorthand, *c.* 1890', p. 22 and p. 34.
93. See article, 'The Real Objective in Education', in *Business Life*, September 1902, p. 27.
94. See the article 'Business as a Profession', Ibid., April 1903, p. 111.
95. Ibid., May-June 1907, p. 439.
96. Ibid., September 1902, p. 27.
97. See UWA RSP/5/4/25, *Polytechnic Magazine*, 23 January 1895, p. 54.
98. See article 'Commercial Supremacy', *Business Life*, August 1902, p. 15.
99. London Metropolitan Archives E0/HFE/9/37, 'Eight Years', pp. 6–7.
100. 'The London Chamber of Commerce, Commercial Education, 1895'.
101. London Guildhall Library, MS-16,460, 'London Chamber of Commerce, General Purpose Committee Book, 1910–14'.
102. London Metropolitan Archives T.E.B. 80/4, 'Report of the Special Sub-Committee of the Technical Education Board', p. xii.
103. E. Green, *Debtors to their Profession: A History of the Institute of Bankers 1879–1979* (London: Methuen & Co., 1979).
104. Ibid., pp. 56–67.
105. Ibid., p. 81.
106. London Metropolitan Archives T.E.B. 80/4, 'Report'.
107. Ibid., 'Appendix II Report of Mr. Fishbourne's interview's with Employers', pp. 25–36.
108. Ibid., p. 35.
109. RBSGA WES/336, 'London County and Westminster Bank, Conditions of Appointments to Junior Clerkships, 1910'.
110. National Archives RAIL 250/746, 'Great Western Railway Staff Committee Papers, Suspension of Advances to Office Clerks Who Fail to Learn Shorthand, March, 1910'.
111. London Metropolitan Archives, T.E.B. 80/4, 'Report', p. xiii, Webb, *London Education*, p. 128.
112. Webb, *The Process of Occupational Sex-Typing*, p. 128.
113. London Metropolitan Archives, T.E.B. 80/4, 'Report', pp. xiii–xiv, Webb, *The Process of Occupational Sex-Typing*, pp. 128–9.
114. London Metropolitan Archives, T.E.B. 80/4, 'Report, Appendix II, Evidence of Mr. Gerard Van de Linde', pp. 25–26, T. Alborn, Quill-Driving: British Life-Insurance Clerks and Occupational Mobility', *Business History Review*, 82:1 (2008), pp. 31–58.
115. 'Eight Years', p. 105.
116. Ibid. The 29,569 clerks in the Report represent 28.4 per cent of the 104,025 clerks in the 1901 Census. Ibid.
117. Borough of Southwark Archives, MS – 1982/117, 'The Diary of Daniel McEwen'.
118. The British Library, Paul Thompson and Thea Vigne's Interviews on Family Life and Work Experience before 1918, QD1/FL WE/262, 'Mr. Frederick Henry Taylor'.
119. 'Report', p. 23.
120. Stevenson, 'Women and the Curriculum at the Polytechnic at Regent Street, 1888–1913'.
121. Greaves, *The Commercial Clerk and His Success*, p. 38.
122. Ibid., pp. 50–1.
123. J. B. Carrington, *The Junior Corporation Clerk* (London: Sir Isaac Pitman & Sons, 1911), p. 128.

124. 'Report', p. 74.
125. UWA RSP/4/1/3, 'Regents Street Polytechnic Prospectus, 1902–3', p. 35.
126. UWA RSP/5/4/15, *The Polytechnic Magazine*, 2 January 1890, p. 16.
127. See Ibid., UWA RSP/5/4/48, May 1910 which included, 'The Polytechnic Holiday Supplement'.
128. Essex Records Office, D/DU418/1, 'The Diaries of George Rose'.
129. See Webb, *The Process of Occupational Sex-Typing*, p. 97.
130. Glynn, 'The Establishment of Higher Education in London', p. 13.
131. Ibid.
132. 'The Diaries of George Rose', 15 January 1902.
133. See Drucker, *Post-Capitalist Society*, ch. 1.
134. UWA RSP/5/4/25, *The Polytechnic Magazine*, 2 January 1895, p. 3.
135. Webb, *The Process of Occupational Sex-Typing*, p. 132.
136. M. Foucault, *The Birth of the Clinic* (London: Tavistock Publications, 1973), *Discipline and Punish: the birth of the prison* (Penguin: Harmondsworth, 1979), *The History of Sexuality: an introduction* (London: Allen Lane, 1979).
137. Report, p. xiii.

8 Clerical Trade Unions, Associations and Collective Organizations

1. For the RCA see M. Wallace, *Single or Return, The History of the Transport Salaried Staffs' Association* (London: Transport Salaried Staffs' Association, 1996). For the NUC see F. Hughes, *By Hand and Brain: The Story of the Clerical and Adminstrative Workers* (London: Lawrence & Wishart, 1953). For the various civil service associations and postal unions see B. V. Humphreys, *Clerical Unions in the Civil Service* (London: Blackwell and Mott, 1958). For NALGO see Alec Spoor, *White Collar Union 60 Years of NALGO* (London: Heinemann, 1967).
2. See G. Anderson, *Victorian Clerks* (Manchester: Manchester University Press, 1976), and D. Lockwood, *The Black Coated Worker* (London: Allen & Unwin, 1958).
3. Ibid., p. 110.
4. See M. Wallace, Single or *Return?*, p. 103, and *Clerk*, May 1914, p. 83.
5. See S. and B. Webb, *The History of Trade Unionism* (London: Longmans & Co., 1920), p. 505.
6. See B. V. Humphreys, *Clerical Unions in the Civil Service*, in particular pp. 231–2.
7. See F. D. Klingender, *The Condition of Clerical Labour in Britain* (London: Martin Lawrence, 1935), p. viii.
8. British Library of Political and Economic Science Archives Division BOOTH F2/3/1–10, 'Booklets Collected as a Result of Charles Booth Survey of Life and Labour in London, 1886–1903'.
9. See London Metropolitan Archives, C. D.Andrew and G.C. Burge, *Progress Report, 1909–1959: The First Fifty Years in the History of the L.C.C. Staff Association* (London: Privately Published, 1959); E. Green, *Debtors to their Profession: A History of the Institute of Bankers 1879–1979* (London: Methuen & Co. Ltd., 1979); W. S. Chevalier, *London's Water Supply, 1903–53: A Review of the Work of the Metropolitan Water Board* (London: Staple Press Ltd, 1953), p. 334. For a report on a proposed merger between the National Union of Clerks and the Law Clerks Association see *Clerk,* February 1908, p. 14.
10. See Andrew and Burge, *Progress Report, 1909–1959*, ch. 1.
11. Green, *Debtors to their Profession*, ch. 3–4.

12. See M. Wallace, *Single or Return*, pp. 39–43.
13. See H. H. Gerth and C. W. Mills (eds), *From Max Weber: Essays in Sociology* (London: Routledge, 1997) pp. 194–5.
14. Anderson, *Victorian Clerks*, p. 16., Keith Laybourn, *A History of British Trade Unionism c. 1770–1990* (Stroud: Alan Sutton, 1992), p. 76.
15. See Webb and Webb, *The History of Trade Unionism, 1660–1920*, ch. VII, and Laybourm, *A History of British Trade Unionism*, ch. 3.
16. Ibid.
17. *Clerk*, January 1908, p. 5.
18. See British Library of Political and Economic Science WIC/B/26, 'Rules of the National Union of Clerks, 1894'.
19. See the A.C.A. magazine *Red Tape*, March 1912, p. 10. See also British Library of Political and Economic Science Coll. Misc. 6/8, 'National Union of Clerks London Central Branch Minute Book, 21 November, 1912'.
20. For examples of memorials sent to the Great Western Railway see National Archives RAIL 258/404, 'Great Western Railway Secretarial Papers: salaried staff, increase in salaries, Sunday pay, grant of concessions, memorials, extract from minute papers, etc., 1904–22'
21. See *Fifty-Sixth Report of the Royal Commission on the Civil* Service, 1912–13 Cd. 6332, Vol.VX..
22. *Red Tape*, October 1911, p. 4.
23. See *Fifty Sixth Report of the Royal Commission of the Civil Service*, 1912–13 Cd. 6332, Vol. XV., particularly the evidence of Mr Stanley M. Leathers, C. B.., First Civil Service Commissioner.
24. See *Red Tape*, October 1911, p. 4.
25. *Fourth Report of the Royal Commission on the Civil Service*, 1914 Cd 7338 Vol. XVI., pp. 7–22.
26. *Red Tape.*, March 1912, p. 4.
27. See *Fourth Report of the Royal Commission on the Civil Service*, pp. 27–39. See *Red Tape*, April 1914, for the response of the A.C.A. to the Report.
28. London School of Economics Library (Pamphlet) HD6 B15, *Progress, Combination and Agreement Amongst Clerks*, 1914, p. 11.
29. Ibid. WIC/B/26, 'Rules of the National Union of Clerks, 1894'.
30. *Railway Clerk*, June 1904, p. 59.
31. See 'National Union of Clerks London Central Branch, Minute Book, 1 May 1911 to 30 June 1914'. See also *Railway Clerk*, 1904, p. 48.
32. See for example, *Railway Clerk*, August 1906, p. 13.
33. Ibid., October 1906, p. 10.
34. See *Clerk*, March 1908, p. 37.
35. See E. Green, *Debtors to their Profession*, ch. 4.
36. See J. B. Carrington, *The Junior Corporation Clerk* (London: Sir Isaac Pitman & Sons Ltd., 1910), pp. 127–8. See also *The London County Council Staff Gazette*, June 1914, pp. 138–9.
37. See National Archives RAIL 258/400, 'Great Western Railway, Clerical Staff: recruiting, examination of, 1877–1914'.
38. *Clerk*, August 1908, p. 105.

39. See *Office*, 10 and 17 January 1891. See also B. V. Humphreys, *Clerical Unions in the Civil Service*, pp. 43–5, and Cohn, *The Process of Occupational Sex-Typing*, p. 148 and pp. 155–6.
40. See *Clerk*, June 1912, p. 88 and April 1914, pp. 61–3.
41. Ibid., August 1908, p. 105.
42. Ibid.
43. Ibid.
44. *Red Tape*, October 1911, p. 2.
45. *Railway Clerk*, January 1911, pp. 4–5.
46. Ibid., January 1910, p. 5.
47. *Red Tape*, October 1911, p. 3.
48. See *Red Tape*, March 1913, pp. 92–3, and Ibid., February 1912, pp. 6–7.
49. Ibid., December 1911, p. 11.
50. Railway Clerks Association, *The Life of a Railway Clerk* (London: Railway Clerks Association, 1911).
51. Ibid., *The R.C.A. and its Path of Progress* (London: Railway Clerks Association, 1928), p. 28.
52. Ibid.. See also National Archives RAIL 258/400, 'Great Western Railway Clerical Staff, 1877–1914'.
53. *Railway Clerk*, January 1906, p. 6.
54. *The R.C.A. and its Path of Progress*, p. 14. See also *Clerk*, January 1908, p. 5.
55. *The Railway Clerk*, 'Portraits of our Leaders', January – July 1904.
56. See Humphreys, *Clerical Unions*, ch. 4.
57. See M. Wallace, *Single or Return*, pp. 31–45.
58. *Clerk*, January 1908, p. 1.
59. See *Red Tape*, October 1911, p. 3.
60. Ibid., pp. 3–4.
61. See ibid., January 1912, p. 3.
62. *Railway Clerk*, November 1911, p. 225.
63. See *The R.C.A. and its Path of Progress*, pp. 15–16, and pp. 20–3. See also Malcolm Wallace, pp. 46–8.
64. *The R.C.A. and its Path of Progress*, pp. 24–6, and p. 31.
65. 'National Union of Clerks London Central Branch Minute Book, 1st May 1911 to 30th June, 1914', 18 August 1912.
66. *The R.C.A. and its Path of Progress*, p. 6.
67. See G. Crossick 'The Emergence of the Lower-Middle Class in Britain: A Discussion', in G. Crossick (ed.), *The Lower-Middle Class in Britain* (London: Croom Helm, 1977), p. 27.
68. See K. Laybourn, *A History of British Trade Unionism c. 1770–1990*, p. 79.
69. Perkin, *The Rise of Professional Society*, ch. 1.
70. See R. J. Morris, *Class, Sect and Party: the making of the British Middle Class, Leeds 1820–50* (Manchester: Manchester University Press, 1990).
71. *Ilford Guardian 1898–1901*. See also London Borough of Redbridge Library, 'Ilford, Including Seven Kings and Goodmayes. The Official Publication of The Urban District Council', 1911.
72. *The L.C.C. Staff Gazette*, July 1914, p. 160.
73. *Railway Clerk*, December 1911, p. 245.
74. Ibid.

75. *Red Tape*, December 1911, p. 3.
76. See L. Davidoff and C. Hall, *Family Fortunes: Men and Women of the English Middle Class, 1780–1850* (London: Hutchinson, 1987). See also R. Q Gray, *The Labour Aristocracy in Victorian Edinburgh* (Oxford: Clarendon Press, 1976), ch. 7.
77. *Fifty-Sixth Report of the Royal Commission*, 2 May 1912, p. 315.
78. See Holcombe, *Victorian Ladies at Work*, pp. 152–62.
79. *Clerk*, November 1908, p. 158.
80. Ibid., p. 168.
81. See M. Wallace, *Single or Return The History of the Transport Salaried Staffs' Association* (London: Transport Salaried Staffs' Association, 1996), pp. 96–8.
82. See I. Aitken, *Film and Reform John Grierson and the Documentary Film Movement* (London: Routledge, 1990), ch. 1 and 8.
83. For a discussion of radical and anti-imperial groups in London see J. Schneer, *London 1900 The Imperial Metropolis* (New Have and London: Yale University Press, 1999).
84. See S. Pennybacker, *A Vision for London, 1889–1914: Labour, Everyday Life and the L.C.C. Experiment* (London: Routledge, 1995), pp. 35–6. and pp. 53–4.
85. Southwark Archives, MS–1982/117, 'The Diary of Daniel McEwen, 1887–1910'.
86. See British Library of Political and Economic Science Archives Division, LNU/5/70, 'League of Nations Union, Staff Standing Committee, 1926–39'.
87. See G. Anderson, *Victorian Clerks*, pp. 110–11.
88. See *Railway Clerk,* October 1911, p. 210.
89. *The R.C.A. and its Path of Progress*, p. 29.
90. Anderson, p. 109.
91. See F. D. Klingender, *The Condition of Clerical Labour in England* (London: Martin Lawrence, 1935), pp. 47–8.
92. *The Life of a Railway Clerk*, p. 16.
93. *Fourth Report from the Royal Commission*, pp. 21–2.
94. Humphreys, pp. 45–7 and p. 57.
95. *Fourth Report of the Royal Commission*, p. 19.

Conclusion

1. *Red Tape*, May 1913, p. 126.
2. Ibid.
3. Orchard, *The Clerks of Liverpool*.
4. C. Booth, *Life and Labour in London, Second Series, Industry, Book 3* (London: Macmillan & Co. Limited, 1903), pp. 277–8., London School of Economics and Social Sciences, *New Survey of London Life and Labour Vol. VIII London Industries II* (London: P.S. King & Son Ltd., 1934), pp. 272–3.
5. William Evans' father Edmund Evans was a carpenter. Out of his four sons, three became clerks. Equally interesting is that both his neighbours in Homerton, Hackney, a working-class area, were artisans, and both had sons who became clerks, London Borough of Hackney Archives Department, DS/EVA/1–3, 'The Diaries of William Evans, 1881–84, 1889–1900'.
6. See *Red Tape*, 'Better Prospects, A Suggestion', January 1912, p. 2., and Ibid., 'Of the Charmed Circle', February 1913, p. 83.
7. *Census of England and Wales, 1911, Volume X: Occupations and Industries Part 2* (London: His Majesty's Stationary Office, 1911), p. 293.

8. See *The Life of a Railway Clerk: Some Interesting Facts and Figures* (London: Railway Clerks Association, 1911), p. 2.

9. For the Inter-war merger movement see J. F. Wilson, *British Business History, 1720–1994* (Manchester: Manchester University Press, 1995), ch. 5. In relation to the railway industry see F. Mckenna, *The Railway Workers 1840–1970* (London: Faber & Faber, 1980), pp. 61–2. In relation to the banking sector see E. Green, *Debtors to their Profession* (London: Methuen & Co., 1979), pp. 97–9.

10. *The County Magazine*, 1913, p. 173.

11. R. Sennett, *The Corrosion of Character The Personal Consequences of Work in the New Capitalism* (New York & London: W.W. Norton & Company, 1998).

12. Ibid. ch. 4.

13. *London County Council Gazette*, September 1912, p. 172.

14. See *Railway Clerk*, August 1906, p. 1. and *The County and Westminster Magazine*, 1914, pp. 76–7.

15. See P. Bourdieu, *Distinction* (London: Routledge, 2002), pp. 109–12.

16. See British Library, QD1/FLWE/183, P. Thompson and T. Vigne, *Family Life and Work Experience before 1918,* 'Mr. Frank Lee' and QD1/FLWE/63, 'Mr. Alfred Pyle'.

17. 'Mr. F. Lee', p. 56.

WORKS CITED

Primary Sources

The British Library

Paul Thompson and Thea Vigne, *Family Life and Work Experience before 1918*.

QD1/FLWE/216, 'Elsie Barralet'.

QD1/ FLWE145/J1–2, 'Percival Chambers'.

QD1/FLWE/300, 'Florence Johnson'.

QD1/FLWE/63, 'Alfred Henry Pyle'.

QD1/FLWE/161, 'Geoffrey Rogers'.

QD1/FLWE/183, 'Frederick Henry Taylor.

Millennium Memory Bank

C900/04111, 'Felix Owen'.

C900/07509, 'Sylvia Ward'.

C900/07507, 'Arthur Whitlock'.

Parliamentary Papers and Government Reports

Report of an Enquiry by the Board of Trade into Working Class Rents, Housing, Retail Prices and Standard Rate of Wages in the United Kingdom; 1908 Cd. 3864 Vol. CVII. 319.

Thirtieth Report of the Civil Service Commission; 1886, Vol. XX. 89.

Fifty-Sixth Report of the Civil Service Commission; 1912–13, Cd. 6332, Vol. XV. 27.

Fourth Report of the Royal Commission on the Civil Service; 1914, Cd 7338,Vol. XVI. 1.

British Library of Political and Economic Science Archives Division

BOOTH F2/3/1–10, 'Booklets Collected as a Result of Charles Booth Survey of Life and Labour in London, 1886–1903'.

BOOTH F2/3/6, 'Pitmans School of Shorthand, *c.* 1890'.

HD6/B/15, 'Progress, Combination and Agreement Amongst Clerks, 1914'.

LNU/5/70, 'League of Nations Union, Staff Standing Committee, 1926–39'.

Misc. 6/8, 'National Union of Clerks, London Central Branch Minute Book, 1st May, 1911 to 30th June, 1914'.

WIC/B/26, 'Rules of the National Union of Clerks, 1894'.

Essex Records Office

D/DU418/1, 'The Diaries of George Rose, 1900–1914'.

General Post Office Archives

POST 30/1017A, 'Burroughs Adding Machine Use in Post Office (Papers 1900–1913)'.

POST 30/4301–02, 'Labour Saving Appliances: use in relation to clerical work in Post Office, Parts 1 & 2'.

POST 30/2625D, 'National Insurance Act 1911: methods of bringing contributions to account, stamp affixing machines and meter machines'.

POST 30/1084, 'Pencil Sharpening Machines: trials of various types'.

London Borough of Hackney Archives Department

DS/EVA/1–3, 'The Diaries of William Evans, 1881–84, 1889–1900'.

London Borough of Redbridge Archives

Ilford, Including Seven Kings and Goodmayes (The Official Publication of the Urban District Council, 1911).

London Borough of Southwark Archives

MS-1982/117, 'The Diary of Daniel McEwen, 1887–1910'.

London Guildhall Archives

MS-11,069D, 'Antony Gibbs and Sons Ltd, Liverpool House: Papers Relating to the Closure of Liverpool House in 1908'.

MS-23,260, 'Heseltine, Powell & Co, Salary and Bonus Payments, 1876–1929'.

MS-28,478, 'Institute of Chartered Accountants, Register of Staff, 1889–1933'.

MS – 15,014 'Law Fire Insurance Society, Salaries 1883–1914'.

MS – 21,276, 'Law Union and Rock Insurance Company Ltd. Register of Salaries Paid to Head Office Branch Staff with Memorandum, 1896'.

MS- 21,277, 'Law Union and Rock Insurance Company Ltd Register of Salaries of Staff at Head Office, 1902–48'.

Pamphlet – 6841, The London Chamber of Commerce, *Commercial Education*, 1895.

MS-16,460, 'London Chamber of Commerce, General Purpose Committee Minute Book, 1910–67'.

MS–16,474, 'London Chamber of Commerce, Salary Books 1911–1950'.

MS-24,698, 'Messers Gillett Brothers, Staff, 1898, 1902 and 1949'.

MS-20,293, 'National Provident Institution, Papers Relating to the Salaries of Office Staff, 1847–1902'.

Closed Access, SL 40:31, *The City of London Day Census, 1911*.

MS-20382, 'The Diary of Andrew Carlyle Tait, 1893–94'.

London Metropolitan Archives

ACC/2558/LA/03, 'Lambeth Waterworks Company, salary records, 1872–1904'.

ACC/3527/179, 'Lyons, Wages for Clerks at Cadby Hall and Olympia, 1895–1901'.

ACC/1559, 'United Law Clerks Society, 1832–1979'.

B/GH/LH/05/03–05, 'General Hydraulic Power Company Salaries Books 1887–1917'.

B/THB/F3, 'Messers Truman, Hanbury, Buxton and Co., Brewer's Clerks Salaries and Rest Expenses, 1898–1920'.

CL/ESTAB/4/59–62, 'Applications for Class II Typists, 1898–1915'.

CL/ESTAB/1/393, 'L.C.C. Establishment Committee Papers, 1894–1913'.

EO/HFE/9/37, 'Eight Years of Technical Education and Continuation Schools, 1912'.

LCC/MIN/4644, 'LCC Establishment Committee Papers, 1898'.

T.E.B. 80/4. 'Report of the Sub-Committee of the Technical Education Board, 1897'.

18.6 L.C.C. Minutes of Proceeding 1890–1914.

18.38 L.C.C.S.A., Andrews, C.D. and G.C. Burge, *Progress Report, 1909–1959: The First Fifty Years in the History of the L.C.C. Staff Association*, Privately Published. 1959.

31.6 LCC 'LCC Statistics 1890–1914'.

National Archives

ADM 116/1008, 'Clerks 2nd Class Pay and Promotion, 1905–11'.

RAIL 258/237 'Great Western (London) Athletic Association, 1900–1947'.

RAIL 253/140, 'Great Western Railway Classification of Station Masters, Goods Agents and Clerks, 1922'.

RAIL 1085/128, 'Clearing House Clerical Staff; salaries, conditions of service, rules, 1873–1912'.

RAIL 258/400, 'Great Western Railway Clerical Staff: recruiting, examination of, 1877–1914'.

RAIL 267/237, 'Great Western Railway Dining Club, 1898'.

RAIL 256/79, 'Great Western Railway, Memorandum to the Chairman and Directors of the Great Western Railway Company'.

RAIL 267/233, 'Great Western Railway, Memorandum to Duties of Accounts and Audit offices, 1883'.

RAIL 264/8–9, 'Great Western Railway Register of Clerks 1835–1910'

RAIL 258/404, 'Great Western Railway Secretarial Papers: salaried staff, increase in salaries, Sunday pay, grant of concessions, memorials, extract from minute papers, etc., 1904–1922'.

RAIL 250/746, 'Great Western Railway Staff Committee Paper, 1909–1937'.

1891 Census, Street Index, Hackney, RG 12/179–207, Acton, RG12/1033–1038 and East Dulwich, RG12/468

Prudential Plc Archives

MS-1295, 'Actuary's Office Papers'.

MS-1152, 'Board Minutes Re. Staff, 1873–1956'.

MS-1264, 'Industrial Branch Managers Register of Clerks, 1858–1879'.

MS-1292, 'Life Claim Department papers'.

MS-1278, 'Register of Clerks, 1885–1909'.

MS – 1263, 'Register of Clerks, 1900–1909'.

MS-1080, 'Staff: Lady Clerks'.

MS-1733, 'Staff: Lady Clerks Memorandum Book 1881–1921'.

The Royal Bank of Scotland Group Archives

GB 1502/GM/947, 'Account Book of Glyn, Mills, Currie & Co Football Club'.

GB 1502/GM/339/1, 'Glyn's Bank, Clerk's Register, 1864–1918'.

GB 1502/GM/2036, 'Glyn's Bank, Regulations Concerning Applications to Clerkships'.

GB 1502/GM/710/1, 'Glyn's Bank Town Office Annual Reports, 1896–1911'.

GM891–2, 'Glyn's Staff Scrapbooks'.

GB 1502/05772, 'H. Archer Letters (London and County)'.

GB 1502/WES/860/1–3, 'The County Magazine 1907–1909'.

GB 1502/WES/860/4–8, 'The County and Westminster Magazine 1910–1914'.

GB 1502/LWB/22/2, 'London and Westminster Bank Staff Register 1897–1919'.

GB 1502/LWB/116/17, 'London and Westminster Establishment Committee Minute Books 1903 to 1904'.

GB 1502/GM/01675, 'London & Westminster Rules and Regulations, 1909'.

GB 1502/20481, 'London and Westminster Sports Club Reports, 1901–1904'.

GB 1502/WES/125/1–11, 'London and County Bank Clerks Register, 1870–1909'.

GB 1502/WES/336, 'London County and Westminster Bank, Conditions of Appointments to Junior Clerkships, 1910'.

GB 1502/WES/271, 'Report comparing the pay, holidays and pensions of staff of London & County Bank and London & Westminster Bank, compiled after the merger of the two banks, c. 1909'.

GB 1502/LWB/159, 'Report of a committee appointed to investigate the policy, direction and staff of the London and Westminster Bank, 17 June, 1904'.

GB 1502/GM/00748, 'Rules and Regulation to be Observed by the Officers of the London and County Banking Company, Limited, 1908'.

Eric Gore Brown, *The History of the House of Glyn, Mill & Co.* (Privately Printed, 1933).

The University of Westminster Archives

UWA RSP/4/1/3, 'Regents Street Polytechnic Prospectus, 1902–3'.

UWA RSP/4/1/18, 'Regent Street Polytechnic Prospectus, 1910–11'.

UWA RSP/5/4/15, *The Polytechnic Magazine*, January–June, 1890.

UWA RSP/5/4/25, *The Polytechnic Magazine*, January–June, 1895.

UWA RSP/5/4/48, *The Polytechnic Magazine*, March, 1910–February, 1911.

Journals and Newspapers

The Acton, Chiswick and Turnham Green Gazette, 1888–91.

Business Life, 1903–12.

Clerk, 1890 and 1908–14.

County Magazine (after 1909 *The County and Westminster Magazine*) 1907–1914.

Great Eastern Magazine, 1911–14.

Ibis Magazine, 1878–1914.

Ilford Guardian, 1898–1901.

London County Council Staff Gazette, 1900–14.

Nibs & Quills, 1898.

Office, 1888–91.

Polytechnic Magazine, 1890–1910.

Railway Clerk, 1911–14.

Red Tape, 1911–14.

Interview

Interview with Jim Hancock at his home, 26 November 2001.

Printed Primary Sources

Anon., *The Story of a London Clerk: A Narrative Faithfully Told* (London: Leadenhall Press, 1896).

Bennett, A., *A Man from the North* (London: John Lane, 1898).

Booth, C., *London Life and Labour* (London: Macmillan and Co, Limited, 1902).

Bowley, A. L., *Wages and Income in the United Kingdom Since 1860* (Cambridge: Cambridge University Press, 1937).

Brown, W. J., *So Far* (London: George Allen & Unwin, 1943).

Bullock, S., *Robert Thorne – The Story of a London Clerk* (London: T. Werner Laurice, 1902).

Cannan, E., A.L. Bowley, F.Y. Edgeworth, H.B. Lees Smith, W.R. Scott, 'The Amount and Distribution of Income (other than wages) Below the Income Tax Exemption Limit in the United Kingdom.' *Journal of the Royal Statistical Society*, Vol. LXXIV, 1910–11, pp. 37–66.

Carrington, J. B., *The Commercial Clerk and His Success* (London: Sir Isaac Pitman & Sons, 1911).

—, *The Junior Corporation Clerk* (London: Sir Isaac Pitman and Sons Ltd., 1911).

Census of England and Wales (London: Her/His Majesty's Stationery Office, 1881, 1891, 1901, 1911).

Church, R., *Over the Bridge, An Essay in Autobiography* (London: William Heineman Ltd., 1955).

Cope, E. A., *Clerks Their Rights and Obligations* (London: Sir Isaac Pitman and Sons, Ltd., 1909).

Crossland, T. W. H., *The Suburbans* (London: John Lang, 1905).

Crouch, F. B., *From School to Office, Written for Boys* (London: Effingham Wilson & Co., 1890).

Davis, J. F., *Bank Organisation, Management and Accounts* (London: Sir Isaac Pitman and Sons, 1910).

Dicksee, L. R., *Office Organisation and Management* (London: Sir Isaac Pitman and Sons Ltd., 1910).

—, *Office Machinery A Handbook for Progressive Office Managers* (London: Gee & co., 1917).

Engineering, V., 'Prospects in the Professions IX. The City', *Cornhill Magazine*, 14 (1903), pp. 620–634.

Gissing, G., *A Freak of Nature or Mr. Brogden, City Clerk* (Edinburgh: The City Press, 1990) (originally published in 1899).

—, *In the Year of the Jubilee* (London: Lawrence and Bulls, 1894).

Greaves, H., *The Commercial Clerk and His Success* (London: Cassell & Co., 1909).

Grossmith, G., *Piano and I* (Bristol: J.W. Arrowsmith, 1910).

Grossmith, G., and Weedon, *The Diary of a Nobody* (Bristol: J.W. Arrowsmith, 1896).

Howarth, W., *Our Banking System and Clearing Houses* (London: Effingham Wilson, 1907).

Howard, H., *The London County Council from Within: Forty Years Official Recollections* (London: Chapman and Hall Ltd., 1932).

Keeble, H., *The Smiths of Surbiton* (London: Chapman and Hall, 1906).

—, *My Motley Life* (London: T. Fisher Unwin Limited, 1927).

Kent, W., *Testament of a Victorian Youth* (London: Heath Cranton Limited, 1938).

Klingender, F. D., *The Condition of Clerical Labour in Britain* (London: Martin Lawrence, 1935).

Laurence, S., 'Moderates, Municipal Reformers and the Issue of Tariff Reform, 1889–1934', in Andrew Saint (ed.), *Politics and the People of London: The London County Council, 1895–1965* (London: The Hambledon Press, 1989), pp. 93–102.

Layard, G. S., 'Family Budgets. II. A Lower-Middle-Class Budget', *Cornhill Magazine*, X (1901), pp. 656–6.

Llewellyn –Smith, H., and Arthur Acland, *Studies in Secondary Education* (London: Percivial & Co., 1892).

London School of Economics and Political Science, *The New Survey of London Life and Labour, 9 Vol.* (London: London School of Economics, 1930–35).

Mansbridge, A., *The Trodden Path* (London: J.M. Dent and Sons Ltd., 1940).

Moseley, S., *The Private Diaries of Sydney Moseley* (London: Max Parish,

1960).

Orchard, B.G., *The Clerks of Liverpool* (Liverpool: J. Collinson, 1871).

Pett Ridge, W. P., *69 Birnam Road* (London: Hodder and Stroughton, 1908).

—, *Outside the Radius* (London: Hodder and Stroughton, 1899).

Railway Clerks Association, *The Life of a Railway Clerk, Some Interesting Facts and Figures* (London: Railway Clerks Association, 1911).

Railway Clerks Association, *The R.C.A. and its Path of Progress* (London: Privately Published by the Railway Clerks Association, 1928).

Walker, G. R., *Commercial Correspondence and Office Routine* (London: W&R Chambers Limited, 1910).

Webb, S., *London Education* (London: Longmans, Green and Co., 1904).

—, *Fabian tract 117: The London Education Act: How to Make the Best of It* (London: The Fabian Society, 1904).

Webb, S., and Beatrice, *The History of Trade Unionism* (London: Longmans & Co., 1920).

Willis, F., *Peace and Dripping Toast* (London: Phoenix House, 1950).

Young, T. E. and Richard Masters, *Insurance Office Organisation, management and Accounts* (London: Sir Isaac Pitman & Sons, 1904).

Printed Secondary Sources

Alborn, T., 'Quill Driving: British Life Insurance Clerks and Occupational Mobility, 1800–1914', *Business History Review*, 82 (Spring 2008), pp. 31–58.

Anderson, G., *Victorian Clerks* (Manchester: Manchester University Press, 1976).

—, 'The Social Economy of Late-Victorian Clerks', in G.

Crossick (ed.), *The Lower Middle Class in Britain 1870–1914* (London: Croom Helm, 1977), pp. 113–33.

— (ed.), *The White-Blouse Revolution* (Manchester: Manchester University Press, 1988).

Attewell, P., 'The Clerk Deskilled: A Study in False Nostalgia', *Journal of Historical Sociology,* 2:4 (1989), pp. 357–387.

Braverman, H., *Labor and Monopoly Capitalism* (New York: Monthly Review, 1974).

Bagwell, P., *The Railway Clearing House in the British Economy, 1842–1922* (London: George Allen and Unwin, 1968).

Bourdieu, P., *Distinction: A Social Critique of the Judgement of Taste* (London: Routledge, 1986).

Breward, C., 'Sartorial Spectacle: clothing and masculine identities in the imperial city, 1860–1914', in Felix Driver and David Gilbert (eds), *Imperial Cities Landscape, Display and Identity* (Manchester: Manchester University Press, 1999), pp. 244–52.

Broadbank, J. G., *History of the Port of London* (London: Daniel O'Connor, 1921).

Byrne, T., *Local Government in Britain* (London: Penguin, 2000).

Chalaby, J., *The Invention of Journalism* (London: Macmillan, 1998).

Chevalier, W. S., *London's Water Supply, 1903–53: A Review of the Works of the Metropolitan Water Board* (London: Staple Press Ltd., 1953).

Clifton, G., 'Members and Officers of the L.C.C., 1889–1965', in Andrew Saint (ed.), *Politics and the People of London: The London County Council, 1889–1965* (London: The Hambledon Press, 1989), pp. 1–26.

Cohn, S., *The Process of Occupational Sex-Typing: The Feminization of Clerical Labor in Great Britain* (Philadelphia, PA: Temple University Press, 1985).

Collini, S., *Public Moralists, Political Thought and Intellectual Life in Britain 1850–1930* (Oxford: Clarendon Press, 1991).

Coustillas, P., and C. Partridge (eds), *Gissing The Critical Heritage* (London: Routledge and Kegan Paul, 1972).

Crompton, R., and G. Jones, *White-Collar Proletariat: Deskilling and Gender in Clerical Work* (London: Macmillan, 1984).

Crossick, G., 'The Emergence of the Lower Middle Class in Britain', in G. Crossick (ed.), *The Lower Middle Class in Britain 1870–1914* (London: Croom Helm, 1977), pp. 11–60.

Crossick, G., and H. G. Haupt, *The Petit Bourgeosie in Europe, 1780–1914: Enterprise, Family and Independence* (London: Routledge, 1995).

Davidoff, L., and C. Hall, *Family Fortunes Men and Women of the English Middle Classes, 1780–1850* (London: Century Hutchinson Ltd., 1987).

Davies, J. W., 'Working Class Make-Believe – The South Lambeth Parliament 1887–1890', *Parliamentary History*, 12:3 (1993), pp. 249–58.

Davis, J., 'The Progressive Council, 1889–1907', in Andrew Saint (ed.), *The London County Council 1889–1965* (London: The Hambledon Press, 1989), pp. 27–48.

Daunton, M., *Royal Mail The Post Office Since 1840* (London: The Athlone Press, 1985).

Dennett, L., *A Sense of Security: 150 Years of Prudential* (Cambridge: Granta Editions, 1998).

Diaper, S. J., 'The History of Kleinwort, Sons & Co. in Merchant Banking, 1855–1961' (Nottingham University PhD., 1983).

Drucker, P. F., *Post-Capitalist Society* (New York: Harper Collins Publishers, 1994).

Dyos, H. J., *Victorian Suburb* (Leicester: Leicester University Press, 1961).

Farrant, S., 'London by the Sea: Resort Development on the South Coast of England 1880–1939', *Journal of Contemporary History*, 22:1 (1987), pp. 137–62.

Feldman, D., *Englishmen and Jews, Social Relations and Political Culture, 1840–1914* (New Haven and London: Yale University Press, 1994).

Flint, K., 'Fictional Suburbia', in Peter Humm, Paul Stigant and Peter Widdowson (eds), *Popular Fiction in Literature and History* (London: Methuen, 1986).

Floud, R., and S. Glynn (eds), *London Higher The Establishment of Higher Education in London* (London: The Athlone Press, 1998).

Foucault, M., *The Archaeology of Knowledge* (London: Tavistock, 1972).

—, *The Birth of the Clinic* (London: Tavistock Publications, 1973).

—, *The History of Sexuality: an introduction* (London: Allen Lane, 1979).

Fulford, R., *Glyn's 1753–1953* (London: Macmillan and Co. Ltd., 1953).

Gerth, H. H. and C. Wright Mills (eds), *From Max Weber: Essays in Sociology* (London: Routledge, 1991).

Gibbon, G., and R. W. Bell, *History of the London County Council, 1889–1939* (London: Macmillan and Co., 1939).

Goldthorpe, J. H., D. Lockwood, F. Bechhofer, and J. Platt, *The Affluent Worker: Industrial Attitudes and Behaviour* (Cambridge: Cambridge University Press, 1968).

Gourvish, T. R., and R.G. Wilson, *The British Brewing Industry, 1830–1980* (Cambridge: Cambridge University Press, 1994).

Gray, R. Q., *The Labour Aristocracy in Victorian Edinburgh* (Oxford: Clarendon Press, 1976).

Green, E., *A History of the Institute of Bankers, 1879–1979* (London: Methuen & Co. Ltd., 1979)

Guerriero W. R., *Disillusionment or New Opportunities? The Changing Nature of Work in Offices, Glasgow 1880–1914* (Aldershot: Ashgate Publishing Limited, 1998).

Harris, J., *Private Lives, Public Spirits A Social History of Britain, 1870–1914* (Oxford: Oxford University Press, 1993).

Harvey, C., and J. Press, 'Management of the Taff Vale Strike 1900', *Business History*, 43:2 (2000), pp. 63–86.

Heller, M., 'Sports, Bureaucracies and London Clerks 1880–1939', *International Journal of the History of Sport*, 25:5 (2008), pp. 579–614.

Hennock, E. P., 'Technological Education in Britain 1850–1926: the uses of a German model', *History of Education*, 19:4 (1990), pp. 299–331.

Holcombe, L., *Victorian Ladies at Work: Middle Class Working Women in England and Wales 1850–1914* (Newton Abbott: David & Charles, 1973).

Hosgood, P., '"Doing the Shops" at Christmas: women, men and the department store in England, c. 1880–1914' in G. Crossick and J. Jaumain (eds), *Cathedrals of Consumption: the European Department Store, 1850–1939* (Aldershot: Ashgate, 1999), pp. 97–115.

Hudson, L., *Almost a Century* (Bexleyheath, Kent: The Alexius Press, 1990).

Humphreys, B. V., *Clerical Unions in the Civil Service* (London: Blackwell and Mott, 1958).

Jackson, A. A., *Semi-Detached London; suburban development, life and transport, 1900–30* (Didcot: Wild Swan, 1991).

Joby, R. S., *The Railwaymen* (Newton Abbott: David & Charles, 1984).

Jordan, E., 'The Lady Clerks at the Prudential: The Beginning of Vertical Segregation by Sex in Clerical Work in Nineteenth-Century Britain', *Gender and History*, 8:1 (1996), pp. 65–81.

Keating, P., *The Haunted Study: A Social History of the English Novel 1875–1914* (London: Secker and Warburg, 1989).

Keeble, S. P., *The Ability to Manage: A Study of British Management 1890–1990* (Manchester: Manchester University Press, 1992).

King, D., *The History of the Hongkong and Shanghai Banking Corporation Volumes I and II* (Cambridge: Cambridge University Press, 1987).

Kynaston, D., *The City of London Volume II Golden Years 1890–1914* (Pimlico: London, 1996).

Lawrence, S., 'Moderates, Municipal Reformers and the Issue of Tariff Reform, 1889–1934', in Andrew Saint (ed.), *Politics and the People of London: The London County Council, 1895–1965* (London: The Hambledon Press, 1989), pp.

Laybourn, K., *A History of British Trade Unionism c. 1770–1990* (Stroud: Alan Sutton, 1992).

Lewis, A., 'The Rate of Growth of World Trade, 1830–1973' in Sven Grassman and Lunberg, Erik (eds), *The World Economic Order, Past and Prospects* (London: The Macmillan Press Ltd, 1981), pp. 11–65.

Lewis, J., 'Women Clerical Workers in the Late Nineteenth and Early Twentieth Centuries', in Gregory Anderson (ed.), *The White-Bloused Revolution – Female Office Workers Since 1870* (Manchester: Manchester University Press, 1988), pp. 27–47.

Locke, R. R., *The End of the Practical man, Entrepreneurship and Higher Education in Germany, France, and Great Britain, 1880–1940* (Greenwich, Conneticut: Jai Press, 1984).

Lockwood, D., *The Blackcoated Worker: A Study in Class Consciousness* (Oxford: Clarendon Press, 1958).

Lowerson, J., *Sport and the English Middle Classes 1870–1914* (Manchester: Manchester University Press, 1993).

Mckenna, F., *The Railway Workers 1840–1970* (London: Faber, 1980).

McKinlay, A., '"Dead Selves": The Birth of the Modern Career', *Organization*, 9:4 (2002), pp. 595–614.

McNay, L., *Foucault: A Critical Introduction* (Cambridge: Polity Press, 1994).

Mangan, J. A., *Athleticism in the Edwardian Public School: The Emergence and Consolidation of an Educational Ideology* (Cambridge: Cambridge University Press, 1981).

Mitchie, R. C., *The City of London* (London: Macmillan Academic and Professional Ltd., 1992).

Morris, R. J., 'Clubs, Societies and Associations', in F.M.L. Thompson (ed.), *The Cambridge Social History of Britain 1750–1950 Vol. 3* (Cambridge: Cambridge University Press, 1990), pp. 395–443.

—, *Class, Sect and Party: The Making of the British Middle Class, Leeds 1820–50* (Manchester: Manchester University Press, 1990).

Olsen, D. J, *The Growth of Victorian London* (London: Batsford, 1976).

Payne, P. L., 'The Emergence of the Large Scale Company in Great Britain, 1870–1914', *Economic History Review,* 20:3 (1967), pp. 519–42.

Pellew, J., *The Home Office 1848–1914 From Clerks to Bureaucrats* (London: Heinemann, 1982).

Pennybacker, S., *A Vision for London 1889–1914: Labour Everyday Life and the L.C.C. Experiment* (London: Routledge, 1995).

Perkin, H., *The Rise of Professional Society: England Since 1880* (London: Routledge, 1989).

Price, R. N., 'Society, Status and Jingoism: The Social Roots of Lower Middle Class Patriotism', Geoffrey Crossick (ed.), *The Lower Middle Class in Britain 1870–1914* (London: Croom Helm, 1977), pp. 89–112.

Roach, J., *Secondary Education in England 1870–1902* (London: Routledge, 1991).

Schneer, J., *London 1900 The Imperial Metropolis* (New Haven and London: Yale University Press, 1999).

Roberts, R., *Shroeders: Merchants and Bankers* (London: Pimlico, 1992).

Savage, M., 'Career Mobility and Class Formation: British banking workers and the lower middle classes', in Andrew Miles and David Vincent (eds), *Building European Society Occupational Change and Social Mobility in Europe 1840–1940* (Manchester: Manchester University Press, 1993), pp. 196–216.

—, 'Discipline, Surveillance and the 'Career': Employment in the Great Western Railway 1833–1914' in Alan McKinlay and Ken Starkey (eds), *Foucault, Management and Organisational Theory* (London: Sage, 1998), pp. 65–92.

Searle, G. R., *The Quest for National Efficiency: A Study in British Politics and Political Thought, 1890–1914* (Oxford: Blackwell, 1971).

Sennett, R., *The Corrosion of Character The Personal Consequences of Work in the New Capitalism* (New York & London: W.W. Norton & Company, 1998).

Sheppard, F., *London A History* (Oxford: Oxford University Press, 1998).

Simmons, J., and Gordon Biddle (eds), *The Oxford Companion to British Railway History* (Oxford University Press, 1997).

Smith, S. R. B., 'The Centenary of the London Chamber of Commerce: Its Origins and Early Policy', *London Journal*, 8:2 (1982), pp. 157–70.

Spoor, A., *White Collar Union 60 Years of NALGO* (London: Heinemann, 1967).

Stedman Jones, G., 'The Determinist Fix: Some Obstacles to the Further Development of the Linguist Approach to History in the 1990s', *History Workshop Journal*, 42 (1996), pp. 19–35.

Stephens, M. D., and G. W. Roderick, 'The Later Victorians and Scientific and Technical Education' in *Annals of Science*, 28:4 (1972), pp. 385–400.

Stevenson, J., 'Women and the Curriculum at the Polytechnic at Regent Street, 1883–1913', *History of Education*, 26:3 (1997), pp. 267–86.

Szreter, S., *Fertility, Class and Gender in Britain, 1860–1940* (Cambridge: Cambridge University Press, 1996).

Thompson, F. M. L. (ed.), *The Rise of Suburbia* (Leicester: Leicester University Press, 1982).

Tosh, J., 'What Should Historians Do with Masculinity? Reflections on Nineteenth Century Britain', *History Workshop*, 38:1 (1994), pp. 179–202.

—, *A Man's Place: Masculinity and the Middle Class Home in Victorian England* (New Haven & London: Yale University, 1999).

Trotter, D., *The English Novel in History, 1895–1920* (London: Macmillan, 1993).

Wallace, M., *Single or Return? The History of the Transport Salaried Staff Association* (London: Transport Salaried Staff Association, 1996).

Wardley, P., 'The Emergence of Big Business: The Largest Corporate Employers of Labour in the United Kingdom, Germany and the United States, c. *1907*', *Business History*, 41:4 (1999), pp. 88–116.

Weber, M., *Economy and Society, Volume 2* (Berkeley, CA: University of California Press, 1978).

Wild, J., *The Rise of the Office Clerk in Literary Culture, 1880–1939* (Basingstoke: Palgrave Macmillan, 2006).

Wilson, J. F., *British Business History, 1720–1994* (Manchester: Manchester University Press, 1995).

Wood, E. M., *A History of the Polytechnic* (London: Macdonald, 1965).

Zimmeck, M., 'Jobs for the Girls: the Expansion of Clerical Work for Women, 1850–1914', in Angel V. John (ed.), *Unequal Opportunities – Women's Employment in England 1800–1918* (Oxford: Basil Blackwell, 1986), pp. 153–77.

INDEX

For Product Safety Concerns and Information please contact our EU
representative GPSR@taylorandfrancis.com
Taylor & Francis Verlag GmbH, Kaufingerstraße 24, 80331 München, Germany